"I learned so much from reading *Strangers and S*... the outsider tells a narrative about how we see our~~selves, what we believe~~, and what we value. We love to talk about diversity and the image of God, but Vos challenges us to consider what that actually looks like, what it costs, and the great reward of extending God's welcome to others. The ultimate freedom is not the ability to serve ourselves but the freedom we give to one another in belonging to Christ."

—**Aimee Byrd**, author of *The Sexual Reformation*
and *Recovering from Biblical Manhood and Womanhood*

"The twenty-first century confronts us with profoundly human issues involving race, gender, immigration, incarceration, and other human realities that take us into uncharted territory where fear can incapacitate us and lead us to divide. We've become better at constructing walls than building bridges—and all too often we are driven more by fear than by faith. In *Strangers and Scapegoats*, Matt Vos shares a wealth of information gleaned from years of scholarship as a sociology professor to help readers better understand the issues. But he doesn't stop with bringing facts to light. His goal is to bring Jesus into the conversation in order to shape our convictions and interactions with others. This bracing book is powerful, eye opening, and hope filled. It empowers us to *be* good news and a healing force in this hurting world."

—**Carolyn Custis James**, author of *Half the Church: Recapturing God's
Global Vision for Women* and *Malestrom: How Jesus
Dismantles Patriarchy and Redefines Manhood*

"A masterful fusion of classic sociology, analysis of contemporary social problems, and personal experience that will support and stimulate Christians toward loving their neighbors. Sociologists have long pondered the nature of modern society: large scale, diverse, and filled with strangers. Vos brings basic sociological concepts to bear on questions of inclusion, mercy, favoritism, and love. Readers will come away strengthened for living Christian faith in the context of today's social challenges and opportunities."

—**Jenell Paris**, Messiah University

"Thanks to Matt Vos for this great exploration of the truth that being considered a stranger is seldom benign. It is too often accompanied by physical, economic, emotional, and psychological harm. Explaining how this plays out in various spheres of social life is a core strength of this book. Furthermore, Vos asks us to see the gospel not as something that provides social and self-justification but as a call to empty ourselves, particularly on behalf of those who are unfairly labeled as strangers and scapegoats."

—**Steve Corbett**, Covenant College

"Weaving personal passion and professional acumen, Vos invites readers to consider the stranger. Vos's integration of Christian faith with sociological theory and research offers a timely response to the widening cultural divides between 'us' and 'them.' This sometimes piercing critique is accompanied with stories, bringing faces and histories to the strangers living near and far, making the stranger less strange. *Strangers and Scapegoats* reminds Christians of our countercultural distinctive to welcome the stranger, to love our neighbor."

—**Lisa Graham McMinn**, George Fox University

"Winsome, accessible, learned, and practical, this is a book I will come back to again and again. Drawing on insights from social identity theory in conversation with the witness of Christian Scripture, Vos develops a fresh lens by which to consider some of the most polarizing issues in the Christian community today related to gender, race, human sexuality, immigration, economic exploitation, and incarceration. In the end, this book will not only deepen your love for the stranger but help you rediscover your own identity in Christ."

—**Amanda W. Benckhuysen**, director of Safe Church Ministry for the CRCNA

"In *Strangers and Scapegoats*, Vos writes a Christian sociological study of the strangers and scapegoats in American and Western culture, holding up both a mirror to show us ourselves and a clear lens to show us how we view others—how we maintain our status by keeping strangers in a position that minimizes their threat to us. While readers may not completely agree with Vos's emphasis or interpretation of events, they will follow his cogent arguments with fascination and find themselves unable to stop reading. He holds us with his thorough research, wide scope of history, vivid narratives and descriptions, overpowering biblical allusions, and depth of insight. This book will be a must-read for sociology courses; it will spark discussion and debate."

—**Mary J. Dengler**, Dordt University (emeritus); editor of *Pro Rege*

STRANGERS
AND
SCAPEGOATS

STRANGERS AND SCAPEGOATS

Extending God's Welcome to Those on the Margins

MATTHEW S. VOS

Baker Academic

a division of Baker Publishing Group
Grand Rapids, Michigan

Published by Baker Academic
a division of Baker Publishing Group
PO Box 6287, Grand Rapids, MI 49516-6287
www.bakeracademic.com

Printed in the United States of America

Library of Congress Cataloging-in-Publication Data
Names: Vos, Matthew, author.
Title: Strangers and scapegoats : extending God's welcome to those on the margins / Matthew S. Vos.
Description: Grand Rapids, Michigan : Baker Academic, a division of Baker Publishing Group,
    [2022] | Includes bibliographical references and index.
Identifiers: LCCN 2021060313 | ISBN 9781540965233 (paperback) | ISBN 9781540965707
    (casebound) | ISBN 9781493436989 (pdf) | ISBN 9781493436972 (ebook)
Subjects: LCSH: Strangers—Religious aspects—Christianity. | Identity (Psychology)—Religious
    aspects—Christianity.
Classification: LCC BR115.S73 V67 2022 | DDC 261.8/32—dc23/eng/20220127
LC record available at https://lccn.loc.gov/2021060313

22   23   24   25   26   27   28   7   6   5   4   3   2   1

For Joan, who stands with the marginal ones in her orbits
and speaks up for those denied a voice. This book would not be,
but for your wisdom that graces its pages.

For my parents, Mark and Rosalie,
who helped me to see the strangers around us
and because of whom I know little of what it means to be a stranger.

And for the strangers in our world.
I am not innocent of the concerns I raise,
but I hope I am changing.

CONTENTS

PART 3

INVITING STRANGERS

ACKNOWLEDGMENTS

In "Child of the Wind" Canadian musician Bruce Cockburn sings,

> Depends on what you look at, obviously,
> but even more it depends on the way that you see.[1]

Sociology is about learning to see old things in new ways, and this book is about learning to see others, especially strangers, in a new light. While I formally began work on this book three years ago as a sabbatical project, many of the ideas it contains have been percolating far longer as I labored to see things in new ways. As inherently social beings, we rarely, if ever, learn to see things anew on our own. Accordingly, I am indebted to countless others for directing my gaze to new places, challenging me to examine lingering prejudices, taking me seriously, encouraging me in my sociological imaginings about the world we share, and offering help when I needed it. While I can only name just a few such people in what follows, I am deeply grateful to so many who have nurtured my thinking and my person in such positive ways. In shaping this project, the ideas it contains, and all the various dimensions of the volume you're now reading, I'm especially thankful for:

- My colleagues in the Christian Sociological Association and the broader Christian sociology circles in which I move. In particular, Dennis Hiebert, Brad Breems, João Monteiro, Tim Epp, Jenell Paris, Val Hiebert, Scott Monsma, Toni Chiareli, Dave and Pat Carlson, Mike Leming, Bruce Wearne, Joshua Reichard, and others. Ours is a strange and wonderful perspective, and any prophetic voice I've developed would not be but for you, dear friends.

1. Cockburn, "Child of the Wind."

- Mark Ward, my father and theologian-in-residence. This book would be a mere shadow of what it is had you not participated in its development. You helped me find my voice countless times, did a lot of behind-the-scenes theological research, read a good many chapter drafts, and modeled a prophetic stance in so many areas of life. I'm grateful for these things you've given me.

- Kelly Kapic, my colleague and friend who so graciously lent me his experience in navigating the world of publishing, helped prepare proposals, and celebrated various milestones with me throughout the process of bringing this book to print. I appreciate your collegiality, generosity, and experience more than you know.

- Jeff Hall, the academic vice president at Covenant College where I teach, who was supportive of the project from start to finish, who provided a variety of much-needed resources, and who has long been a source of encouragement to me in my teaching and writing. Also Cliff Foreman, a colleague who read and edited early chapter drafts, from whom I have learned a great deal, and whose enthusiasm for humor in scholarly discourse has left its mark on me.

- Chris Robinson, my sociology colleague in our two-person department who shares my strange sociological view of the world and offers friendship and collegiality on a daily basis.

- Carolyn Custis James, who speaks for the marginal ones in our world and who has been such a blessing and model to me as I struggle to emulate her prophetic voice. Your friendship and support have been a gift to me. Also Frank James, who supported and advocated for this project in its earlier stages.

- Steve Glass, my college roommate and friend, who has shaped me in innumerable ways and who generously donated his significant talents in taking promotional headshots of me for the project (Steveglassphotography.com).

- Bob Hosack at Baker Academic. I'm thankful that you extended yourself to a new author. Quite literally, this book would not be but for your initiative, counsel, and support. And Melisa Blok, my editor at Baker. You are a truly kindred spirit, and I've become such a better writer for having worked on this project with you. I very much enjoyed the entire editorial process. And Sarah Gombis and Brandy Scritchfield and the rest of the good people at Baker. Many thanks.

INTRODUCTION

Strangers among Us

Three Stories of the Stranger

Like a Good Stranger . . .

A few years ago, my family and I drove our Mercury Sable to my parents' home in Ontario, Canada. As I made the final left turn onto their road, a motorcycle that had pulled out to pass me in a residential no-passing zone struck the driver's side front quarter-panel of the car, propelling its two riders and their machine over our hood, through the air, and onto my parents' neighbor's lawn. It happened fast—probably a couple hundredths of a second and the crash was over. While my wife worked to reassure our car-seat encumbered young daughters, I pulled over to the curb, jumped out of the vehicle, and tried to figure out what to do. Someone came out of the house whose lawn we'd just relandscaped and telephoned the police. As various people began coming out of their residences to see what the commotion was about, I walked over to where the driver of the wrecked motorcycle lay. He was on his back, semiconscious, mumbling incoherently, and trying to remove his helmet. I sat near his head and, being careful not to touch him, tried to prevent him from removing it lest he hurt himself more. He had been wearing flip-flops, and I could see that his bare feet were broken and badly bruised, with blood pooling just under the skin. The passenger seemed to be less hurt than the driver. The ambulance quickly arrived, lifted both men onto stretchers, and carted them off to the local hospital. My wife and I stayed to give statements to the police officer who arrived at the scene.

That evening I had difficulty falling asleep. I desperately wanted to know whether the young men from the accident had been critically injured or just shaken up. It's a terrible and unsettling thing to be involved in an accident where people are hurt. As you can imagine, privacy acts and such prevent nonfamily members from finding out injury details. In fact, three years went by before I learned anything about the injuries sustained by these young motorcyclists. Then, one day, I was served papers inviting me to participate in a lawsuit designed to relieve me of a sum of one million dollars for a variety of shortcomings including failure to maintain my vehicle, reckless endangerment, and a laundry list of personal vices that were seen as causing the accident. Frightening. Long story short, the motorcycle driver and defendant in the lawsuit did not have any permanent injuries other than post-traumatic stress, and eventually, after I flew to Toronto to give a deposition, my State Farm (insurance) appointed attorney disposed of the lawsuit, and I avoided losing a million dollars I didn't have.

Since the accident, I've thought a lot about the character of the relationships involved. All of the ways I'd been taught to communicate with other human beings seemed inaccessible in this accident and its aftermath. In short, I couldn't address the young man as one human being to another. There were powerful forces at work that colluded to keep the motorcycle driver a stranger to me. I didn't even learn his name until I was served the lawsuit. On my insurance card, it clearly instructs me not to admit fault, not to say "I'm sorry," not to act as a concerned and compassionate human might act. "Like a good neighbor, State Farm is there" goes the jingle. But make no mistake, State Farm and its attorneys are my so-called neighbor in this scenario, not the young man hurt in an encounter with me. In the end, the accident seemed mostly about money, attorneys, maneuvering, self-protection, and self-righteous posturing. I remember a moment of elation when I heard that the defendant (a term used between strangers) was possibly fighting a DUI in a separate case. Elation? I'm glad about this? He's the stranger—faceless, far away, without humanity, and not deserving of my compassion. After the initial shock of the accident, and then being sued, I found myself softening toward this young man, and even wishing him well. I wanted to hear that he was restored to health, that his life was good—and not just so I might be absolved of liability. But the lawsuit, anonymity, and big money at stake turned our backs on each other, and we remained strangers. Never say you're sorry? Never admit fault? What kind of world is that? As part of the legal arrangement closing out the case, I had to agree never to stalk him or try to contact him. We're legally obligated to remain strangers.

Women on the Margins

The Roma people, sometimes referred to as "Gypsies," are an ethnic minority who trace their origin to the Dalit community in India (often referred to as "untouchables"). Historically a nomadic people, the Roma are primarily concentrated in central, southern, and eastern Europe. Every year in Bulgaria (and undoubtedly in other countries as well) there are bride markets for the Roma community. Young women and girls as young as twelve will wear their best clothes, layer on makeup, and travel with their fathers to the market to be sold to future husbands. During this mortifying and frightening ritual, the girls will simply stand there while men circle them, visually sizing them up as they choose a promising wife. The most beautiful go first and tend to fetch the highest prices for their families. In the Roma communities, a beautiful newborn girl may mean future fortune for her family. As deals are struck in the bride markets, suitors will pay fathers an agreed-on amount in either money, livestock, or property, after which plans commence for the wedding.

While attending a vacation Bible school with her grandchildren, an elderly Roma woman named Nadeshda shared her life story with a former student of mine whose family operates a Christian ministry in Bulgaria.[1] Nadeshda was sold as a child bride at age fifteen.[2] Her husband was thirty when she married him, and she had her first baby just after she turned sixteen. Nadeshda remembers being angry at her father for selling her to a man—a stranger—who lived in a village so far away she would never again see her brothers or sisters. She remembers the feeling of having no control over her life and not being able to make choices about her future. Of the eight children Nadeshda went on to birth, she had contact with only one. Her husband, who had died years earlier, had been a lazy drunk (her words) who did nothing for his family.

Nadeshda teared up as she expressed thankfulness to the people running the vacation Bible school. They were teaching her grandchildren the sort of things she never had the opportunity to learn herself. She hadn't been able to go to school to learn to read and write, but she felt hopeful that her grandchildren would learn these things and more at the school that was part of this new church.

Echoes of Nadeshda's story reverberate around the world—her situation is not atypical. Poverty, early forced marriage, little autonomy or access to power, and the constant threat of interpersonal violence are the lot of many women. Absorbing the lion's share of global suffering, girls and women are

---

1. The story is real, but the name is fictitious.
2. Worldwide, an estimated fifty-one million girls have been married before the age of consent. End Slavery Now, "Half the Sky Movement."

frequently cast in the role of the stranger, and they are far more likely than men to be marginal in the social worlds they inhabit. Around the globe, women are more likely to be oppressed, exploited, and victims of violence. Their incomes are lower, they own less property, and they have far less access to power. Consequently, to "observe" gender is to observe inequality and, by extension, oppression.

Girls and women are routinely denied power in our global society. They are hurt. They are discarded. They are used. They are strangers and almost universally unwelcome, especially in the parts of social groups where power is wielded and negotiated. Consider the following:

> Women are present in most social situations. Where they are not present, the reason is not because of their lack of ability or interest but because there have been deliberate efforts to exclude them. Where they are present, women have played roles very different from the popular conception of them (e.g., as passive wives and mothers). Indeed, as wives and as mothers and in a series of other roles, women have, along with men, actively created many situations being studied. Yet though women are actively present in most social situations, scholars, publics, and social actors themselves, both male and female, have often been blind to their presence. Moreover, women's roles in most social situations, although essential, have been different from, less privileged than, and subordinated to, those of men. Their invisibility is only one indicator of this inequality.[3]

I'm increasingly aware of how easy it is for me to stand, to direct, and to interact with people in the central and powerful parts of the social worlds I inhabit. I'm White, I'm male, I'm educated, and I'm middle class. I'm no stranger. By contrast, I've begun to see the extent to which my daughters and my wife are so frequently marginal to, yet governed by, the realms of power that are readily accessible to me. My minority, adopted daughters (one Roma, from Bulgaria, and the other Chinese) witness few female authority figures in the institutions that shape their young lives. They rarely see people like them (female, of a racial minority) making weighty, authoritative, and consequential decisions. Women are everywhere, but they're frequently strangers to the parts of society wielding power.

There's a Church Nearby Where You'll Feel More Comfortable

There's a church in the midwestern United States that some of my relatives attend, where I've worshiped a good many times, and of which I'm quite fond.

---

3. Ritzer and Stepnisky, *Modern Sociological Theory*, 291.

The church is situated in a small agricultural town that has grown considerably in recent years. In the past two decades, agribusiness dairy has become the defining industry in this growing community. A number of these large dairies are owned by Christian families who hold membership in, or are closely associated with, this church or similar churches located in the town. Mexican laborers (mostly men) work these farms, many of them saving money and sending it back home to their families. In the decades since these farms moved in and began employing Mexican workers, I've never heard one of these men called by their name. In my presence they've been referred to as "technicians" or "the Mexicans" but never by name. I've heard stories about how hard they work, and how diligent, honest, and devoted they are, but I've heard little else about them. And lamentably, I've never seen a Mexican worker or family attend a service at my relatives' church. There is no Spanish on their church sign, and little evidence that Spanish-speaking people would fit in there. There's no visible antagonism, but there's no invitation either. Sociologist that I am, a few years ago I took it upon myself (and this is why no one likes sociologists!) to ask a minister at the church why I never saw Mexican people in attendance. He told me that "the Mexicans would feel nervous attending church here, but we're building a facility for them down the road a bit where they can worship together." I asked whether they had considered the possibility that Mexican people might like to come to this church if it offered basic headphone translation services (something we did at my church). He replied, "We've already spent our money on the new building down the road." Shortly after this, a Mexican man showed up at this church, and a friendly and genuinely well-meaning elder escorted him back out, explaining how to get to the other church where he might feel more comfortable . . . with his people: Mexicans, laborers—strangers. And sometimes the church youth group raises money for mission trips to Mexico.

These stories—and you probably have your own—illustrate how pervasive the stranger role is in our lives. In the first story, money replaces human compassion, and the system and those who benefit from it *demand* adoption of the stranger posture. The second story shows what pervasive and negative effects can result when a category of people—women, in the example—stand outside the realms of power and are relegated to the role of the stranger. The third story reveals a benevolent and perhaps unintended enforcement of the stranger identity. Be grateful, stranger: We can help you! But we're off to Mexico on our mission trip. . . . See you soon.

I wonder how Jesus might reimagine these stories. I wonder whether he'd stop and say he's sorry to the wounded young man on the motorcycle, not really caring about lawsuits and such. I wonder what he'd think of our world of men at the center of wealth and power, and of the marginalization of women, so shamefully obvious on the global stage. Would he reinforce male power monopolies, or would he invite women into the center of things? I wonder whether he would start attending the Mexican church instead.

I wonder.

Slave Shackles, Harley Riders, and Mean Girls

For the most part, we experience strangers as naturally occurring phenomena. We know some people; we don't know others. In a world where we face all kinds of risks, it just makes good sense to be wary of strangers. We've all heard stories of elderly people who were duped into giving out their Social Security number or other personal information and who were then exploited. Of course we cringe at the thought that our children could fall into the hands of a stranger, and we diligently instruct them about stranger danger. And there's little doubt that unseen nefarious strangers invade us online, placing us at risk of identity theft. When we think about such strangers, they are mostly people who are disconnected from us—who stand outside our communities, who are inaccessible to us, and who have little chance of engaging us in neighborly contact.

This book is not about such distant strangers, the mythical, shadowy ones who lurk about and want to do us harm and take our things. Rather, this is a book about how we cultivate identity by actively constructing out-groups or strangers around us. Strangers, seen this way, are those "others" who we work to distance ourselves from, often in symbolic ways, not because they pose a danger to us but because our contrast with them—our superiority against their inferiority—affirms our dominant and desirable position in the social hierarchy. Think about how the identities of White people in the antebellum South were established and maintained through their contrast with the Black people around them. During this time, and right up through the Jim Crow[4] era, when Whites lynched Blacks, the perceived offense frequently came down to Blacks "not knowing their place."[5] The so-called offense was blurring the lines between groups—not maintaining "proper" distance between identity camps. If you glance through the lengthy list of Jim Crow laws (separate bathrooms, a Black may not address a White by their first name, a Black man

4. *Jim Crow* is a name for the state and local laws that enforced racial segregation after Reconstruction in the Southern United States.
5. For a sobering experience, examine the map in this article: Lewis, "This Map Shows over a Century of Documented Lynchings."

may not touch a White woman, and so on), they all pretty much boil down to maintaining a well-defined out-group contrast that was favorable to White identity and that subordinated Black culture and identity.[6]

A few years ago I visited the Lest We Forget Museum of Slavery in Philadelphia as part of a Christian sociology conference.[7] At this small, modest, privately owned museum, there was an impressive and sobering collection of slave shackles, branding irons, bill-of-sale documents, and other slavery-era artifacts. Combined, these items functioned as cruel and coercive identity props for the dominant White group. And oh the lengths the dominant racial group went to in order to maintain and augment the racial contrast and prevailing social order. One of the final displays in the museum was a large whiskey barrel with the words "Barrel of Laughs" written on its side. When we inquired about this we were told that, during Jim Crow, some cities placed these barrels on street corners. If Black people felt like they were going to laugh or otherwise express emotion in public, they had to put their head in the barrel until the impulse had passed or the emotion was spent. When the individual came up out of the barrel, they were to display a sober, emotion-free face. For emotion reveals humanness. In this way, and a host of others, Whites were able to maintain social distance between themselves and Blacks—"Look, we're completely different." In effect, Whites depended on Blacks being strangers in their midst. If you were White, you were not free to be friends with Blacks—in fact, you would be required in formal and informal ways to clearly demonstrate your unmitigated support of the social inequality established between the racial groups. And those differences became normal. Failing to uphold important racial distinctions would result in sanctions, whether you were Black or White (though the sanctions against Whites were usually gentler). All this, though differences between Blacks and Whites do not exist in a "real" way—there is no credible scientific definition for race. In fact, a Black person shares no more genes with another Black person than with a White person, and we all have most genes in common. But the identity functions that exaggerated racial difference have, for the dominant group, arguably made the struggle surrounding Black/White constructed differences the defining characteristic of American history.

The social distance between Blacks and Whites during Jim Crow and beyond is one thing, but what about the other, less significant, less important identities we maintain? We go through life with a variety of identities, many

6. A list of Jim Crow laws can be found at this website: https://www.nps.gov/malu/learn/education/jim_crow_laws.htm.
7. "Lest We Forget Slavery Museum."

of them operating concurrently in our lives. I'm a father, college professor, motorcycle driver, PC (not Mac!) user, Presbyterian, husband, heterosexual, White male, with a PhD in sociology. Oh, and I only own Fords (my father-in-law was a diemaker for Ford his entire career, and my brother-in-law owns a Ford dealership!). What a quiver of identities! And that's not the half of them. How do I maintain all these identities that, combined, give my life its distinctive character? They show my preferences, loves, and hates. We don't go through life in amorphous ways as though there's no difference between being a father, an uncle, or a high school teacher. These identities (sociologists call them "statuses") help us understand ourselves, and they make our actions intelligible to those around us. The common thread tying them together is that they are established and maintained by creating and sustaining favorable out-group contrasts. Take my "Ford owner" identity (if you think that trucks are an insignificant part of a man's identity in North Georgia, where I live, spend a little time in the South!). People who own Ford F-150s frequently root an important part of their identities in their trucks. Such people actively scan the world for evidence of Ford quality. They resolutely believe the commercial slogans proclaiming such truths as "At Ford, quality is job #1!" And they (we?!) delight in locating information—true or not—that Chevy or Dodge trucks are inferior. Attaching ourselves (I write as a dedicated Ford owner, and my extended family may someday read this book!) to the Ford symbol aligns us with quality, good decision-making, and a host of other admirable social attributes. We're aligned with a winner, and that makes us winners! Have you ever seen the truck window decal of Calvin (from *Calvin and Hobbes*) peeing on a Chevy insignia? Ford owners take that seriously! And Chevy owners have an equivalent decal with Calvin relieving himself on a Ford.

The important point here is that our identities, in all their glorious dimensions, are generally established in opposition to less desirable out-groups. Look back through the list of my identities. I'm a Presbyterian—thank God I'm not a Baptist! I'm a college professor—no blue-collar job here! I'm a father—with this identity the out-group contrast does not fall on non-fathers, but rather on bad fathers. It's pretty easy for me to see my own enlightened parenting tactics in contrast with those of less prodigious fathers. You've probably seen the friendly wars between those who home-school and those who don't. Often, the mode of schooling you endorse as a father (or mother) functions as an identity platform that serves to remind you of your own diligence and morality in the face of those who use other, "lesser," educational approaches with their children (my insecurity leads me to make a lot of homeschool jokes!). I have a PhD in sociology, and we (sociologists) quickly correct well-meaning people who confuse us with psychologists. The very thought! Finally, I noted that I am a motorcycle driver. While you would think that there would be a friendly bond among motorcycle drivers (and in many respects there is), Harley-Davidson owners (I own a Honda) generally do not see those of us who motor along on Japanese bikes as "real" motorcyclists. If you've ever driven a motorcycle, you know that bikers wave at each other as they pass going opposite directions. I've recently learned, much to my dismay, that there is a growing movement among Harley riders to only wave at other Harley riders! And some people are serious about this! How thinly we slice our identities. Try riding a Suzuki to a Harley-Davidson rally and see if you feel safe! I sometimes drive around on my brother-in-law's Harley just to see how the "real" bikers live!

The 2004 movie *Mean Girls*, starring Lindsey Lohan, provides an instructive example of the ways people construct identity by creating out-groups.[8] In the movie, after being homeschooled somewhere in Africa for fifteen years, Lohan's character, Cady Heron, moves with her family to an American town where she must learn to navigate the cruel cliques, factions, in-groups, and out-groups of a large public school. While Heron fairly quickly forms friendships with a small group of "unpopular" teens (you know the type caricatured in movies), she finds herself pulled toward the dominant clique of beautiful, fashionable girls who her new friends call the "plastics"—"the A-list girl clique at her new school," as the movie's promotional blurb puts it.[9] The plastics rule the school—people are envious of them and many want to be noticed, praised, or accepted by them. But the plastics construct their identities through bullying, degrading, and cultivating envy. Their identity is in the contrast (there's really not much more to them), and they actively look for ways to belittle "inferior" others. Most of their time is spent making strangers. The movie's lesson emerges when Cady Heron recognizes how easily she is drawn away from her kinder, gentler, more vulnerable group of friends toward the plastics. The redemptive turn in *Mean Girls* comes when Cady casts off her plastic identity and renews her previous friendships. This movie was a popular success in part because we all recognize these various cliques in high school settings (and beyond), we know the damage they can do, and we simultaneously feel their pull. The plastics would not exist without subordinated groups to prop up their identities. If we're honest, our own identities have plenty of plastic parts.

8. Waters, *Mean Girls*.
9. Waters, *Mean Girls*.

The Eyes of a Stranger

And so, our world takes on an oppositional cast, and we come to live among strangers in a zero-sum identity game—they lose, we win. As social psychologist Ken Gergen laments, "We scan the world to ensure we are better than all."[10] So many stranger categories are required to maintain our identities: Black/White, Christian/non-Christian, gay/straight, blue-collar/white-collar, American citizen / noncitizen, Republican/Democrat, college-educated / high school dropout, male/female, Protestant/Catholic/Jew/Muslim, Tennessee/ Alabama (Southeastern Conference Football rivalry), fat/thin, tall/short, plastics/nerds, blue eyes / brown eyes, and so on.

This last contrast—blue eyes / brown eyes—was explored in a famous third-grade classroom experiment conducted by Jane Elliott on April 5, 1968, the day after the assassination of Martin Luther King Jr.[11] Elliott wanted to help her young students understand the experience of racism and discrimination. She divided the students into two groups—those with blue eyes and those with brown eyes. Blue-eyed students were given all kinds of privilege over brown-eyed students. For example, blue-eyed students got to sit in the front of the classroom while those with brown eyes were banished to the back, and blue-eyed students were encouraged to play *only* with other blue-eyed students. Elliott didn't let the two groups drink from the same water fountain. She gave blue-eyed students extra time at recess and extra helpings (of delicious cafeteria food?!) at lunch. Furthermore, she used brown-eyed students as negative examples when she taught, and she even gave the brown-eyed students misinformation, telling them that the superior intellects of blue-eyed students came from higher levels of melanin in their bodies. Full-grown adults have accepted supposed biological realities about race on thinner scientific evidence!

The effects of this little experiment were dramatic. Blue-eyed students, in response to their superior position in the classroom, rose to the occasion, becoming bossy and mean-spirited toward their former brown-eyed friends. They completed phonics drills in about half the time it previously took them. "The very first day I taught the lesson," Elliott recalled, "it seemed to me that students in the so-called 'superior' group were performing academically in ways that would have been impossible for them the day before."[12] In contrast, brown-eyed students became timid and subservient, and they scored poorly on tests. They also isolated themselves on the playground during recess. The next week, Elliott reversed the experiment, privileging the brown-eyed students.

10. Gergen, *Relational Being*, 16.
11. Peters, *Eye of the Storm*.
12. Peters, *Class Divided*, 108.

While she did witness some of the behaviors present in the first iteration of the exercise, the effect was much less intense (probably because the original experiment sensitized the children to what was going on).

If a teacher, in the space of one day, can cultivate stranger identities among groups of students who had been friends in an elementary school classroom, and if group identity can be established with such trivial criteria, how much more do *we* fortify our important identities by pushing strangers out of our various playgrounds? This same process, so decisively demonstrated by Elliott in her effort to help White students understand racism and discrimination, operates simultaneously on many identity fronts in our lives. The stranger phenomenon occurs at international levels, where nations jockey for superior position (just think about the rhetoric of war continually bouncing back and forth between the US and North Korea). It happens in schools. It happens among groups defined by race and social class. And it happens in churches. The Sunday after the Supreme Court decision about gay marriage, I attended an adult Sunday school class. I don't recall the subject of the lesson, but we were talking about the implications of the court's decision. As I listened, I heard comments like the following: "Before you know it *they'll* be teaching in our schools, and there won't be a thing you can do about it." "I'm so sick of *them* pushing their agenda on us." I was curious about this animosity, so I looked up church signs about LGBTQI+ people[13] and read things like, "Turn or burn," "God is good, gays are bad," "Homosexuals must repent or go to hell," and "God created man & woman; Satan made gays & transgender." These have not a hint of Christian hospitality or neighborliness about them. And to a desperate world, the church can seem fixated on its in-group identity, extending little grace to the strangers nearby. Yet we who were once far away have been brought near (Eph. 2:13). . . . . We who were strangers have been declared sons and daughters.

Inviting Strangers

This book is about learning to see "strangers" in new ways and, in so doing, to see ourselves with fresh eyes. It's about opening ourselves to strangers—some quite near to us—who we've never before noticed. It's about recognizing the myriad ways our own thirst for identity is slaked by keeping "them" away from "our" drinking fountain. And it's about just how much of the "plastics"

13. The media generally use the now familiar acronym LGBTQ+ to refer to sexual minorities. In this book, on advice from guest author Val Hiebert, I use LGBTQI+, with the "I" representing intersex people who sometimes feel invisible, even in contexts addressing sexual minorities.

still live in us. While we (and I write primarily for people of faith) wrest identity for ourselves through oppositional relationships and social comparison, being heralds of the good news of Jesus Christ requires a different posture toward others and a different basis for identity. The gospel itself is a story of how strangers became neighbors and friends—it's a story culminating in the great wedding feast of the Lamb (Rev. 19:9) to which all who are thirsty are invited (22:17), in a city whose gates are always open (21:25). Imagine that. If we're in the habit of stranger-making, engaging in downward social comparison, and keeping "them" away from "us," we offer but a pale gospel to a desperate and identity-impoverished world. Plus, we'll miss many of the good things that "strange" others can bring into our lives. We are the people of God, not for ourselves but for the world—a world that we must know, love, and nurture. We people of God are exhorted to avoid the "patterns of this world." Finding identity at the expense of others—by making strangers of them, guarding resources for ourselves, and taking the seat of greater honor—is *the* dominant pattern of this world. It's the pattern at work, in sports, in our neighborhoods, in international politics, at church, in school, and just about everywhere else. Opening ourselves to others in new ways can make for a safer and more just world, and it moves us closer to the sort of identities that commend us as the people of God.

In working toward these goals, I will draw on a number of sociological and theological frameworks that illuminate some of the unseen ways we interact as human and social beings. As I bring these frameworks to bear on the myriad ways in which we create and maintain strangers, I hope that they will complement and bring new understanding to some of the things you've already read in the Scriptures. Sociology has some remarkable things to offer the person of faith who looks to the Scriptures for wisdom and illumination. Finally, I hope that by the end of this book you will have learned to recognize some of the ways that we (sometimes intentionally, sometimes inadvertently) push others outside the boundaries of our various worlds, where they remain strangers to us. As you learn to edge toward those who stand outside the bounds of your worlds, I invite you to a new boldness about who you are, as you embrace and embody an identity that is rooted in Christ, worked out among God's people, and lived for the sake of his kingdom. "So then you are no longer strangers and aliens, but you are citizens with the saints and also members of the household of God" (Eph. 2:19).

PART 1

STRANGERS AND SCAPEGOATS IN SOCIOLOGICAL PERSPECTIVE

CHAPTER ONE

CONSTRUCTING IDENTITY

The Self, the Social, and the Stranger

On September 26, 2017, Saudi Arabia's King Salman bin Abdulaziz Al Saud issued an order that opened the way for Saudi women to obtain driver's licenses.[1] This story caught my eye as I sat in my North Georgia home browsing the news. At the time, my wife was in Grand Rapids, Michigan, attending a work-related conference. Two days earlier she'd taken her driver's license, started her car, driven to the airport, and headed out. All on her own! She'll be back tonight, and I don't even have to go to the airport to pick her up as her car is waiting in the long-term parking lot! I should probably buy flowers and show up in baggage claim, but after twenty-five years of marriage, I'm pretty sure she'd rather come home to a clean house and kids who've finished their homework. I better get to work. I can't imagine what life would be like for us—with our three kids and frenetic lifestyle—if she were not able to legally drive a vehicle. Were her license revoked for some reason, my life would become considerably more complicated. It's difficult to imagine what I'd gain from a moratorium on women's driving here in the US.

King Salman's edict leaves many questions. Will women need their husband's (or some other male's) permission to get a license or drive a vehicle? Will women's driving infractions be penalized more harshly than men's? Will social

---

1. Hubbard, "Saudi Arabia Agrees to Let Women Drive."

pressures discouraging women from driving outweigh the potential benefits to them? In 1990, forty-seven Saudi women challenged the ban, whereupon they promptly lost their jobs, were shunned, and were banned from traveling for years. It was challenged again in 2011, when activist Maha al-Qahtani became the first Saudi woman to receive a ticket—but the effort fell apart after a few women were jailed for driving.[2]

The Saudi driving ban and the new order that rescinds it exist in a complex context. When Saudi women get behind the wheel, they do so in a social space where traditional meets modern, religious meets secular, freedom meets restriction, and where even things like driving must be done in compliance with Islamic law. King Salman's decision was backed by a majority of members of the Council of Senior Scholars, Saudi Arabia's highest religious body.[3] Women are allowed to be members of the council, but they must sit in a different room from their male counterparts.[4] No mixing. In this and in so many other dimensions of Saudi life, we see clear boundaries drawn between men and women, insiders and outsiders, actors and those acted on, centrals and marginals. My guess is that even with the license victory, women will still stand in the shadows of Saudi society.

Nonetheless, both Saudi women and other women who posted comments on websites that carried the story see this new direction as a major victory. And it is. They recognize that profound change won't happen overnight, but as one woman, Manal al-Sharif, an activist who has been jailed for driving, stated on Twitter, "Saudi Arabia will never be the same again. The rain begins with a single drop." She also explained that the driving ban's removal is "just the start to end long-standing unjust laws that have always considered Saudi women minors who are not trusted to drive their own destiny."[5]

When activists press for women to access rights and privileges equivalent to those enjoyed by men, they're challenging social arrangements in which some people are insiders and others are outsiders. When one group actively violates or simply ignores the rights of another, often more is going on than simple cruelty or resource guarding. Usually the identity of the dominant group is at stake. Why won't Saudi men allow women to drive? Why can't women sit in the same council room with their male "colleagues"? The basic answer is that, in important ways, Saudi male identity is established and sustained in its contrast with the subordinated and inferior status of women. Humans identify as group members, and a dominant group's identity exists in how it stacks up

2. Kennedy, "Saudi Arabia Says It Will End Ban."
3. Human Rights Watch, "Saudi Arabia."
4. "Women Can Be on Council."
5. Kalin and Paul, "'Rain Begins with a Single Drop.'"

against a relevant subordinated group. In effect, in this and other contexts, a man is a man because he's not at all like a woman. We even learn to refer to men and women as the "opposite" sex. When women's status improves, the distinction between men and women is reduced, and a primal identity threat for males rears its head. Some men feel threatened when women begin to "invade" their turf, especially in cultures that maintain great distinction between men and women. I've heard men talk in derisive tones about the "feminist agenda"—not acknowledging that the so-called feminist agenda is mostly a push for the things men already enjoy. But since men constitute the dominant group, no one speaks of the "masculine" agenda. . . . It's just "normal." Thus for the sake of a positive identity, the male group, Saudi or otherwise, maintains an out-group—a group of female "strangers." If you google pictures of Saudi women driving, you'll see no recognizable faces—they are veiled, hidden, invisible. They're strangers—different, less than, maligned, controlled. And for trying to advance in status and move into the circles where they may be known, they have paid, and will continue to pay, a high price.

It's not just gender identity that functions this way. The driver's license story underscores a process that governs and characterizes interactions between many dominant/subordinate human groups (Black/White, citizen/noncitizen, white-collar/blue-collar, etc.). In short, and as I'll develop presently, we identify as group members, and group identity is established through positive contrast with relevant out-groups. Groups look for, create, and maintain those "less than," and use such oppositional relationships to establish themselves.

Connecting and Disconnecting

Humans are eminently social beings. We spend vast portions of our lives trying to connect with others. In fact, social connection is pretty much the sum of our life's activity. We join clubs and sports teams in school, we marry and have children, we join churches, civic organizations, and bowling leagues. We cultivate followers on Twitter and Instagram. And that's not the half of it. Even when we're alone, we have inner conversations about our relationships. When I'm by myself, I think constantly about my children or my wife, and I wonder what my students thought about my most recent lecture. As I write this chapter, I pause frequently to ask myself how readers will connect to it and thus to me. Even something as mundane as looking in the mirror is done with a view to social comparison—"Mirror, mirror, on the wall, who's the fairest of them all?" In our myriad attempts to connect with others, we're insiders (accepted group members) in some settings and outsiders or "strangers" in others. I've watched my children (and myself on occasion!) fantasize about what it would be like to be a celebrity—a famous musician, actor, or sociologist (one can dream!). We're enchanted with celebrities, in large part because they seem so universally embraced by the people around them. Who doesn't want to have lunch with George Clooney, Julia Roberts, Bono, or Beyoncé? Celebrities always have a place at the table—everyone knows their names. They're insiders. They fit. Conversely, we're frightened of being outcasts, of being shunned, stigmatized, or embarrassed by others—especially groups of others. Many movies aimed at teens develop the theme of fitting in, in one way or another. And we've all been saddened by a story about someone who committed suicide, in part, because they just couldn't connect with others.

Our abiding need to be embraced by the social groups that compose our worlds, and our relentless push to connect, testifies to a fundamental feature of human existence: for us, there is no such thing as "alone." In important ways, we just don't exist apart from others. I'm not saying that we don't go off by ourselves from time to time. Rather, humanness itself is something social. We're always located within a social group, always sustained by the social, and everything that holds value for us is of social origin. Despite our feelings of autonomy and individuality, we humans are the product of relationships (with God, with others), dependent from first to last. In fact, most of our efforts to stand apart, stand alone, distinguish ourselves from others, or achieve independence from those around us have pathological and damaging effects (more on this later). We were made to connect; we were made for fellowship—self *with* others. Alone we are not.

However, we normally think about self and identity in atomistic ways. I just "am." I have my preferences, hopes, fears, doubts, and so on. This sort of thinking envisions the people and groups around me as fundamentally separate from me. I engage with them, but there is a distinct line of separation between "me" and "them." And our (Western) world supports this individualistic view of the self. Our legal system champions the rights of the individual. In school our individual academic achievements are recorded (to the second decimal!) on a report card. When I win the hundred-meter sprint, I stand alone on the podium. This view of the self—the dominant view at present—positions a person against others. And in such a world, the goal of most people becomes social distinction—separating oneself. Accordingly, we try to beat, dominate, control, destroy, and crush many of those who would occupy the sacred space of the self with us. We learn to think of others as opponents because a win for them feels like a loss for us and vice versa. Ever watch the disappointment on the face of an Olympic silver medalist? She failed to stand alone, to set herself apart from others, to be the best in the world. Social psychologists tell us that silver medalists are less satisfied with their performance than athletes who won bronze. Barely missing the distinction of being the best continues to haunt them. Jerry Seinfeld parodies this in a comedic sketch where he explains how we all know the name of the guy who won gold, but silver . . . never heard of him! "What happened? Didn't he hear the gun go off? Forget to tie his shoe?"[6] So much of our world promotes this view of the self—a view where a person's value is found in their ability to disconnect from, to be set apart from, those around them. I win and you lose. Shirl James Hoffman laments that many collegiate sports teams no longer eat lunch with "opposing" teams because seeing other players as friends inhibits the killer spirit that athletes need to crush their opponents on the field—a field where "losing is not an option."[7]

The competitive "I win, you lose" view of humanity is, though it doesn't have to be, fundamental to the way we conceptualize the Western self. A consequence of this way of understanding identity is that we establish ourselves as the antithesis of others, learning to see ourselves favorably in comparison. And efforts at comparison can become ridiculous. In an episode of *Seinfeld*, the character Kramer is found taking karate and dominating in his dojo. When Jerry goes to witness this, he finds Kramer sparring with much younger opponents. Says Jerry, "You're beating up ten-year-olds," poignantly illustrating the absurdity of our compulsion to win, to dominate, and to stand alone.[8]

Social comparison as a means to positive identity is itself rooted in intergroup (between group) dynamics. Social identity theorists (which we'll get into later) explain that we see ourselves as group members (my family, my school, my church, my team) and that group identity is established through favorable comparison with relevant out-groups. So, to be a Presbyterian might not be primarily about a group's commitment to distinctive Presbyterian beliefs as much as it's about theological superiority over, say, Southern Baptists or Roman Catholics. When I was in a graduate program in education administration and taking a course on multiculturalism, we, the students, had the opportunity to invite leaders from our religious communities to serve on a panel. What a great opportunity! Only none of us actually listened to anyone but our own guest on the day of the panel. It was like an athletic contest. We students organized ourselves into little religious communities of two or three, and we rooted for our invited leader. We groaned when one of the infidels made an illogical point, and we grinned when our own saint voiced some unassailable truth. Rather than really learning something about the impressive

---

6. Seinfeld, *I'm Telling You for the Last Time*.
7. Hoffman, *Good Game*, 152–53.
8. Ackerman, *Seinfeld*.

array of religious perspectives represented in the room, we mostly squandered the opportunity, rooting for our champion in a religious tennis match.

Social identity theorists explain that we don't simply "encounter" groups that seem to be inferior to our own; rather, we actively look for them, and when we can't find them, we take measures to construct out-groups. And out-groups are everywhere. Think about the social gulf between men and women, Presbyterians and Baptists, athletes and band nerds, Whites and Blacks, Americans and terrorists, homeschoolers and public school kids, and so on. Witness the reaction of a dominant group when a subordinate group moves ever so slightly in the direction of equality. As we saw in the story about Saudi women and the right to drive, gender functions as a critically important organizing structure. Think about the insult intended when someone describes a man in "feminine" terms. "You throw like a girl" stands as the ultimate insult to a male athlete. The request, "We need a few strong men to carry tables over to the fellowship hall after the service" performs a similar identity function for men, affirming them for their strength in contrast with women who are, ostensibly, weaker. In-group/out-group. And these biased, group-based comparisons take place along every conceivable dimension of human life.

The point is that our identities rest on comparing favorably with out-groups. Who we are and how we see ourselves depends on the presence of strangers, real and implied, in our lives. All of the categories by which we measure our worth—race, gender, social class, education, athletic ability, intelligence, attractiveness, and so on—take on meaning, become valuable, and are maintained through social comparison. And though we might know those who provide our out-group contrast, I'm referring to them as strangers. Strangers, in this sense, are others who we, for one reason or another, push away or hold at arm's length because inviting them into full and equal fellowship would cast doubt on our own fragile identities. Of course, Jesus invited strangers and social pariahs into his inner circle all the time—think here of the woman with the issue of blood, lepers, children, or the woman caught in adultery. Jesus always found identity in something other than out-group comparisons. "Zacchaeus, I'm coming to your house today. You'll be no stranger to me" (Luke 19:5). And the Pharisees were always worried about eating with sinners.

Some strangers are easy to identify. Perhaps "illegal" immigrants come to mind here. "They" take our hard-earned resources, and in our often caustic words about "illegals," we draw attention to our own virtue and worthiness. Increasingly, appealing to a voter constituency depends on vilifying an out-group. "Illegal" immigrants became an identity linchpin in the 2016 US national election. Some strangers are less visible to us because we've accepted social distance from them as a normal part of everyday life. Gender provides a good example of "familiar" strangers. A wife, for example, can be stranger to her husband when her assumed inferiority augments his identity.

The rest of this chapter will examine some ways that our identities are inseparable from the groups we are members of. As we explore this, we will focus on the destructive character of an ethic of individualism that establishes identity on the basis of disconnection from others. The last part of the chapter will provide an overview of German sociologist Georg Simmel's now classic treatise on the stranger. Simmel helps us understand just where strangers "fit" in the context of a group, and he draws attention to the benefits that accompany the stranger.

Let Me Introduce Myself

Next time you're asked to introduce yourself, try the following: In your introduction, make no reference to any groups in which you hold membership. Just talk about yourself. Try it! You'll find this quite impossible, and the results will be puzzling to your audience. Since you can't talk about your family, school, a football team you love, a church, or a nation to which you're loyal, you'll be reduced to identifying a few idiosyncratic quirks, such as "I like pizza." And then it will dawn on you, as your sociological instincts kick in, that liking pizza isn't something that originated inside of you. Rather, it began in the groups (your family, youth groups, etc.) where you learned to like pizza—groups that also instructed you about which foods to regard as disgusting.

Then start over and introduce yourself again but with one difference. This time, refer to any groups you wish—no restrictions. Now you can talk about your family, school, church, a person you're in love with, the Chicago Cubs, and so on. Notice how, in the absence of group ties, you were hard pressed to explain who "you" were. Also notice that outside of referring to groups, you really can't talk about what you love. To know yourself is to locate yourself within the boundaries of a variety of social groups, and to love something or someone is to locate yourself in culture and tradition. Even the enjoyment we have of certain objects (I have a motorcycle of which I'm quite fond) derives from their cultural history, from their place in traditions that have given them value. And, of course, "tradition" is a by-product of a group. In an important way, there is no "you" outside of engagement with and immersion in groups. Groups create you; groups sustain you. It's fascinating that in a culture that so highly prizes individualism (I write as an American here), it is through groups that we establish and maintain identity. To stand alone, apart from others, is to have nothing and to be nothing. Having money, enjoying social position or success, and possessing impressive talent, strength, or striking good looks all derive their value from groups—from relationships. What's the point in being really good looking if there's no one to admire you?!

Social groups predate us (we're born into them) and will be there long after we're gone. Sociologists like to point out that humans, as social beings, are more reflective of things outside us than inside us. Accordingly, much sociology is focused on how group bonds that are too weak or too strong can have negative and pathological effects on people. When they're too weak, we have difficulty knowing who we are—think about how your identity is rooted in a family, a marriage, a workplace, a soccer team. Take away a person's job and the previously attempted introductions become a bit more difficult—consider how quickly people ask each other what they do for a living. And on the opposite end of the spectrum, when group ties are too strong—like in a cult—we lose our identities as individuals, as the collective overwhelms any sense of the importance of self. In short, personal identity is a function of a tenuous balance between the group and the individual. And viewed sociologically, individual identity proceeds from the group, not the group from the individual.

We spend vast portions of our lives asking the simple question, "Who am I?" Liminal points in life—those murky, in-between places where we transition to new identities—generally move us to ponder who we are. Going off to college, getting married, having a child, tackling a new career, having your last child leave home, or learning to function with a newly diagnosed chronic illness all compel us to pause and ponder our identities. "Who am I, and what do these changes in my life mean for the person I am becoming?" And the above list contains pretty normal things that many, if not most, people go through. You can, undoubtedly, think of other identity markers I haven't noted. Look at my short list again. What is common to these transitional experiences? They all demarcate a change in the individual's stance within, or in relationship to, one group or another. For example, think about a student leaving home to go off to college for the first time—something I observe each year in my role as a college professor. From the moment (usually one anticipated for some time) that their parents drop them off in front of their new dormitory, peel out of the parking lot, and head home to convert the empty bedroom into a reading room, a new college student is thrust, very suddenly, into crisis as the identity he or she built over the past eighteen years shudders and buckles. Familiar worlds fall away. Former restrictions like curfews simply vanish. Don't want to get up in the morning? Then don't! Exciting? Yes and no. We humans don't deal well with rapid change. A change in our fortunes, whether it's a good change or a bad change, can upset our equilibrium, sometimes quite severely.

Why? Again, it goes back to our relationship with the familiar groups that structure our world. Fast-paced change upsets, obliterates, strains, and alters our ties to the groups in which we are members, thwarting predictability. Going off to college, which may turn out to be a very good thing for a person, severs old ties (not permanently, but fairly radically nonetheless) and initiates new ones almost overnight. There's little transition and little space to regain balance. And abrupt transitions can overwhelm us. Accordingly, it's not at all unusual to find depression and homesickness lurking just behind the "Isn't this great?" façade of the new college student. By second semester, generally, relationships are established, and identity is again secure, albeit an identity that is different from before.

Winning the Lotto, Losing Yourself

The life stories of lottery winners provide interesting, yet unsettling, examples of how rapid changes in someone's relationship to a group can have detrimental effects on their life. Wouldn't you like to win the lottery? Who hasn't fantasized about that a time or two? Wouldn't your problems just evaporate? Well . . . probably not. In fact, the suicide rate for lottery winners is significantly higher than the rate for the general US population. And this seems strange. But think about what winning an impressive amount of money would do to your life. It would change everything—and not necessarily for the better.

On August 23, 2017, Mavis Wanczyk won the $758.7 million Powerball jackpot—the largest single lottery jackpot in history.[9] Wow! The first thing fifty-three-year-old Mavis did was to quit her job—not an unusual move among big lottery winners. Remember the old Johnny Paycheck song "Take This Job and Shove It"? Who wouldn't quit their job? Even if Mavis had wanted to remain in her present employment, it would be all but impossible. How would she take direction or orders from a boss who could no longer hold a paycheck over her? Where would the motivation to show up at 8 a.m. come from? But the important thing to notice is that abruptly quitting a job severs ties to a group that has, for better or worse, structured one's life. And that's only the beginning. All of the groups and people that formerly had regulatory power over Mavis now have no influence at all. And while that sounds great, think about how much of our lives are lived amid negotiating with others. Our lives exist in the midst of the mundane. Émile Durkheim, a French sociologist who lived from 1858–1917, saw the group (or the social) as producing the individual, not the other way around. Seen this way, society gives birth to you, rather

9. Isidore and Kaufman, "We Have a Powerball Winner!"

than you to society. To be cut off from society (or from community) and free from social restraints is like being a child with no parents or family. Though a child may feel constricted by the rules enforced by their parents, what may feel coercive is necessary if they are to flourish. "For Durkheim, freedom came from without rather than from within."[10] We are most content when we are most bound to (and restrained by) the groups around us.

I conduct a simple exercise with freshman college students in my Principles of Sociology class that requires them to respond to such a scenario. Imagine you've won $100 million (pocket change for Mavis Wanczyk!). Where would you live? How much would your house cost? Would you stay in college? This college? Would you tithe at your church? Would you give money to your parents? What about to the uninsured family of one of your dorm-mates whose mother was just diagnosed with an aggressive cancer? Who would you not give money to? What kind of car would you buy? (You'd be surprised how often I hear "Honda Civic" in response to this question.) Would you travel? Commercial or chartered flights? Where would it all stop?

Now, these all sound like great problems to have. Who wouldn't want the "burden" of giving money to friends and family, or the freedom to quit a tedious job? It's the American dream, is it not? But think again. Winning a lottery would disrupt all of the settled patterns in your life. When I ask my students various questions about what would change in their lives if they won a huge lottery jackpot, I almost always find that they intend to live about the same lives, with the same relationships, but with more money stirred in. And that simply wouldn't happen. Winning a lottery would profoundly change the character of a person's relationship to almost all the groups of which they are members. For example, think about church. Would you tithe (or give any percentage) on $100 million? What if you didn't? What if you gave what you give now? Wouldn't that raise a few eyebrows? The point is that your relationship with your church (or your college, family, friends, significant other, soccer team, workplace, or . . .) would change whether you liked it or not because $100 million makes all your relationships negotiable. It weakens your ties to the groups presently constraining you. Must you listen to your parents when you have that kind of coin? Only if you want to. Do you put up with a boss who doesn't seem to respect you or treat you well? Probably not. And whenever there was romantic attraction between you and another, you would always have that nagging question about love and money. Because you aren't just you when you have $100 million. But oddly, it's not having the money that would push you to the breaking point; it's the speed at which

10. Ritzer, *Sociological Theory*, 99.

you came into the money. Earn that money slowly, over forty years or so, and you have a much better chance at maintaining equilibrium. Win it overnight and you don't have time to adjust to the changes in your relationships with other people. And huge money won overnight separates us from others in profound and unseen ways. In effect, winning the lottery pushes the people around us outward toward the "stranger" end of the human spectrum. The dismal statistics on lottery winners testify to what happens when the bonds that tie us to others are abruptly loosened.

Simmel's Stranger

Imagine living in a really close-knit community. In this place almost everyone would be familiar. Other community members would know most things about you, and for the most part you would feel safe. Life in such a place would be fairly predictable, and you would feel included and needed by the people around you. Sound good? We're drawn to scenarios that feel familiar and nostalgic. I think this is the reason that television programs like *The Andy Griffith Show*, *The Jeffersons*, *Cheers*, *Friends*, and *Saved by the Bell* can still be found in syndication or on streaming services years after they've ended. Though they appeal to different demographics, they offer a safe respite from a world where strangers press in. *Cheers*, which ran for eleven seasons and revolves around people who frequent the same bar in Boston, features the theme song, "Where Everybody Knows Your Name."[11] This bar is a place without strangers, where almost everyone's a friend or a neighbor. In the twenty-first century, where it sometimes seems like everyone's a stranger, escaping into a thirty-minute program where we can live vicariously among friends and neighbors for a bit is a welcome relief.

But what would a place with no strangers be like? Would it really be a good place to live? Also, do you ever wish that you were, even for a short time, in a place where *you* were the stranger—where not everyone knew you? Of course there's the other extreme as well. Some people live in places where everyone's a stranger to them. David Riesman's famous book *The Lonely Crowd* gets at this idea of being lonely while surrounded by people—by strangers.[12] And German sociologist Georg Simmel, who we'll encounter presently, writes, "Under certain circumstances, one never feels as lonely and as deserted as in this metropolitan crush of persons."[13]

11. Burrows, Ratzenberger, and Beren, *Cheers*.
12. Riesman, *Lonely Crowd*.
13. Simmel, *On Individuality and Social Forms*, 334.

Strangers present a difficult conundrum for us. On the one hand, they pose a threat. They may intrude on our safety, but perhaps more unsettling, they can weaken our solidarity, bringing new, unwelcome, and destabilizing ideas into "our" midst, forcing us to reconsider who we are, how we act, how we live. Think about Harrison Ford's character—detective John Book—in the 1985 movie *Witness*.[14] To protect a young Amish boy who has witnessed a murder, Book moves into an Amish community with the boy and his widowed mother. Though Officer Book is there to protect the boy from police corruption, as a stranger in town he represents a serious threat to the Amish and their countercultural way of life. Before long he's romantically inclined toward the boy's mother, getting in fistfights with other outsiders who bully the community members (strict adherents to a doctrine of nonviolence), and bringing guns into the settlement. As a stranger, John Book, with his modern, worldly ways and attitudes, is perhaps a greater threat to the Amish than the original threat against the young boy. For his ways can undo their ways. His ways raise difficult questions. His ways make their ways look quaint and ineffective. Their orthodoxy is not his orthodoxy, and he erodes the plausibility structures that support their way of life. In the movie, leaders of the Amish community want nothing more than for Book to leave them so they can go back to the way things were. Saving them from threat? He is the threat!

On the other hand, don't we want to live in a world that's welcoming to strangers and that sees a benefit to including outsiders? It's an ugly thing when wealthy countries refuse to admit desperate refugees fleeing persecution. And isn't it refreshing, every so often, to take on the role and persona of the stranger ourselves? After attending a small (first through eighth grades in two classrooms) elementary school, a Christian high school of around 120 students, and a Christian college that matriculated about five hundred students a year by the time I graduated, I was glad to be on the huge campus of the University of Tennessee at Knoxville for graduate school. The anonymity felt wonderful. It was good to be the stranger, the outsider. The experience was freeing, and I felt like I could think clearly and without restriction or public commitment to "our" worldview.

I visited a "no strangers" community a few years ago during an outing for an annual Christian sociology conference I attend. Our midwestern host college set up a visit to a nearby Hutterite colony. The Hutterites are an Anabaptist group (an offshoot of Protestantism coming out of the Radical Reformation of the sixteenth century), similar in a number of ways to the Amish and the Mennonites but with several important distinctions. To the naive

14. Weir, *Witness*.

observer, Hutterites look like the Amish, wearing simple, handmade clothes, with women always in long dresses and donning head coverings. One of the key differences between the Amish and the Hutterites is that the Amish shun most technology but live out "in the world," while the Hutterites selectively use much of the technology you find in the outside modern world (albeit in heavily filtered ways) but sequester themselves in colonies, away from secular society. In a way, the groups simply choose different modes of sequestration.

These differences between how the Amish and the Hutterites position themselves relative to the modern world significantly affect the posture each group takes toward strangers. Many of the Amish feel called by God to take in any needy person who comes to them for help. On the way to the Hutterite colony, we visited several Amish homes, where we were able to ask questions and talk with families. In one of these homes, there were non-Amish adults who had varying degrees of intellectual disability or some form of mental illness. Our Amish host explained that when people show up looking for help, they simply take them in, out of obedience to God's call to care for those (strangers) in need. The Hutterites, in contrast, were less likely to have strangers show up on their doorstep, mostly owing to their geographic distance from other cities and towns and to the gated character of their compounds.

We had to drive quite a distance, down long, straight gravel roads, to find the Hutterite colony we were to visit. And the community we visited was definitely gated—in both physical and symbolic ways. Being far away from any city, store, or neighborhood is itself a kind of gate. Upon arrival we were met by our host, who handed us off to a small group of charming young women (somewhere around age nineteen or twenty), clothed in long dresses they had sewn themselves, who led us on a tour of their facilities. Different from what I expected, this colony made its livelihood from an impressive, highly technological, and fully automated agribusiness turkey farm—didn't see that coming! We got to walk through the barns and see and hear about their various operations. Everything was clean and well organized—well, as clean as ten thousand turkeys can be!

Lunch consisted of grilled hamburgers from home-grown beef, on home-made rolls—it was really good food. As we finished our lunch and completed the tour, I remember a warm feeling about the place. It felt good. It seemed to be the sort of arrangement that we envision when we say things like, "We need more community in our lives." People were closely bonded, life was simple, and the path forward was clear. While we were there, we saw several teenage girls proudly wearing brightly colored Crocs (inexpensive molded shoes) and chatting excitedly about their recent acquisitions. Inquiring, we learned that girls were permitted to leave the colony only about twice a year—and one of those outings was for shoe shopping. This colony did not permit girls to get driver's licenses or leave the compound without preapproved male accompaniment. The group was governed by a minister and a business manager—both men. Furthermore, everyone—some eighty people—in this colony had the same last name, and we glimpsed some evidence of the genetic anomalies that can enter into closed societies with a narrow gene pool.

Nonetheless, I concluded the tour with a positive feeling about this "traditional" community, its simplicity, and its care for its members. It wasn't what I'd want for my own life, but it did have a certain appeal. As we boarded our van and drove back to the college to resume our hectic modern lives, we chatted about our outing. Many of my colleagues shared my cozy feelings about how the colony resonated with warmth and respite from the pressures of the modern world. But one woman in our group—a long-term and well-respected member—emerged from the experience livid with anger. She reminded the rest of us sociologists that social environments that prevent people from accessing the "outside" world, that keep them wholly bound up in the insular group, and that prevent others from entering in are dangerous and produce fertile conditions for abuse. And we should have recognized this. For girls and women to be denied the agency afforded by a driver's license, for them to be required to gain prior male approval to seek help (medical or otherwise), and for them to have no formal or powerful role in decision-making is a formula for oppression and abuse. A community without strangers is a dangerous community. When no stranger is permitted in to inspect, observe, advise, or protect, low-status people in "closed" and gated communities are at risk. Strangers provide something essential for a community, whether in the form of police, medical personnel, guidance counselors in high schools, or peers working teen-help hotlines. Just think about how important it is that your doctor—the person who asks you to take off your clothes and put on one of those paper gowns with no back—*shouldn't* be someone in your circle of familiars! And the thing strangers provide is precisely what Georg Simmel develops in a famous sociological essay titled "The Stranger."[15]

Simmel was a German social philosopher who lived from 1858 to 1918. He was interested in the ways that society exists as a number of "social forms" that develop as humans interact with each other. Once established, these social forms exert influence over the individuals who inhabit them. In other words, we humans develop various patterns (which become our institutions), and those patterns or institutions then act back on us in controlling ways. Examples include family, fashion, education, and religion. Simmel wrote on

15. Simmel, *On Individuality and Social Forms*, 143–49.

a diverse array of topics, and his most important insights center on the inevitable and necessary conflict between the individual and society, or "the group." He was most interested in the contradictions that existed within, yet also formed the basis for, particular forms of social life. For example, if individual motivations are at the root of most of our social interactions, and if such individualism is of paramount importance, how is society even possible?

Simmel's now famous excursus develops a typology of the stranger as an individual who is simultaneously an insider and an outsider to the group in which he or she stands. Here's an example: In the sociology department where I teach, every ten years we are required to invite a sociologist from outside our college to visit us to conduct a comprehensive review of our program. When we invited such a person about five years ago, he came in and spent three or four days at our college. He attended sociology classes, taught a class or two himself, met with administrators, had lunch with students and local alumni, and so on. Why do we do this? Well, for one reason, we are required to do it as a stipulation of our accreditation. But another, more important reason is that it has potential to give us insight into what we are doing—insight that we can't obtain on our own. I graduated from the college in which I now teach. If people like me run around evaluating the effectiveness of our programs, we will overlook important things because we lack the capacity to be truly objective. An outside reviewer has no (or few) preexisting allegiances to the college or our sociology program, and thus can help us insiders begin to see our blind spots. Here's the other thing: As this outside reviewer interviewed me (which he did quite extensively), I found myself opening up to him, telling him things that I might not have told my colleagues, and certainly not my administrators. To an outside reviewer—a stranger—with little or no permanent ties to our community, I could reveal my misgivings, places where I questioned parts of our orthodoxy, areas in which I felt inadequate. And he could advise me. Save for the stranger coming into my world, I would have kept my less-than-orthodox thoughts to myself. And in the end, while some of the reviewer's conclusions prodded a few of our beloved ideas, we gained valuable perspective on ourselves and avoided the easily indulged, group-based tendency toward self-congratulation.

Simmel recognizes the stranger not as idiosyncratic and trivial but as an important feature of a group. The stranger occupies a particular position in a group's structure. The strangers that Simmel are concerned with are those who come into a group and stay for a while—not just those passing through who have a cup of coffee and move on. Such strangers are "fixed" within the group but not fully committed to it. They have the potential to move on but haven't done so. Simmel writes, "[The stranger] is, so to speak, the potential wanderer: although he has not moved on, he has not quite overcome the freedom of coming and going. He is fixed within a particular spatial group, or within a group whose boundaries are similar to spatial boundaries. But his position in this group is determined, essentially, by the fact that he has not belonged to it from the beginning, that he imports qualities into it, which do not and cannot stem from the group itself."[16] This last part is important. The stranger can offer group members something they cannot acquire on their own. That something is perspective, or objectivity.

Strangers of the sort Simmel writes about are both far and near to those in the group, allowing them to be more objective. As Simmel says, the stranger "is not radically committed to the unique ingredients and peculiar tendencies of the group, and therefore approaches them with the specific attitude of 'objectivity.'" Simmel provides an example of how it was common in his day for some Italian cities to call their judges from the outside, "because no native was free from entanglement in family and party interests."[17] Makes sense. We do this sort of thing when we make sure that potential jury members have no ties to or prejudices about the person on trial. Furthermore, Simmel explains, such objectivity can be seen as a kind of freedom in that the stranger isn't constrained by the group's particular prejudices and consequently is free to offer an honest opinion on some matter. The stranger owes the group no loyalty to their particular ways of thinking and being. In this way, though not something Simmel mentions, the stranger is more prophet than priest.

Consider the Old Testament prophets. They were frequently (though not always) positioned as strangers to the Israelites—they were coming from the outside and were not usually involved in the day-to-day life of the group. Lacking intimate ties to the group, they could bring a word from the Lord—often a critical word that suggested (or commanded) that the group change its ways or prepare for the consequences. The prophets, partly enabled by their status as outsiders, owed no allegiance to the patterns, loyalties, or shibboleths of the group. For example, the prophet Amos, an outsider who lived in Judah, came to pronounce God's judgment on Israel (the Northern Kingdom). Speaking for the Lord, Amos says

> I hate, I despise your festivals,
>   and I take no delight in your solemn assemblies.
> Even through you offer me your burnt offerings and grain offerings,
>   I will not accept them;
> and the offerings of well-being of your fatted animals
>   I will not look upon. (Amos 5:21–22)

16. Farganis, "Georg Simmel," 138.
17. Farganis, "Georg Simmel," 139.

Note Amos's lack of concern for the ways of life that the Israelites have come to adopt and value. He has no entrenchment with the group (Israelites) or attachment to their ways that would prevent him from delivering to them a stern warning from the Lord. Because of his unique position as a stranger on the margins of the group, Amos, like other biblical prophets, could offer valuable insight to the people he addressed—insight unencumbered by material interests and other entanglements that might distort the counsel offered by an insider.

Whether in reference to Old Testament prophets like Amos or prophetic voices that address us today, Simmel's work can help us better understand just how important strangers are to the proper functioning of a group. Accordingly, we should more readily notice when a group has excluded (consciously or otherwise) outsiders from entering group life in meaningful ways. Consider how insular and self-referential churches, governments, colleges, political parties, and armies can become when no stranger is permitted input. How can denominations have their perspective challenged if all theological judgments are made by religious insiders who derive material and social benefits from their monopolies? What happens when a nation permits no other nation to offer outside perspective? And so on. Simmel reminds us not to discount the stranger. For where there are no strangers, there is no prophetic voice. And where the prophets have been excluded, there is no justice.

CHAPTER TWO

A STRANGER WORLD

In-Groups, Out-Groups, and the Space Between

Early in my career as a professor, in addition to my full-time duties teaching sociology, I taught adjunct evening classes for the adult degree-completion program (DCP). Most students in this program were working adults between the ages of twenty-five and sixty-five, with an average student age of thirty-eight. At the time, I was newly credentialed and fairly young—perhaps twenty-nine or so. Though enthusiastic about teaching, I wasn't having much success with these adult students. I couldn't always put my finger on it, but I frequently had the feeling that they were resisting me—that we weren't on the same page. At the same time, I was having a fair bit of success in the traditional classroom where I worked with nineteen-year-old undergraduates, who appreciated my jokes, complied with my directions, and generally followed my lead.

One time a male student in his mid-fifties went to the director of the DCP to take issue with one of my assignments. The assignment required that he address an interpersonal conflict at work using some of the theories and approaches we'd learned in the classroom. He just didn't want to do that. And that's a pretty reasonable thing to want to avoid—who wouldn't? After their meeting, the DCP director explained to me that he heard something more than simple concern over an assignment in the subtext of the student's concerns. There was something more personal, something relational, something between us.

As the next couple of years clipped by and I gained more teaching experience, I continued to feel just a little off with some of the adult students. One day it dawned on me that the ever-so-slight tension I felt with the adult students had little to do with my assignments and quite a bit to do with me—or rather with what I represented. Look at it this way: Imagine that you went to a community college and got an associate's degree when you were nineteen or twenty. Following that, you got a job with, say, Blue Cross Blue Shield, a large insurance company in town. Thirty years ago there was far less pressure than there is now to get a bachelor's degree in order to keep your job or advance in an organization. But as the years passed, bachelor's degrees became prerequisite to having a job at all. And you didn't have one. Eventually, at age fifty or so, you're being managed by some twenty-three-year-old upstart who managed to get an MBA—someone young enough to be your own child! Someone who could fire you for not being qualified. What would that feel like? How would you continue to see yourself as valued and as valuable in your organization? So you go back to school, and your professor is some newly credentialed "kid" who thinks he's hot stuff and who tries to make you perform academic tasks that seem a bit intrusive. Get the picture? I, the young professor, was not "one of them." I was a member of a completely different group—an out-group. Not only was I a humbling presence in their lives—I had degrees, they didn't—I also had coercive power to direct and control them. I could even delay them from attaining their goals.

So I tried something. I created a new out-group with the goal of deflecting student angst away from me and onto something else. With a new class, I entered the room, introduced myself, and then said something like the following:

> Hi. I'll be your instructor for this research class. As we get started, let me tell you why I like teaching DCP students. It's because you know a lot of stuff, and I always come away having learned something myself. When I'm not in the classroom with you people, I'm teaching youngsters up at the college. They're great people, but bless their hearts, the research projects they choose are always pretty much the same. They like to write about relationships. And that's about it. They just don't have life experience that goes much beyond their parents' home, their time in school, or maybe playing sports. You folks do. One time one of my DCP students who worked with the Life-Force helicopter program at the big hospital here in town used his research project as the basis for a grant proposal, and he secured a $500,000 grant that was used to outfit the helicopters and hospital with new GPS based technology that allowed them to fly under low-visibility circumstances. This resulted in far fewer incomplete flights and more trauma victims actually making it to the hospital. A DCP research project that continues to save lives. Isn't that something?! Pretty cool to be involved with that as an instructor.

Another of your fellow students worked as a nurse at a nearby OB-GYN clinic that served Hispanic women who didn't speak English. She noticed that the nursing staff seemed somewhat biased against Spanish-speaking people. Think about this—the women come to this facility for the most intrusive of medical treatments. Many of them, according to this student, suffered from advanced conditions because they had waited far too long to make an appointment—a consequence of the language barrier and the challenges of navigating an English-speaking culture. And in a context where those in authority seemed prejudiced against them, they may not have felt safe or welcome. But they had few other choices. So they endured it because they had to. For her DCP project, this student researched prejudice and discrimination in medical settings, administered a questionnaire to the clinic staff, and identified a measure of prejudice against the women they served. In her project recommendations, she suggested that they hire at least two bilingual nurses. She gained administrative support for this, and the clinic implemented her recommendation. What a great thing! A DCP research project that protected very vulnerable people and perhaps saved lives along the way.

I just don't get projects like this from my nineteen-year-old undergrads. And while I learn something from just about every DCP project I'm involved with, it's pretty rare that I take away something like this from my younger students. They're great folks, but they're young. . . . What they know is quite limited. Not so with you folks. Every one of you has the ability to come up with a project topic that will demonstrate your depth of experience. And when you've finished your research, you'll have something you can really be proud of. And I'll have learned something interesting along the way! And that's why I keep teaching in this program. Let's begin.

Using this new approach, occasionally varying the research topics I talked about and tailoring it for different student groups, I found the results nothing short of astonishing. Praising and admiring a group of adult students while denigrating an out-group (my younger, less experienced students) recategorized me as a kind of honorary in-group member. I was still different from them. I still had a couple of advanced degrees and they had their associate's, but we were all in the category of adult students, and I had helped transform that identity from something to be ashamed of to something that held value. As the leader, I had privileged their in-group. By the end of my opening-night monologue, I was one of the group, and we were a "we." Once the identity threat that stood in their way dissolved, we could get on with our work and even enjoy it a bit.

Several features of this account merit closer inspection. First, it didn't take much to help the groups think positively about themselves and about my involvement with them. I simply reminded them of the main thing they had going for them—life experience. Second, I created an out-group that they'd never be in contact with—really an out-group that didn't matter much. This wasn't an out-group against which they could retaliate or to whom they could direct threats or insults. This was simply an imagined out-group. They could imagine they were better than their younger, less experienced counterparts, and that edge gave them what they needed to feel good about themselves and about me. And I was no longer the stranger in the group. Things got a lot better.

Minimal Groups, Maximal Strangers

Social psychologists use experiments to try to identify the bare-minimum conditions under which a group will form and then discriminate against another group. This research method, first employed by European social psychologist Henri Tajfel, the founder of social identity theory, is known as the "minimal group paradigm."[1] Before experiments like those conducted by Tajfel, researchers had studied prejudice and discrimination in the context of long-standing groups who were well-known to each other and who were in conflict over scarce resources. In these earlier studies, prejudice and discrimination were the logical result of struggles between established groups—over time, and through prolonged conflict, "we" learn to dislike "them." Discrimination directed against Black people by White people during slavery in the antebellum South provides a good example. However, using the minimal group paradigm, researchers like Tajfel were able to demonstrate that someone didn't have to have a history with, or even prior knowledge of, a group to show in-group favoritism or to voice prejudice and discriminate against an out-group. In fact, an individual might share more features with out-group members than with in-group members and still discriminate against them. In short, people like Tajfel found that when an individual for some reason categorizes him- or herself as a group member, the resultant group, or "social," identity becomes more salient (pronounced, important) for that individual than his or her "personal" identity. Of course, we have all sorts of group affiliations, each of which becomes more or less salient under particular circumstances. For example, I'm a college professor. When I'm making a presentation at the Southern Sociological Society's annual conference, my professor identity is salient and very important to me. If I'm lifting weights in a gym (it could happen!), it may be that my male identity is salient, and the professor identity slides into my cognitive background. Other times, my identity as a father is front and center.

1. Tajfel, Billig, Bundy, and Flament, "Social Categorization."

In some ways, these minimal group experiments simply elaborated ideas explored by earlier researchers. For example, in his 1946 book *Problems in Prejudice*, Eugene Hartley explores prejudice through the lens of what has been called "we/they theory." This theory helps explain the human tendency to accept those who are similar to oneself and to be suspicious of those perceived as different. In his investigation, Hartley adapted the Bogardus Social Distance Scale, an instrument used to measure prejudice against ethnic groups. The original instrument, developed by sociologist Emory Bogardus, asked respondents to think about a person of a different race and then indicate agreement or disagreement with the following statements:

1. Would marry
2. Would have as regular friends
3. Would work beside in an office
4. Would have several families in my neighborhood
5. Would have merely as speaking acquaintances
6. Would have live outside my neighborhood
7. Would have live outside my country[2]

Bogardus instructed that by taking the lowest number checked (agreed with), one can obtain a Group Racial Distance Quotient. So, for example, a Black person who would be willing to *marry* a White person would show less social distance from that racial group than someone who draws the line at number 3, "Would work beside in an office." The scale can be adapted to just about any group—immigrants, gay people, Catholics, and so on.

Using Bogardus's scale, Hartley asked respondents (college students from eight northeastern universities) to evaluate actual racial/ethnic groups.[3] But he also added three fictitious groups into the mix—Danireans, Pireneans, and Wallonians. Oddly, Hartley found a high degree of prejudice against these nonexistent groups—no one wanted to marry a Danirean (would you?)! Nearly three-quarters of respondents who were prejudiced against a specific racial/ethnic group also showed antipathy toward these fabricated minority groups. From these data, Hartley concluded that prejudice is not caused by stereotypes, which are frequently based on rigid and exaggerated images of a category of people, for no stereotypes existed for these made-up groups. Rather, the negative reaction by respondents derived from something far more

2. Bogardus, "Social Distance Scale," 269.
3. Hartley, *Problems in Prejudice*.

trivial—the made-up groups simply sounded "unlike" the respondents. "The name Pireneans sounded more like one of 'them' than one of 'us.'"[4]

Hartley's findings go a long way toward explaining the animosity that some Americans express toward "illegal immigrants." Being both "illegal" and an "immigrant" pits not just one but two identities against any similarity with a "legal American": "I've never met you, but I'm pretty sure I don't like you." These findings also help explain why businesswomen hit the proverbial glass ceiling (to begin with, men and women are conceptualized as the "opposite" sex) and why my Chinese son is fairly regularly teased about his Asian eyes. We are predisposed to dislike those who we perceive as unlike us—whether they are or not.

These findings hold up in experiment after experiment. In fact, psychologists have found that we prefer mirror-image photographs of ourselves more than "regular" photographs.[5] If you place reasonably equivalent pictures of an individual, one of which is in mirror image, before a person and ask which they like most, that person will most likely pick the transposed one. We generally only see ourselves in the mirror and thus "normal" pictures of us are less familiar and different from what we're used to (hair parted on the wrong side, etc.). Have you ever recoiled at the sound of your own voice on a recording? "I sound like that? How embarrassing! I'll never speak again." Our recorded voice doesn't sound like the voice in our head. The familiar is comforting, and we work hard to distance ourselves from the different and the strange(r).

In one minimal group experiment, researchers divided subjects into two groups and led them to believe that their in-group was either similar to or different from them in their beliefs. At the same time, they set up conditions where subjects believed that the out-group held either similar or different beliefs from theirs. They found that subjects showed high levels of in-group favoritism under all conditions—identifying with a group was a powerful motivator. Subjects even favored in-group members who held beliefs at odds with theirs over out-group members who held their same beliefs. Furthermore, personal similarities between in-group and out-group members had no impact at all on the extent to which an in-group would discriminate against an out-group, but in-group similarity produced greater discrimination against an out-group.[6]

In another of these experiments, researchers investigated whether in-group cohesiveness mattered when it came to discriminating against out-groups. And

4. Quoted in Roberts and Yamane, *Religion in Sociological Perspective*, 268.
5. Mita, Dermer, and Knight, "Reversed Facial Images."
6. Tajfel, *Social Identity and Intergroup Relations*, 24.

again, while there were in-group benefits to highly cohesive groups (most of us know what it's like to be with a group that really gets along well and in which members enjoy each other), in-group cohesiveness made no difference at all in how subjects discriminated against out-groups. In-groups discriminated against out-groups simply because they were out-groups.[7]

What do we learn from these rather simplistic experiments? For one thing, they clearly demonstrate the extent to which group identification biases our perceptions. Even when people in our group aren't like us much at all, and when people in our out-groups are very similar to us, we favor our own groups. Irrationally so at times. About minimal group experiments, prominent social identity theorist Michael Hogg writes, "The robust finding is that the mere fact of being categorized as a group member produces ethnocentrism and competitive intergroup behavior."[8]

When I was in college, I attended a church that had an intentional and very effective ministry to young Black men in the inner city. The minister of this church was White, his wife was Black, and together they had an adopted Black son, a biracial son, and a biracial daughter. Once, while volunteering at a youth camp, our minister's wife told me a curious story about her younger, biracial son. To understand the story, you need to have a sense of just how focused this church was on racial integration and on narrowing the social space between Black and White people in their city. They were highly committed to achieving racial integration in the church and in the city. Accordingly, the church and surrounding religious community were strongly committed to racial equality and took great pains to walk the walk in addition to talking the talk. This young boy was the offspring of a White father and Black mother, and he also had a Black adopted older brother, so he was immersed in multiracial situations all the time. But one day while playing at an inner-city park, his mother noticed that he seemed uncomfortable. She asked him what was wrong. And, to her surprise, he replied, "I want to go home. I don't like it here—there's so many Black people." She didn't know whether to be amused or dismayed. "But son, you're Black!" Although this young boy was Black, looked Black, and was immersed in multiracial situations every single day—even in his own family—he saw inner-city Black children as out-group members. Perhaps this was partly because he attended a private Christian school with mostly White teachers and mostly White classmates. Who knows? But, despite his physical similarity to other children in the park, he was not drawn to them. And, oddly, he may have felt much more comfortable at a park

7. Tajfel, *Social Identity and Intergroup Relations*, 24.
8. Hogg, "Social Identity Theory," 6.

filled with middle-class White kids. Recall your own discomfort in situations where you've been thrust into unfamiliar groups. I grew up in Southern Ontario (Canada), and after moving to the American South to attend college, I was surprised by how many people introduced me to Canadians they knew with the assumption that we would get along, like each other, and have much to talk about, *Eh*!

In light of these findings and a host of others like them, John Turner offers the following summary: "We may not form a group with individuals we like so much as like people because they belong to our group."[9] Minimal group findings are both profound in their revelations and frightening in their implications, for "naturally" occurring groups. If it's so easy to bias individuals toward in-groups in experimental situations, leading them to show favoritism to groups with whom they have no history or future, and equally simple to prejudice those individuals against recently constructed out-groups, how difficult must it be to control those tendencies in the more naturally occurring groups that matter in our real lives. We/they tendencies confront us in every social environment we inhabit. They lurk in gender, racial, social class, religious, educational, familial, political, and occupational groups, and a host of others. And the very mechanism that makes groups and communities attractive and comforting is also the mechanism responsible for our prejudices and worst tendencies. For example, we join churches, sink ourselves into the community and fellowship they offer, and then get about the business of denigrating religious groups that aren't like us. The following bit of church humor from comedian Emo Philips illustrates this perfectly:

> Once I saw this guy on a bridge about to jump. I said, "Don't do it!" He said, "Nobody loves me." I said, "God loves you. Do you believe in God?"
>
> He said, "Yes." I said, "Are you a Christian or a Jew?" He said, "A Christian." I said, "Me, too! Protestant or Catholic?" He said, "Protestant." I said, "Me, too! What franchise?" He said, "Baptist." I said, "Me, too! Northern Baptist or Southern Baptist?" He said, "Northern Baptist." I said, "Me, too! Northern Conservative Baptist or Northern Liberal Baptist?"
>
> He said, "Northern Conservative Baptist." I said, "Me, too! Northern Conservative Baptist Great Lakes Region, or Northern Conservative Baptist Eastern Region?" He said, "Northern Conservative Baptist Great Lakes Region." I said, "Me, too!"
>
> "Northern Conservative Baptist Great Lakes Region Council of 1879, or Northern Conservative Baptist Great Lakes Region Council of 1912?" He said,

9. J. Turner, "Towards a Cognitive Redefinition of the Social Group," 25.

"Northern Conservative Baptist Great Lakes Region Council of 1912." I said, "Die, heretic!" And I pushed him over.[10]

We are who we're not. Turner's self-categorization theory (an elaboration of social identity theory) is rooted in our desire to achieve a positive social identity.[11] Identification with a group is the primary means by which we craft a positive identity. Furthermore, intergroup (between group) discrimination on the basis of social categorization (we/they; us/them) appears to be associated with increased self-esteem. The solution is the problem. We feel positive about ourselves through our enmeshment with groups. Sounds good; we talk about the need for community all the time. But it's not so good for subordinated groups or strangers who exist on the periphery of our communities. And, as we'll see in the next chapter, out-grouping and denigrating the stranger are not an acceptable basis for the identity God intends and requires for those who would be known as his people.

Between Worlds: Sociology's "Cake of Custom" and Marginal Man

We might think of sociology as the science of the stranger. How do people become strangers? How is the stranger-status of groups maintained over time? How do people move from being strangers to occupying more desirable parts of the social strata where there are more resources (upward mobility) and opportunity? Accordingly, a great deal of sociological theory can be viewed through the in-group/out-group, we/they "stranger" lens we have been developing. Much of the stratification and many of the problems we see in the social world around us can be reduced to the basic processes illuminated by social identity theory and the minimal group paradigm.

Robert E. Park was an American urban sociologist who played a leading role in the development of the sociology department at the University of Chicago during its 1920s–1930s rise to prominence in American sociology. Park began his career as a journalist and later moved into sociology. It's easy to see how his early journalistic interests and methods influenced his later academic work. As a sociologist, he focused on cities, human ecology, race relations, human migration, social movements, and a host of other similar phenomena. Mid-career (he worked at the University of Chicago from 1914 until 1933) he wrote a now-famous monograph titled "Human Migration and the Marginal Man." In this essay, Park explores the phenomenon of human

10. Philips, "Best God Joke Ever!"
11. J. Turner, *Rediscovering the Social Group*.

migration with an eye on the benefits that immigration and other stranger influxes bring to a host culture.

Park examines how the "cake of custom" is broken when one group enters another through immigration, war, or some other means of cultural infiltration. This cake of custom is a reference to social order—the culture, patterns, cycles, and routines that characterize and regulate a group of people. Park argues that cultures change and advance through contact with strangers and stranger-groups. Without influence from outside the group, culture stagnates and becomes dormant. For example, Park argues, war serves a social function in that it disrupts the settled (and stagnant) routines of a group of people. War puts previously separate people groups into contact, which over time can result in beneficial sharing of knowledge and experience. In effect, war puts a group of people into contact with strangers. In developing this effect of war as a type of migration—and, of course, noting the obvious downside of war—Park cites anthropologist Theodor Waitz, who writes, "Whenever we see a people, of whatever degree of civilization, not living in contact and reciprocal action with others, we shall generally find a certain stagnation, a mental inertness, and a want of activity, which render any change of social and political condition next to impossible. These are, in times of peace, transmitted like an everlasting disease, and war appears then, in spite of what the apostles of peace may say, as a saving angel, who rouses the national spirit, and renders all forces more elastic."[12]

It's frightening to think of war as a "saving angel"! Park notes how Waitz writes of peace and stagnation as a "social disease"—not in the sense that we should avoid peace but rather to point out that society needs some "ferment" in it "to break up stagnation and emancipate the energies of individuals imprisoned within an existing social order."[13] Park continues, "When the traditional organization of society breaks down, as a result of contact and collision with a new invading culture, the effect is, so to speak, to emancipate the individual man. Energies that were formerly controlled by custom and tradition are released."[14] If you read between the lines a bit, you'll see Park drawing attention to the importance of the stranger. Strangers enter a culture through war and through migration. And their presence breaks the cake of custom, cutting through stagnant tradition and stimulating new and innovative ways of thinking and behaving.

The maxim "Christianity flourishes under persecution" reflects the same idea. When Christianity has few strangers to oppose or challenge it, when

12. Quoted in Park, "Human Migration," 884.
13. Park, "Human Migration," 884.
14. Park, "Human Migration," 887.

Christians have erected impermeable boundaries around themselves and their communities, they tend to direct their energies toward maintaining familiar tradition. Without the presence of challengers, of strangers, of those not like-minded, Christianity easily becomes just another formerly sectarian group that hunkers down, congratulates itself, and focuses on boundary maintenance. Jesus's prayer that God the Father enable and protect his followers as they are in the world but not of the world (John 17:14–16) reveals how necessary it is for people of faith to be accessible to those who are not like-minded. God calls the faithful to be separate but not to separate themselves from others. When the stranger cannot enter the community, the community stagnates and withers. This is counterintuitive to how we, people of faith, often think. Oddly, the danger to a community of faith lies as much in keeping people out as in letting them in. Walls, boundaries, and borders are both necessary to distinctive communities and destructive of them. Barricades that prevent strangers of various types (sexual minorities, immigrants, the poor) from entering change the purpose of a community of faith, and not for the better. Without the presence of strangers, people of faith become an end to themselves, doing little more than eating the cake of custom baked from a recipe found in the same cookbook the rest of the world uses. For the people of God to act repulsed or repelled by the stranger, and to take measures to avoid contact, is to forsake the gospel itself, disparaging what it means to be the bearers of God's good news. Under stranger-free conditions, peace can function as the social disease against which Waitz cautioned.

Another noteworthy feature of Park's essay is contained in his description of the "marginal man." The marginal man is, of course, the stranger. Here Park is writing about how the immigrant is caught between worlds. He writes of such a person as having an unstable identity. A recent immigrant has not yet assimilated to patterns of the new world nor completely abandoned those of the old. Immigrants have broken with the old world as an exclusive in-group. However, recent immigrants are strangers to the customs, traditions, and orthodoxies of the new world. Park explains that this produces a kind of spiritual distress—a soul in turmoil. He notes how immigrant autobiographies reflect the tension present in the "divided self," between the old self and the new. Here again we find a resonance with the identity that the Christian is called to take up. The Christian should be a person divided, not in the double-minded sense cautioned against in James 1:8 but in the sense of living in the world but not being of the world. In other words, the follower of Christ is to approach life from two perspectives—as a member of this world but as one not fully committed to its norms and culture. In effect, the Christian is called to function as a stranger in the world, not in the sense of being dissociated from or indifferent to it but in the sense of having perspective on it and resisting full allegiance to it. Groups, Christian or otherwise, need strangers lest they choke on the cake of custom.

The "world" as described in Scripture stands in need of a perspective that only the stranger can offer. When Christians become little more than morally accented versions of the world around them—feasting on the same cake, reveling in the same festivals—their ability to provide an alternative perspective or prophetic voice diminishes. Likewise, when Christians take up the stranger role in the sense of adopting an "otherworldly," this-world-is-not-my-home perspective, turning up their noses at the world's cake and seeing the world as a pollutant, they are equally unable to be bearers of *good news* who offer a new way of seeing. Neither posture—"all in" or "all out"—is of much use. God's people should not simply be fans of the world's dominant patterns. Fans are not strangers; fans are all in. Christians ought not to go to the Super Bowl (a cultural tradition of the dominant culture) as the world does, nor should they refrain from attending it at all. Rather, a measure of spiritual cognitive dissonance must always be present in communities of faith. The Christian, like the immigrant, must always ask what involvement in some behavior means both in terms of this world and in the context of the other world. The people of God are called to be strangers, who, with "in-not-of" the world identities, are able to offer something new, fresh, and nourishing to a world subsisting on moldy cake. Strangers to worldliness, yet strangers for the world.

A Double Consciousness: The Stranger in Sociological Theory

Once you think of sociology as the science of the stranger, the stranger theme comes into focus across the great breadth of sociological theory. For example, the sociology of Karl Marx, a staple in sociological theory books, is rooted in the concept of alienation and the two-class (proletariat and bourgeoisie) economic structure. Marx finds that the class structure (owners and workers) under capitalism produces a number of alienating effects.[15] Under capitalism the worker is alienated from the product he makes, from his fellow workers, from the productive process itself, and from his own human nature. The concept of alienation—of being alien to something—is quite similar to the concept of the stranger. The alien is the stranger. For the most part, Marx's entire sociology rests on this concept. Marx is concerned with the portion of humanity he sees occupying the stranger role, as well as with how people are designated strangers and what structures and forces contribute to

15. Fromm and Bottomore, *Marx's Concept of Man.*

their subordination. Marx's vision for communist society is one where the structures that divide people are removed, people can come into their "true" human nature, and there are no strangers. Utopian? Sure. But note how concern for the stranger lies at the very heart of Marx's writings and vision.

Here's another exploration of the stranger in sociology. French sociologist Pierre Bourdieu's theory shares a number of emphases with Marx, but where Marx saw oppression and alienation as a result of the economic class structure, Bourdieu views culture itself as the arena of alienation and oppression. In his work, Bourdieu develops the concept of cultural capital. For example, I'm a sociology professor. My class or economic position is relatively low compared with, say, that of an investment banker. But, because I hold academic degrees and teach in a college, I'm well positioned to rub shoulders with people who have access to the sort of resources society values. In my various interactions, I learn how to talk, walk, shake hands with, and tell jokes to people who can increase my cultural capital and thus my ability to control and direct resources. In fact, in limited ways, I can pull off being a member of the upper classes if I have to (though I'd probably need new shoes!).

Bourdieu suggests that our class position becomes inscribed on our very bodies. The ways I walk, talk, eat, smile, and drive reflect my position in society. Accordingly, I would have a difficult time fooling people into thinking that I was a member of the urban underclass. If I attempted such a deception, people would quickly see that something was off. Likewise, someone from the urban underclass could not pull off being me. A few people are able to have a foot in both of these groups. For example, I interact in both white-collar/college-educated groups and in blue-collar groups with less formal education. I find it easier and more natural to pull off my role in the white-collar groups—the vocabulary and mannerisms come easily to me because I practice them every day. I can pull off blue collar, but I have to watch my body language and word choices.

People whose arena of interaction is primarily among those who are not in possession of the sort of cultural capital that society values have ways of walking, talking, dressing, eating, and doing their hair inscribed on their bodies. These ways of being prevent them from successfully interacting with people who can help them "get ahead" and move up the social ladder. In fact, because of these kinds of differences, people from the lower classes often shy away from interacting with people with "greater" cultural capital. These habits reinforce cultural stratification in a society. People simply come to embody—in their flesh-and-blood bodies—their class position and remain there. Bourdieu calls this embodied cultural capital, which we internalize and effortlessly act out, the "habitus."[16] The habitus is a major factor in what divides people into familiars and strangers. Come watch me at church and you will see how easily I gravitate toward interacting with my fellow professors—colleagues who share my social class, manner of dress, vocabulary, and life goals. In our clique, we interact with our similar vocabularies, mannerisms, goals, and dislikes—and good luck breaking into our little group!

Marx and Bourdieu are just two examples of how sociological theorists search for and explain the stranger. Though there are dozens more such examples, I conclude this chapter with a brief examination of the work of W. E. B. Du Bois. Du Bois was the first African American to earn a PhD from Harvard University. He finished his PhD work and graduated in 1895, right in the middle of the Jim Crow era—a time when US laws enforcing racial segregation still prevailed (they weren't overturned until 1964, at the beginning of the civil rights movement). As you can imagine, Du Bois knew what it was to be a stranger, and his writing so clearly reflects the tension he felt while living in America. Du Bois's work reads differently from other, more dispassionate and scientific sociology. It resounds with emotion, longing, vision, and a keen sense of the spiritual. In his book *The Souls of Black Folk*, he, referring to the African American experience, poses the question, "How does it feel to be a problem?" He might have substituted the word *stranger* for *problem* with the same effect. In an emotionally moving passage, Du Bois describes an early school experience where he awoke to consciousness of his "strangeness." Listen to the following:

> In a wee wooden schoolhouse, something put it into the boys' and girls' heads to buy gorgeous visiting cards—ten cents a package—and exchange. The exchange was merry, till one girl, a tall newcomer, refused my card—refused it peremptorily, with a glance. Then it dawned upon me with a certain suddenness that I was different from the others; or like mayhap, in heart and life and longing but shut out from their world by a vast veil. I had thereafter no desire to tear down that veil, to creep through; I held all beyond it in common contempt, and lived above it in a region of blue sky and great wandering shadows. That sky was bluest when I could beat my mates at examination-time, or beat them at a foot-race, or even beat their stringy heads. Alas, with all the years all this fine contempt began to fade; for the words I longed for, and all their dazzling opportunities, were theirs, not mine.[17]

This stands as one of the most plaintive laments you'll find in a sociological theory text. Of all the readings my students encounter in their classes with me,

16. Bourdieu, *Distinction*, 169–225.
17. Du Bois, *Souls of Black Folk*, 2.

this is the one that stays with them the most. Our modern equivalent would be the practice of exchanging Valentine's Day cards in elementary school and having your "Be My Valentine!" card rejected . . . with a sneer thrown in for good measure. To be different. To be a stranger. To be outside and marginal. How difficult—especially for a child.

Du Bois goes on to explain how this experience, and doubtless many others like it, shaped his motivations. He writes of being driven by contempt, in hopes of "showing them." He writes of wanting to "beat their stringy heads" in foot races, in his writing, as a lawyer, as a doctor. This diatribe culminates in the "bitter cry," "Why did God make me an outcast and a stranger in mine own house? The shades of the prison-house closed round about us all: walls strait and stubborn to the Whitest, but relentlessly narrow, tall, and unscalable to sons of night who must plod darkly on in resignation, or beat unavailing palms against the stone, or steadily, half hopelessly, watch the streak of blue above."[18]

Further explaining the condition of being a "stranger in mine own house," Du Bois writes the following:

> The Negro is a sort of seventh son, born with a veil, and gifted with second-sight in this American world—a world which yields him no true self-consciousness, but only lets him see himself through the revelation of the other world. It is a peculiar sensation, this double-consciousness, this sense of always looking at one's self through the eyes of others, of measuring one's soul by the tape of a world that looks on in amused contempt and pity. One ever feels his twoness—an American, a Negro; two souls, two thoughts, two unreconciled strivings; two warring ideals in one dark body, whose dogged strength alone keeps it from being torn asunder.[19]

With these words, Du Bois begins to sound like Simmel and Park, two of the sociologists we discussed earlier. As strangers, African Americans have special qualities—qualities that, though very costly for them, are much needed by the culture that excludes them. He refers to the African American as a sort of "seventh son, born with a veil, and gifted with second sight." The "seventh son" is a folk-reference to someone with special powers—a seventh son born to a seventh son in an unbroken line. Likewise, the veil—or "birth caul"—of which Du Bois speaks holds spiritual significance. In some births, the inner fetal membrane tissue doesn't rupture, and it covers the head at delivery. This "caul" appears in about one in one thousand births. Due to its rarity, some traditional cultures consider such a birth spiritually significant, and the caul

18. Du Bois, *Souls of Black Folk*, 2.
19. Du Bois, *Souls of Black Folk*, 2.

is kept for good luck. Finally, "second-sight" is a reference to clairvoyant or prophetic vision.[20]

All of these qualities coalesce in the concept of double consciousness— seeing oneself simultaneously from two perspectives. To be in possession of double consciousness is to be divided, in tension. And for the African American, double consciousness has both constructive and destructive properties. On the destructive end, Du Bois observes how African Americans can internalize self-loathing, as they are continually forced to see themselves from the perspective of the dominant culture. Du Bois was critical of some of the ways that Black people worked to tone down their "Blackness," making themselves more palatable to White culture, as this represents a form of agreement with the dominant group. On the constructive end, African Americans, by virtue of their status as "strangers," offer a critical prophetic voice by which the dominant culture may begin to cast off its "false consciousness" and see themselves and others anew.

Recall Simmel's discussion of the stranger as a specific, positive form of social relation in a group. Strangers possess objectivity that in-group members do not have, and accordingly they are able to offer insight that otherwise eludes the insular group. Recall Park's words about how immigrants or "strangers" bring ferment to a group, breaking the cake of custom. African Americans, with their double consciousness—their simultaneous stance both inside and outside the group—are uniquely positioned to challenge the dominant culture of oppression. Accordingly, Du Bois would not have Black people solve their problem simply by adopting White ways, stating, "He would not bleach his Negro soul in a flood of White Americanism, for he knows that Negro blood has a message for the world. He simply wishes to make it possible for a man to be both a Negro and an American, without being cursed and spit upon by his fellows, without having the doors of Opportunity closed roughly in his face. . . . This, then is the end of his striving: to be a coworker in the kingdom of culture."[21]

The blood of people of color—the blood of strangers—has a message for the world. Without the stranger, a group of people cannot understand who they are. Without the stranger, group identity becomes a fetish—something dry, empty, and destructive. Without the stranger we are condemned to live lives of false consciousness. And blood with a message for the world . . . well, that is something Christians are familiar with.

20. Allan, *Social Lens*, 199.
21. Du Bois, *Souls of Black Folk*, 3.

CHAPTER THREE

NO MORE SCAPEGOATS

A Stranger Theology

The Bible says a great deal about strangers. Once you start to see them, they'll jump off the pages as you read. Sometimes strangers aren't called strangers as such. Instead, they're referred to as aliens, women, lepers, sinners, the poor, tax collectors, unbelievers, immigrants, eunuchs, those possessed by demons, the blind, prostitutes, the lost, gentiles, the uncircumcised, or children. And those are just the obvious ones. It's all but impossible to comprehend the message of the Bible without significant reflection on strangers. Much Christian theology revolves around some understanding of the atonement, which hinges on the idea that "apart from Christ" we remain "strangers to God" (Eph. 2:19). Acts of compassion prescribed in the Bible usually require extending oneself to strangers, and to withhold mercy, resources, or hospitality from a stranger in need is to risk igniting God's wrath. The people of God are to be especially sensitive to strangers who fall outside the protective structures of society. Jesus, for example, has harsh words for Pharisees (religious in-groupers) who make a spectacle of their VIP status through long (and presumably showy) prayers, while devouring widows' (strangers to the realms of power and resources) houses (Matt. 23:14; Mark 12:40; Luke 20:47). Hmm. Best beware if you're acting religious while abusing or neglecting the stranger! In fact, caring for strangers in their various manifestations—the poor, widows, immigrants, orphans—is prerequisite for the sort of worship God accepts. The

New Testament gospel message—the good news about Jesus Christ—is the story of God drawing in strangers. The book of Ephesians, a book written to *gentile* believers, emphasizes reconciliation. In it Paul proclaims, "But now in Christ Jesus you who once were far off have been brought near by the blood of Christ" (Eph. 2:13). You who were strangers need be strangers no more. Christ's unique sacrifice offers humanity the possibility of rooting identity in something other than social comparison, out-groups, and scapegoating.

As you might expect, the focus on strangers begins back in the Old Testament with the story of the "fall" of humankind. That fall from grace—a shattering event rooted in a desire for status and culminating in the man's scapegoating of the woman—propels humanity into an identity crisis that becomes the defining feature of human social existence. After the fall, the people who had enjoyed close camaraderie with their creator and with each other become strangers, both to God and to each other. Since that fall from grace, human beings have struggled with knowing themselves and with being known by others. In effect, our lives typically appear as the working out of identity crises—"Who are we and what will become of us?" Unfortunately, our primary way of addressing these questions is through social comparison, cultivating strangers to whom we compare favorably. I am because you're not. We are because they're not. Such identity issues lie at the heart of racism, sexism, social class bias, and other divisions. Consequently, we live lives of alienation from God, from each other, and from ourselves.

But it doesn't end there. The Bible tells about much more than alienation. It tells a story of God reaching out to reconcile with humanity, to atone for their alienation through Jesus, whose sacrifice offers human beings the possibility of new identities not dependent on scapegoating and social maneuvering. Through Jesus we have the possibility of recoupling with God—of anchoring our identities through a spiritual move the New Testament refers to as being "in Christ." No out-groups, no strangers, no scapegoating. And this is good news—this is the gospel.

This good news is not universally accepted. Human beings go on scapegoating one another, finding ourselves at the expense of strangers. And "identity in Christ" becomes little more than a pithy catchphrase. But it doesn't have to be this way. A big part of being people of God involves imitating God—acting as God acts and loving what God loves. One reading of the Old and New Testaments finds the truest expression of imitating God reflected in how we regard and treat the stranger. And strangers are everywhere. Oddly, one of the greatest barriers preventing churches from caring for strangers may come from the way they construct fellowship. Fellowship, or spiritual camaraderie, is good, but for whom is it fellowship?

Given our tendency toward homophily (birds of a feather), we easily establish boundaries that deter those unlike us (remember the Wallonians?) from approaching and feeling welcome. Such boundaries can be moral (for example, the way "we" talk about sexual minorities), social class–based and evidenced by the cars we drive and the clothes we wear, racial ("wouldn't they prefer to worship with their own people?"), gendered, and so on. Our "fellowship" may deter Christian hospitality and mission. Embracing strangers requires a willingness to accept a measure of *strangerhood* ourselves as we push against in-group bias and work to make fellowship boundaries more permeable. Seeking out and caring for strangers is required by the Old and New Testament Scriptures—to do so is the defining feature of the people of God. Scripture insists that disregarding the stranger is forsaking the worship of God. True worship is to care for widows and orphans (vulnerable strangers in society) in their distress (James 1:27). In the absence of this "stranger ethic," God hates our assemblies, our worship is not accepted as such (e.g., Amos 5:21), and we fall under judgment.

Sociologists like to talk about social location. We all have a physical location, but we also have a position, or location, in the social world. For example, to be a woman is to occupy a lower or lesser social location than a man in most societies. In the US, being Black has historically relegated one to a marginal social location relative to Whites. To be in the upper classes, and thus protected from many of the economic fluctuations that hurt those in the lower classes, is to be in an advantageous social location. Each of these social locations is associated with having more or fewer life chances.

The concept of social location is related to the concept of the stranger in that those in privileged social locations are able to separate themselves from their lower-status counterparts, in effect keeping them as strangers. The rich can live in gated communities inaccessible to the poor and thus not see or feel their suffering. Men can enjoy and reserve for themselves the choice and powerful parts of social institutions, never concerning themselves with how women have to contend with less of most things. White plantation owners in the antebellum South could avoid contact with much of the suffering endured by their Black slaves. And Marie Antoinette could famously say "Let them eat cake" as she looked to her own needs and ignored those with no bread.

The writers of Scripture consistently call those in privileged social locations to be sensitive to those impoverished by their social position. But the call goes beyond mere benevolence. Taken as a whole, the Bible's message is not only to care for the stranger but to love the stranger. As we'll see later in the chapter, loving the stranger is presented in the book of Deuteronomy as an unconditional command, a distinctive ethic required of God's people. It seems that God is pleased when his action toward us is mirrored in our action toward others. God is honored when we seek out, love, and privilege the strangers among us. I delivered you . . . you deliver others. Would we cling to a theology of adoption without participating in the real, flesh-and-blood practice of caring for parentless children (a specific and protected class of strangers in the Bible) ourselves? Would we praise God for his provision and then not provide for the widow on the edge of our community? Apart from such things, our worship is just in-group lip service. Loving the stranger makes it genuine.

In thinking about the stranger as a central figure and social type in the Bible, consider the examples that follow.

The story of Ruth and Naomi is a story about strangers. Ruth is an undocumented immigrant who comes to a new country as an unprotected, powerless, and apparently infertile widow. Boaz, a powerful and prominent man who stands to lose much should he step forward as Ruth's kinsman redeemer, steps back from patriarchal privilege and shows *hesed* (mercy, kindness, loyalty, love) to them, exemplifying what it means to love the stranger.

Jesus creates a great deal of scandal by going out of his way to make contact with strangers. Lepers (the ultimate social pariahs in biblical times), tax collectors ("Zacchaeus, I'm coming to your house today"), the woman caught in adultery ("which of you religious in-groupers wants to cast the first stone?"), eunuchs (a type of intersex person in the Scriptures), the man born blind, the woman with the issue of blood ("who touched me?"), children ("suffer the little children to come unto me"), women (in a highly patriarchal society), the gentile woman at the well (not one but two "stranger" statuses), and the man with the withered hand (clearly a stranger to the Pharisees "fellowshipping" with him in the synagogue) were all strangers who Jesus touched, healed, approved of, acknowledged, affirmed, or stood up for. Jesus also reversed the violence against the Roman soldier whose ear Peter cut off, thus refusing out-group stranger scapegoating even en route to his death.

A number of Jesus's parables explicitly focus on a stranger. The parables of the lost sheep, the prodigal son, the good Samaritan, the persistent widow, the Pharisee and the tax collector, and the sheep and the goats all highlight a stranger as one of their central characters. In the parable of the sheep and the goats in Matthew 25, Jesus makes specific reference to the stranger, saying, "Then the righteous will answer him, 'Lord, when was it that we saw you hungry and gave you food, or thirsty and gave you something to drink? And when was it that we saw you a stranger and welcomed you, or naked and gave you clothing? And when was it that we saw you sick or in prison and visited you?' And the king will answer them, 'Truly I tell you, just as you did it to one of the least of these who are members of my family, you did it to me'" (Matt. 25:37–40). And conversely, "Then he will answer them, 'Truly I tell you, just as you did not do it to one of the least of these, you did not do it to me'" (25:45).

Paul opposed Peter when he required gentile converts (the strangers) to observe in-group Jewish customs such as table regulations. Peter was afraid of what the circumcision party (the Jewish religious in-group) would think and do (Gal. 2:11–14). Paul's ministry was to Jews *and* gentiles (in-groups and stranger groups, a multiracial church), for all are one in Christ Jesus. Paul's inclusive vision for the church is clearly expressed in Galatians 3:26–29: "For in Christ Jesus you are all children of God through faith. As many of you as were baptized into Christ have clothed yourselves with Christ. There is no longer Jew or Greek, there is no longer slave or free, there is no longer male and female; for all of you are one in Christ Jesus. And if you belong to Christ, then you are Abraham's offspring, heirs according to the promise."[1]

In Revelation 21, the New Jerusalem is described as having twelve gates that are never closed—gates that aren't gated, a city with no strangers.

With these images in mind, let's return to the Old Testament to see where this New Testament focus on strangers comes from.

Christian Faith and the Stranger Paradox

Communities are odd things, and religious communities are even odder. On the one hand, the word *community* has a welcoming, "come join us" feel to it. But on the other hand, communities are entities that self-consciously maintain boundaries between themselves and nonmembers. A community that has no boundaries ceases to be one of distinction, while a community with overly rigid and aggressively policed boundaries suggests privilege and exclusivity, and taken to extremes is a cult. Religious communities like churches face the tension inherent in maintaining a distinctive identity while being accessible and welcoming to those who are not like-minded—to strangers. Churches have particular beliefs, moral codes, worldviews, and traditions. They have books of church order that copiously detail their policies, theological positions, disciplinary formulae, and other boundaries. Furthermore, most church congregations like to consider themselves distinct from "the world." These identity markers make for a fairly narrow and selective membership roll. The

---

1. While the NRSV says "You are all children of God through faith," other translations including the pre-2011 NIV, ESV, and NKJV use "sons" rather than "children." Some suggest that this inclusion of women as "sons" of God nullifies patriarchal privilege as holding any currency in the kingdom of Jesus.

temptation to support the in-group (congregation) and to denigrate the out-group (worldly strangers) is formidable. As we saw with the earlier material on the minimal group paradigm, we're all but hardwired to discriminate against out-groups. The paradoxical task to which the people of God are called might be stated as follows: "Do not love the world," yet "Really love the world." What's a church to do?

Many of the terms that Christians use to describe themselves and their activities reflect an outward focus. For example, when churches engage in "ministry," they (ideally) move resources outward to people who are not presently part of their fellowship—to strangers. Though using the word *ministry* to describe activities *within* the congregation is right and proper (after all, churches employ "ministers"), the term is most appropriately applied to efforts the church makes on behalf of others. The body ministers to those not yet a part of it. Likewise, the label "evangelical" describes Christians (and churches) who feel called to tell others, presumably strangers, the good news of Jesus Christ. Evangelicals aren't simply in the business of heralding the good news to fellow believers that they run into in the church foyer. Rather, to introduce oneself as an evangelical Christian (the culture wars notwithstanding) is to identify oneself as an ambassador (one sent as an official representative to a foreign country) for Christ and his kingdom. It makes little sense to consider intra-church activity as evangelical—that interaction is better called "fellowship." Lamentably, the term *evangelical* has picked up so much political baggage that it has become more associated with walls, boundaries, and moral platforms than with heralding the good news. The term *missionary* is another label claimed by Christians that projects a definite outward focus. To embark on a mission is to leave familiar surroundings and people and venture out to "strange" places where one can care for, or minister to, strange(r) people. Finally, the term *witness*—used by Christians as a verb to describe an activity they engage in—makes sense only in the context of strangers. Witnessing for Christ—bearing witness—has little meaning as an activity undertaken between church members. Witnessing, rather, is for the sake of strangers. And witness is mute when accompanied by little love for the stranger.

Outward-focused terms that many Christians use, like *ministry*, *evangelical*, *mission*, and *witness*, reflect identities that are other-oriented, or stranger-oriented. And rightly so. An other-orientation reflects the ethic and heart of God. Accordingly, Christians must not be a people unto themselves. Christians, rather, are an evangelical people—a people who go out of their way to bring good news to strangers.

Why is love and care for the stranger essential to an identity as the people of God? Here's where we go back to the Old Testament. Understanding the origins of the "stranger ethic" requires digging into the Israelites' story from their days as wanderers, to their enslavement and escape from Egypt, to their coming into their identity as the people of God in the Promised Land. Instructions to love the stranger cap off the story and function as the central and distinctive way that the Israelites can remember and honor God's deliverance and provision for them. Consider the exodus . . .

Love the Stranger . . . for You Were Once Strangers

The exodus is a defining story of Jewish identity, told and retold even in the present day. It is a story of deliverance, a story in which slaves are redeemed, identity as the free "people of God" is restored, provision is made, and the future looks good. It is a story that reminds the Jewish people that God had not forgotten them and that God does keep promises. Its significance is expressed in Miriam's song, just after the harrowing experience at the Red Sea:

> Sing to the LORD, for he has triumphed gloriously;
> horse and rider he has thrown into the sea. (Exod. 15:21)

You can find the stranger theme throughout the story. The Israelites were strangers, slaves, subject to oppressive rule, and continually on the low end of social comparison. But God delivered and restored them.

The book of Deuteronomy picks up the story just as the Israelites are poised to move into and take possession of Canaan, the Promised Land. Settling in an unfamiliar land brings new challenges. The Israelites will have to establish new customs, cultural patterns, and ways of relating to others. With a new identity comes the necessity for new ways of living. These new ways of living and this new identity must be grounded in the imitation of the God who delivered them. And so Deuteronomy reiterates the Ten Commandments, states numerous other commands that people of God must observe, reminds them to remain distinct from the nations around them ("Do not intermarry with them . . ."; Deut. 7:3), and warns them not to forget that it was "the LORD" (YHWH) who did all these things; it wasn't you. In addition, Deuteronomy reminds the Israelites that they are not God's people because of some desirable quality they possess—they are not inherently righteous in God's eyes—but because of promises God made to Abraham, Isaac, and Jacob.

In Deuteronomy 10:19 we find an unusual and unconditional command— the Israelites are to love *the stranger*: "You shall also love the stranger, for you were strangers in the land of Egypt." This brief statement summarizes an ethic that must characterize the people of YHWH as they settle into life in the Promised Land and develop norms and customs that reflect their identity and commitment to imitate God. This ethic, inseparable from their identity as the people of God, has two parts. First, they are to *love* the stranger. Fleur Houston explains the significance:

> The transition in Deut. 10:19 to the unconditional command to "love the *ger*" [Hebrew for "stranger"] is as sudden as it is remarkable. The emphasis now is not so much on the poverty and need which the *ger* shares with the fatherless child and widow, as on his particularity as a stranger. As perspective moves from the *ger*-fatherless child-widow in their collective need to the *ger* who is singled out in his distinctiveness, "royal" responsibility extends to the people of Israel. Just as YHWH does justice to the *ger* and loves him, so Israel too must treat the *ger* justly and love him—with the love of Abraham for Isaac, the love of Isaac for Rebekah, the love of Ruth for Naomi, and the steadfast love of God to the thousandth generation of those that love him.[2]

The Israelites are not simply to be hospitable to strangers or to tolerate them; they are to *love* them and for no other reason than that they are strangers. Their obligation to love is not further qualified.

Second, the Israelites are to be people of memory: "For you were strangers in the land of Egypt" (Deut. 10:19b). Being people who imitate God has to mean something. The events of the exodus and the appropriation of the Promised Land must continue to define Israelite identity. For these events to hold meaning, the Israelites must *remember*. To malign or mistreat those who are foreigners or strangers in their new land—when they themselves had suffered and been mistreated while strangers in Egypt—is to disparage YHWH's provision. To act only in collective self-interest, disregarding or even harming the stranger, is to act like the Egyptians had acted. And Israelite identity must be distinct from "Egyptian" identity. Remembering that they "were once strangers" should move the Israelites to treat strangers as YHWH had treated them. To remember is to show gratitude. Thus, loving the stranger both is a defining cultural practice that sets the Israelites apart from "the nations" surrounding it and functions as an act of memory.

And so, loving the stranger becomes the distinctive and defining feature of the people of YHWH. The Christian church is called to intentionally practice an ethic like that. Nonetheless, the natural human tendency, Christian or otherwise, has been to scapegoat the stranger, to preserve "our" collective identity at the expense of the other. It's the wrong sort of other-orientation.

Consider the scapegoat . . .

2. Houston, *You Shall Love the Stranger as Yourself*, 75.

Fifteen Hundred to One: The Simplistic Morality of Slaying a Stranger

At the local Family Tire where I buy tires, the little TV in the corner is always playing some Spaghetti Western. And while I wait, I'm drawn into the drama. Sometimes my car is ready a bit too quickly, so I linger a bit, just to see how it turns out. Part of the appeal of Westerns, I believe, is that they offer moral simplicity in a morally complex world. There seems to be a clear right and a clear wrong. There are good guys and bad guys. And when a fair maiden goes missing, a bad guy is quickly identified, whereupon the outraged community (represented by a posse in Westerns) rises up and hunts him down. And when the body of the transgressor is killed, we're led to believe that justice has been done—that good has triumphed, evil has been vanquished, and the community can again go about their business. Watching these dramas, it can be easy to forget that there was no real investigation and no real trial—just over-the-top retributive violence. We may even experience a little catharsis in the mob violence perpetrated against the one assumed guilty. And we should know better. The basic plot of most Western movies centers on how a community tries to purge itself of evil by unleashing violence on one presumed guilty. Insiders and outsiders. Those who belong; those who don't.

Émile Durkheim writes about something he calls the "collective conscience"—a group's sense of itself.[3] For example, if you're an American, or a "Southern" American, you probably have some sense of what that identity means, even if you can't quite put your finger on it. Durkheim explains that communities in earlier, more traditional societies held together because of the similarity of their members—everyone had a similar sense of the "we." In those societies, someone with a different religion, from a different race, or with a different way of thinking about things was seen as a threat, and the solution to such threats was to purge them so the community could continue. Durkheim calls this form of social organization—that based on sameness— "mechanical solidarity." *Solidarity* is another word for *bond* or *cohesion*, and you can think of *mechanical* as a repetitive, machine-like sameness, like an electric motor that goes around and around and around. This sort of bond stands in contrast with the kind of social bond we see in the pluralistic societies we live in today. Our modern societies are characterized more by interdependence and tolerance of difference than by enforced sameness. Durkheim refers to this more complex, modern form of social organization as "organic" solidarity. "Organic" is a reference to an organism that has many component parts and only holds together if each different part is doing its job. Get rid

3. Durkheim, *Division of Labor in Society*.

of a part because it's different, and the whole thing falls apart. Mechanical solidarity is a stronger and simpler type of community bond, one character- ized by a strong collective conscience. Communities are moral in character (defined by their sense of right and wrong), and a simple, clear morality is easier to wrap our heads around than the kind found in the complex, plural- istic, give-and-take societies we live in nowadays. But in their stark, absolute morality and intolerance of difference, societies characterized by mechanical solidarity easily devolve into mob brutality when threatened by an outsider. Part of the reason that movies (Disney films, for example) can be so exhilarat- ing is that they avoid the moral complexity that we have to deal with in our real, modern lives. We long for simplicity, when all it took to right a wrong was the slaying of an outsider. First-person shooter video games owe much of their popularity to the same sort of ethic and worldview.

Some of the most chilling examples of expunging the outsider for the sake of the collective conscience can be seen in the 4,743 lynchings that took place in the United States between roughly 1882 and 1968. The majority, though not all, of these lynchings were committed against Black people (73 percent).[4] Consider the following example of a lynching that took place some twenty- five minutes from where I live—on the Walnut Street Bridge in Chattanooga, Tennessee.

In 1906, Ed Johnson, a twenty-four-year-old Black man, was lynched on Chattanooga's Walnut Street Bridge for a rape he didn't commit. His alleged victim was a young White woman—nineteen-year-old Nevada Taylor. Johnson was convicted by an all-White jury, despite the fact that Taylor, the victim, couldn't definitively identify him and refused to swear in court that he was her assailant, preferring to state her "belief" that he was her attacker. Taylor lost consciousness during the attack and could only remember that her rapist had been Black, had approached her from behind, and had put a leather strap around her neck. A Black man named James Broaden, who had been seen in the area, was also taken into custody. On the night Johnson was arrested, a mob of fifteen hundred White Chattanoogans gathered around the prison in an attempt to lynch him. Anticipating this, authorities had already moved Johnson to a Nashville prison. The mob in Chattanooga dispersed only after Hamilton County Judge Samuel D. McReynolds, who would later preside over the trial, promised that the legal system would deliver swift justice. After a time, Johnson was returned to Chattanooga to stand trial. Just three days into the proceedings, he was convicted and given the death penalty. His public defenders did not file an appeal, thinking that it probably wouldn't do any

4. NAACP, "History of Lynching in America."

good anyway and would cause a major disruption in Chattanooga, given the widespread animosity against Johnson.[5]

Two local Black attorneys filed an appeal on Johnson's behalf. It was quickly denied, as were subsequent appeals, but in the end a stay of execution was granted by the Democratic governor of Tennessee. During this stay, one of Johnson's attorneys, Noah Parden, traveled to Washington, DC, where he met with US Supreme Court Justice John Marshall Harlan, the circuit judge of the Sixth Circuit, which contains Tennessee, who agreed to have the Supreme Court hear their appeal. The Court ordered a second stay of execution in order to facilitate this.

But later that same evening, in defiance of the high court, Johnson was murdered.

Although Hamilton County Sheriff Joseph Shipp's chief deputy had recommended that extra guards be placed around the Chattanooga prison to prevent mob violence, Shipp sent all law enforcement agents home, leaving only one elderly nighttime jailer on duty. Before the others left for the night, they transferred all other prisoners, save Johnson and one White woman, off the third floor. Using an ax and a sledgehammer, a group of men broke through three sets of third-floor doors, a task that took more than three hours. Shipp showed up and "implored" the gathering mob to cease their activities and let the law run its course. Several men, annoyed with Shipp, took him to a bathroom and told him to stay there. Though unguarded, Shipp did not attempt to return to his duties until after the lynching was over.

The mob took Johnson to the nearby Walnut Street Bridge and hanged him from one of its beams. When he hadn't died after two minutes, some of the onlookers became impatient and began shooting at him. One report indicates that he was shot more than fifty times. One of the bullets severed the rope from which he was hanging, whereupon a deputy sheriff in attendance fired five additional shots directly into his head. Johnson's last words were, "I am ready to die, but I never done it" and, "God bless you all! I am innocent."

Johnson's final words are inscribed on the top of his tombstone. On the bottom is written "Blessed are the dead that die in the Lord."[6] And so ends the story of how a mostly Christian mob murdered an innocent Christian man.

Sheriff Shipp was later tried by the Supreme Court and found guilty of contempt. He was sentenced to a mere ninety days in prison for his role in Johnson's murder.

5. Wikipedia, s.v. "Lynching of Ed Johnson."
6. "Ed Johnson Project."

Ninety-four years later, in 2000, Hamilton County Criminal Judge Doug Meyer overturned Johnson's conviction. On Sunday, September 19, 2021, a memorial to Ed Johnson was unveiled at the south end of Chattanooga's Walnut Street Bridge—a structure that some Black residents still don't cross. My son, Alec, and I were in attendance. While standing in the drizzling rain right near the spot where this terrible injustice occurred, we heard a dramatic account of the story of Ed Johnson, listened to poetry and music written for the event, meditated on the "proclamation of apology for the miscarriage of justice" read by Chattanooga's mayor, and pondered a lecture given by a professor of African American studies. And we mourned.[7]

Mimetic Rivalry and the Scapegoat (Stranger) Solution

The harrowing account of Ed Johnson's lynching that you just read is chilling, haunting. There is no happy ending. No one in the febrile crowd tried to save him or make things even slightly more humane. No one thought their actions were premeditated murder. More likely, the mob saw their collective action as the hand and will of God purging evil from their midst. Ed Johnson's murder assuaged something that lay deep in their collective hearts. He was their scapegoat, his guilt beyond doubt. He became the stranger, who (from our modern perspective) bore the penalty for their sins—for all that festered in that turn-of-the-century Chattanooga community. With no regard for his humanness, let alone his innocence, a mob of people sacrificed Johnson on the altar of a bridge that I still walk on from time to time. And life goes on, until tensions ferment and the ritual is repeated with a new sacrifice.

We're used to reading about sacrifices in the Old Testament, and to seeing them depicted in movies that feature mythic, premodern tribes. Blood gets spilled, the community draws together, the community goes on, tensions build up, new blood gets spilled. But just a hundred years ago? For we moderns, sacrifices are seen as primitive and archaic, something we think we've moved beyond in our enlightened condition. We have better ways of addressing tensions in our culture . . . or so we think.

In his study of sacrifice, French historian, literary critic, and theological anthropologist René Girard (1923–2015) asks the reader to think about the invisibility of the victims of sacrifice.[8] After the description just given of the false accusations, trial, appeals, and murder of Ed Johnson, most of us come away burdened about what has happened. We see Johnson as a victim. He

---

7. University of Tennessee, "Chattanooga Dedicates a Place of Remembrance."
8. Girard, *Scapegoat*.

has a name. He has a grave with an inscribed headstone. We wonder about his family or what he did for a living. Nothing about it seems justified. The newly unveiled Ed Johnson memorial commemorates the terrible thing that took place on the evening of March 19, 1906. The group responsible for the memorial, the Ed Johnson committee, worked for years in hopes of restoring his name, making it known, and making him visible. They labored so that his lynching no longer stands as a "victimless" crime—so that he won't be just another statistic on the altar of human sacrifice. They made him visible so that we may mourn and remember. But this isn't how the sacrifice of the innocent has traditionally been regarded. For much of human history, the victims of sacrifice have been invisible. They are nameless and faceless. Think here of a child sacrifice or the sacrifice of a virgin. When a sacrificial victim is referred to as "child" or "virgin" or "slave," that flesh-and-blood person is not seen. What child? What virgin? Who are their parents? What was their name? What were the things they most loved? In sacrifice they become invisible—nameless and faceless strangers. They are no longer unique persons but are reduced to their functionality as elements in ritual murder.

Girard observes that human sacrifice—scapegoating—has been all but universally practiced across the great expanse of history, even up to the present day.[9] The central stories of many cultures—their myths—prominently feature sacrifice and its invisible victims. Greek myths (Oedipus), Inuit/Eskimo myths (Sedna), Native American myths (Ojibwa clans' origin myth), Jewish myths (Isaac), Christian myths (Stephen), and a host of others recount stories where one dies for the many—the scapegoat for the people. In fact, Girard contends that the practice of sacrificial scapegoating is the cornerstone of human religion and society itself. Why is scapegoating so ubiquitous across the great expanse of human society? What is it about sacrificial bloodletting that assumes a role of such centrality in so many of the world's cultures?

According to Girard, communities solve their internal problems by "uniting against a victim."[10] Communities are always at risk of coming apart as they grapple with various tensions, guilt, and sin. One of the central questions sociologists explore concerns social order—how does society hold together? This Hobbesian problem of order (from seventeenth-century philosopher Thomas Hobbes) is succinctly stated in the question "What prevents the war of all against all?" How is it that we are able to maintain this thing called "society"—or even a community within a society—when its members face conflict and tension at every turn? Why doesn't it all just disintegrate? In

9. Girard, *Scapegoat.*
10. Girard, *Scapegoat.*

dissecting this fundamental social problem, Girard offers the insight that society is mimetic.[11] In our lives we mimic or imitate each other, and from this mimicry, culture, identity, and human life take shape, as well as the forces that threaten those things.

Consider fashion as a basic example. How does something become fashionable? It's difficult to predict what styles will come into fashion in a given year. Nothing is inherently fashionable. To figure out what's in fashion, we watch others to see what they seem to like, and then we imitate them. Have a look back at your high school yearbook and you'll marvel that you were duped into hairstyles that now seem little more than a cry for help. After a time, as all kinds of people internalize and pursue the things they see others desiring, a consensus emerges that a particular hairstyle or style of clothing is fashionable. Soon we have hordes of middle-aged people wearing skinny jeans! Furthermore, in fashion, as in all of life, people compete relentlessly for things perceived as socially valuable. And out of the competition to be fashionable emerge envy, bullying, mockery, slander, and the like—all forces that threaten to undo a group. Fashion unites; fashion disintegrates. Don't believe me? Go watch ninth graders interact at school.

Here's an additional example: While humans and animals share many qualities, they also have marked differences. For one thing, animals are largely one with their environments (as I write, my dog is a few feet away living in the moment, operating on instinct and with no thought to the past or the future), but humans transcend the natural environment through sophisticated symbol systems like language. Language, which itself depends on mimicry, allows us to interact in uniquely human ways. We humans are dependent on relationships in ways that animals are not. When babies in orphanages have too little interaction with a caring parent figure, they often fail to thrive, sometimes dying, even when they have enough food, shelter, and warmth. We humans simply cannot make it without others. And so we always live in reciprocal relationship with other people, knowing and being known by them and constantly bouncing various stimuli off each other. This human dynamism has potential for great good and great evil.

Because we are so highly attuned to and dependent on others, we imitate them, and our desires start to converge. Girard calls this "mimetic desire."[12] For example, think about our tendency toward covetousness—the desire for something we don't possess. When one person has something, others around them become interested and begin wanting that thing too. Think here about

11. Girard, *Scapegoat*, 63–64.
12. Girard, *Scapegoat*, 64.

school athletics. When children are young, they are more prone to play than to compete. For most young children, the initial goal of sports is simply to have fun and to be accepted by a group. Outside of adult involvement in their play, young children don't think much about dividing themselves by gender or ability. At these early stages of life, children rarely approach their games thinking that losing is not an option or hoping they crush it.

Perhaps you remember early games of hide-and-seek or low-stakes playground soccer or four-square games that were simply fun. However, our culture (and indeed most cultures) has constructed sports around the concepts of rivalry, drama, dominance, and standing alone on the podium. And the well-publicized rewards (a trophy symbolizing social recognition) for those who dominate and crush their opponents (and along the way demonstrate superiority over their own teammates) become highly valued and tirelessly sought after. Children learn increasingly early (by middle school, sports are high-stakes) that success comes not through cooperation but through dominance via competition.

I well remember from my daughter's middle school basketball days just how easily a group of friends on the same team became rivals in the quest for the coach's blessing, playing time, recognition, and other rewards both tangible and intangible. Girls who were previously friends began seeing mixed motives in each other, and friendship sometimes became more exclusive and guarded. Parents joined in the fray, and to my shame I can even remember a time or two where my own thoughts ran to criticizing some eleven-year-old who received more playing time than my daughter. And when you add to this the pressure on coaches and schools to win, you can see how school sports become arenas for mimetic rivalry. What originally drew a group of girls together becomes fraught with envy, dissension, maneuvering, slander, and criticism. In sports it's amplified to a fever pitch.

As you can see, this mimetic rivalry threatens to undo the group of friends who, before the competitive stakes were raised, may have been good friends who enjoyed playground basketball together. Taken to extremes, the team (or community or society) may rupture beyond repair. So what prevents this war of all against all?

A scapegoat does.

Mark Heim, a contemporary theologian who draws Girard's ideas about the scapegoat into a cogent theology of the cross, explains that despite all the good that "mutual responsiveness" can bring into human communities, mimetic rivalry has a powerful destructive potential. Anger, fear, suspicion, jealousy, envy, and a host of other covetous tendencies can ricochet through human communities, wreaking discord, violence, and death. And communities can be undone. Heim notes that animals rarely fight to the death with their own species. Have you ever seen the way that venomous cobra males neck-wrestle for mates, so the loser can slink away unbitten and alive? Humans have no similar genetic limit for their rivalry and tests of dominance. We kill each other—sometimes on a massive scale. If you have any doubts, go read *Lord of the Flies*.[13]

Humanity's great upside, our wonderful human ability to communicate through symbol systems and to build a life together in infinite ways, has a powerful, destructive downside. Not only do we respond to threats of violence by meeting force with force, but we are also sensitive to slights, perceived intentions, and even the distant memory of a callous act. We are always poised to make strangers of others—to escalate violence, to rupture our bonds. It is at this point, when some escalating feud threatens to dissolve the community, that something must be done to rescue it, stabilize it, and return it to order. That something is sacrifice. And according to Girard, the reason history so routinely evidences bloody sacrifice mediating social crisis is that it works. Sacrifice works.

Heim dissects Girard's reasoning as follows:

> As human communities struggle with this crisis, the means to break this vicious cycle appear as if miraculously. No one thought out this prescription. The antidote comes without planning, and (a key point for Girard) its continued effectiveness depends upon a certain obscurity about how it works. At some point escalating feud threatens to dissolve the community—a moment of "sacrificial crisis" in Girard's terms. Spontaneous and irrational collective violence rains down upon some distinctive person or minority in the group. The conflict rending the community is said to be all their fault, because of their "evil eye" perhaps, or because of some offense that has brought pollution and punishment to the group on their account. They are accused of the worst crimes the group can imagine, crimes whose very enormity would be sufficient to cause the terrible plight the community now experiences. They are lynched.[14]

And the lynching works. The guilty-beyond-doubt sacrifice of the one deflates the group's fixation on violence and mutual destruction, and the community continues on. "The contagion of reciprocal violence is suspended; a circuit breaker has been thrown."[15] A peace (at least compared with before the sacrifice) settles over the community. And this dramatic result only confirms the guilt of the scapegoat and the assumed rightness of the sacrifice.

13. Golding, *Lord of the Flies*.
14. Heim, *Saved from Sacrifice*, 43.
15. Heim, *Saved from Sacrifice*, 43.

Think back to Ed Johnson's lynching. His alleged crime was the rape of a White woman. In the American South in the early 1900s, social divisions between Blacks and Whites were absolutized in ways it's now hard to imagine. Whites widely believed racial differences were biological and immutable, and those beliefs were part of a sacred order seen as essential if society were to move forward according to "God's plan." Pretty much everything, including all institutions in the South, contributed to the maintenance of this highly racialized system: education, religion, the government, the military, the courts, restaurants, and families, to name just a few. Everything in the society supported and testified to the rightness of such a system. Racialized beliefs ran deep, and to many Whites—maybe to most Whites—to blur race distinctions represented an unthinkable breach in reality itself.

This sort of thing is not unusual. Ponder a few contentious issues in society at present. Think about how homosexuality is deeply threatening to many heterosexual Christians. It blurs previously clear social divisions. Consider how much energy many churches expend discussing the place of women in the church. When women move into parts of the church or social structure previously monopolized by men, it can feel, for some, like a tear in the cosmos. And, perhaps the most unsettling social "violation" of all, think about the difficulty many have understanding intersex or transgendered people. The very presence of people who don't fit into traditional sex and gender categories is destabilizing and disconcerting to those for whom sex and gender have rigid and immutable theological roots.

Sacrifice happens most commonly when sacred divisions are transgressed—when a community's most extreme taboos are broken. So, in a community like Chattanooga in the early twentieth century—one filled with racial tension, mimetic rivalry, and the envy, hatred, and lack of compassion produced in societies with sharp racial divisions—when a Black man was accused of raping a White woman, it represented not just a crime but a transgression of the ways of God. In an important way, it didn't matter that it was Ed Johnson . . . any Black man would do. To breach this social division was to invite the end of society itself. Had a White man been accused of raping a White woman, racial taboos would not have been challenged, and there would have been no reason for over-the-top retributive violence, such as that leveled against Ed Johnson. A sexual act between a Black man and a White woman, however, was (sadly) regarded like an interspecies union—unthinkable. Johnson's alleged crime served as a challenge to the sacred racial division on which the community was based.

For Girard, rituals of sacrifice originated as tools to fend off social crisis. The racial ferment in Chattanooga and its destructive potential had but one solution: sacrifice. Ed Johnson was lynched, not by an angry individual but by an entire community. All against one. The ritual scapegoating of Johnson reaffirmed crucial in-group boundaries for the dominant group, and as a result tensions within that group dissipated, the hole in the cosmos sealed up, and the "community" could continue. Of course, their actions showed little concern for the traumatized African Americans among them. Rather than love the *ger*, the people of Chattanooga killed the *ger*, which served to reapportion the world into their desired in-group/out-group arrangement. This sort of collective violence works as a way of holding the community together, fortifying the collective conscience . . . but not once and for all. It must be repeated again and again and again. And this pattern of scapegoating, where the one is ritually sacrificed for the "needs" of the many, is seen over and over across human history.

Long before Ed Johnson's time, but after centuries of sacrificed and scapegoated victims, Jesus comes along. And, after living as a stranger to the things of this world, dying a scapegoat's death, and then rising from the dead (a rejection of ongoing sacrifice as a solution if ever there was one!), Jesus breaks the pattern and compels us to look at victims, such as Ed Johnson, in a new way. After the resurrection, we can no longer accept as legitimate scapegoating solutions and the cultural myths that surround them.[16] A myth is a form of cultural memory that reminds a people of important social principles—of what they must do to ensure their collective survival. In many prominent myths, like those of Oedipus or Sedna, that come before Jesus, we see the scapegoat as guilty—someone who appears deserving of their death. Furthermore, we see the victim at the myth's center as "invented"—as part of a fiction designed to teach us something important. The real victim from which the myth developed is forgotten or disregarded altogether. Girard, however, contends that the real, historical sacrifice of a flesh-and-blood person stands at the center of cultural sacrifice myths. The lesson supplied by the myth obscures the invisible victim. We just accept the lesson offered by the myth, remembering the stabilizing social principles it illuminates and move on, the real victim forgotten.

Consequently, murder becomes allegory; death a lesson about the circle of life. We don't see scapegoated victims who, though not innocent like Jesus was, are innocent of the community's sin for which their sacrifice temporarily atones. Before Jesus, the victims of scapegoating are invisible, eclipsed by the powerful myths that cover their faces. But the Gospel writers compel us to look at Jesus's death in a particular way: they never concede that he deserves to die. They maintain his innocence from start to finish. In this way, Jesus's death dismantles and deconstructs the scapegoating myths before him. He is

16. Heim, *Saved from Sacrifice*.

the truly innocent one—the Lamb of God who delivers the sacrifice to end sacrifice (note how an innocent lamb brings an end to scape-*goat*ing). The Gospel writers' insistence that we see the *innocent* Jesus hanging on the cross forces humanity to recognize scapegoating for what it is—the murder of innocent victims and a weak and ultimately ineffective solution for the problems of human sin and guilt. Violence can no longer be seen as a legitimate solution for the tensions, uncertainty, brokenness, and other problems communities must address. And with Jesus's death as the sacrifice to end sacrifice, for those who would be "in Christ," there is a new basis for identity—one that doesn't require scapegoats, out-groups, or a continual supply of strangers.

The End of Sacrifice and a New Identity

Mark Heim writes that "Jesus' death is one aspect of his saving work, and liberation from scapegoating sacrifice is one aspect of the new life it intends."[17] "Liberation from scapegoating sacrifice" is resonant with our "stranger" theme. Scapegoats either are strangers to begin with or are those who are turned into strangers for the sake of the community and the identity boundaries it seeks to protect. In effect, if Jesus is the sacrifice to end sacrifice, saving us from the need for further scapegoating, his death and resurrection provide us with a new basis for identity. Consequently, rooting identity in Jesus requires that we dispense with scapegoating, or to state it more sociologically, dispense with anchoring our identities in an out-group. Christ's once-and-for-all sacrifice means that the people of God no longer need to define themselves in opposition to strangers. We are freed to instead love strangers, to embrace them, to work for their good, and to include them in our fellowship. We are not, however, free to scapegoat them—either physically by killing their bodies through disregard or neglect, or symbolically by positioning ourselves against them. An identity that rests on scapegoating—individuals or out-groups—stands in opposition to an in-Christ identity. If not, for what did Jesus die? To identify with Jesus, claiming his name and identity as your own, is to stand with the scapegoat in his sacrifice. In identifying with the innocent one who became a stranger for the sake of humanity, we can be liberated from making strangers of others.

It's one thing to think about Jesus illuminating the practice of scapegoating as a form of ritualized murder and serving as the sacrifice to end all sacrifice. Most Christians grasp that idea quite well and have no intention of lynching or burning someone at the stake. If excising ritual murder from our future plans is all we get from this, its usefulness is fairly limited. As Girard explains,

17. Heim, *Saved from Sacrifice*, 134.

in Jesus's *death* he made victims visible, forever changing how we must think about scapegoats.[18] But, to extend Girard's idea a bit, Jesus also made victims/scapegoats/strangers visible during his *life*. Recall the beginning of this chapter, where I suggest that Jesus creates scandal by going out of his way to commune with strangers. When Jesus draws attention to strangers, honoring them, forgiving them, offering them "living water," and healing them, he is also bringing their hurt, exclusion, and longing to public expression. In effect he is telling the community, "You must embrace these people. . . . If you want to act like the people of God, you must not position yourself against them or scapegoat them. These people must not remain strangers." Consequently, the woman caught in adultery goes away forgiven and condemned by no one. The leper is cleansed and able to rejoin the community. The woman with the issue of blood is healed and drawn back into the community's worship. The eunuch is praised as being someone special from whom others can learn. The man with the withered hand is restored, right there in the temple. No more victims. No more scapegoats. No more strangers. Instead, living water and a new identity. No need for out-groups.

Heim offers one further idea that I find particularly compelling and that provides ample summary for this chapter. He suggests that for the early Christians living in the shadow of the resurrection, the sacrifice motif is not eradicated but changed in form. He writes:

> What difference does it make that Christ "died for us"? What does it mean to live without sacrifice? The answers to these questions involve personal conversion and a new form of social reconciliation. The resurrection of the crucified one brought with it not righteous vengeance but the formation of an odd new community that gathered around him. This community deployed a whole range of elements to substitute for scapegoating. Christians celebrated their ritual remembrance of Jesus' death not with copycat killings or new sacrifices, but with a meal of bread and wine. This was the "sacrifice of praise" that they believed powerful enough to do what violent scapegoating had hitherto done in human history. They celebrated not their unanimity against a victim, but their identification with the crucified one, and so with all those placed in a similar position. They remembered that at this death Jesus' disciple had played the roles of betrayer, deserter, and denier. Therefore they faced a reminder that they too were not free of the sin that leads to the cross, and were in need of conversion.[19]

No sacrifice of strangers . . . but a sacrifice of praise.

18. Girard, *Scapegoat*, 202–3, 207–8.
19. Heim, *Saved from Sacrifice*, 18.

In the rest of the book I invite you to join me in meeting a variety of strangers who reside in our world(s)—some familiar, some not—with the hope that in recognizing them, learning about them, and seeing them with fresh eyes, we might invite them into our fellowship, move more into theirs, come to think of them as neighbors and friends, and better understand what it means to have an identity in Christ. And who knows, along the way you may meet someone like Ruth the undocumented immigrant, the woman at the well, the eunuch, a fellow like Zacchaeus, someone caught in adultery . . . possibly even a Wallonian! Some version of these people, each honored, supported, and included by Jesus, exists in our world today. It's up to us to find them. It's up to us to welcome them. It's up to us to love them. What would Jesus do?

PART 2
STRANGERS
ON THE MARGINS

CHAPTER FOUR

STRANGERS IN THE PEW
Girls and Symbolic Exclusion

Recall some social situation where you felt like you didn't belong. Perhaps you remember the awkwardness of being the new kid in a middle school after your family had recently moved. Maybe middle school fashion was different in the place you came from. Maybe you had an accent that seemed funny to them or at least felt funny to you. Or maybe you were the first African American kid in a White school. Have you ever seen the picture of Ruby Bridges, the young African American girl who was the first to desegregate the all-White William Frantz Elementary School in New Orleans in 1960—the one made famous in the Norman Rockwell painting? If you haven't, google her name and feel the hostility that exudes from those iconic pictures. Schools should be welcoming. This one isn't. There's no welcome banner for young Ruby. Everything in the scenario proclaims that Ruby doesn't belong, that she's in the wrong place, that she shouldn't get too comfortable. Or else. Some teachers refused to teach while six-year-old Ruby was present in their classroom. Some White parents pulled their kids out of school. Just imagine. In that environment, and at that point in American history, the symbols surrounding young Ruby were overwhelmingly White, and there was no mistaking their violent and exclusionary meaning for a Black child.

Have you ever thought about female student wrestlers who petition school athletics to wrestle on the boys' team? Or female kickers who work to gain a position on the school's football roster? They stand peripheral to the worlds they wish to join. Or what about some of the first women to join military combat units? What in those worlds of military machinery, violence, brotherhood, and male camaraderie was welcoming to them, supported them, or proclaimed that they were needed or wanted? How did they ever develop the fortitude to attempt such a thing in the first place?

And finally, think through your experience at a church you have visited. Was it welcoming? Would you go back? Did you want to join? Was it a place where your gifts and talents would be nurtured—where you could contribute? Chances are that if you wanted to join, it was, at least in part, because you could see yourself there. It felt like a place where you could fit—a place where the people were like you in important ways, where they valued the same things, where you felt comfortable. The well-known "birds of a feather" maxim aptly describes most of us. We seek out people and situations where we feel embraced, and we avoid those that oppose us or raise questions about our identities. This is why the Sunday morning worship hour is correctly labeled the most segregated hour in America. And it's not just racial segregation. We typically go to church with those who share our social class, education level, and (here in the American South where I live) even sports allegiances. Furthermore, many churches are deeply divided along gender lines, and frequently male statuses and roles are clearer, more pronounced and more important, and more readily accessible than the more sideline roles designated for women.

My wife and I have three children—a daughter (now twenty) adopted from Bulgaria, a daughter (now sixteen) adopted from China, and a son (now fourteen) adopted from China. As I've watched our daughters grow up in church, I've tried to notice what about it would lead them to conclude that their presence and involvement is crucial if the church is to continue on in faithful witness. And I fear that my/our daughters could easily conclude that the church could continue on quite well without them. It's nice to have them, but nothing crucial or of a public nature is required of them. When they don't step up to the plate, no one seems alarmed. They're seldom compelled to take leadership or responsibility. Without them the show goes on. And week after week, year after year, my daughters, and perhaps your daughters, remain spectators in the pew.

For my son the reality is very different. Each week he sees people like him, like his dad, who plan, perform, and carry out the service, who serve the Communion, and who pick up the offering. Each week my son has ample opportunity and compelling stimuli through which to imagine himself doing, saying, being, all of those things(whether he does so is quite another matter) that are crucial and important if the church is to continue in its established pattern. It's easy for me to imagine my son hearing a message to "step up and contribute," but it's somewhat difficult for me to imagine my daughters hearing the same message with the same urgency. Who is alarmed when our daughters aren't leaning in to lead? In fact, when some women step up in church, they are met with symbolic threats, possibly less intense but not wholly unlike those experienced by Ruby Bridges.

The symbols in many churches in the circles in which I move support identities like mine—White, male, educated, and middle class. When I hear sermon references to theologians, they're usually White males (as an exercise, ask yourself which female or other minority theologians have affected you most). Even the pictures I see of Jesus (in children's Bibles and in other Christian art) portray him as a kindly, middle-aged, tall White man. In fact, there's almost no place in the church in which I do not feel a resonance with the symbols that mediate my experiences. But for my minority daughters, it feels quite different. It's a whole different world. I fit . . . they don't.

If we continue to structure the church around the identities of people like me—largely people already committed to a life in the institutional church—our daughters and young women may find other social worlds where they can more readily locate themselves and nurture and exercise their gifts and talents. At present, women are leaving the church at a higher rate than their male counterparts. In this chapter, I argue that the church's failure to retain women reflects failure at the level of symbols. In effect, people like me (described in the previous paragraph) have cultivated churches where we can see ourselves and our contributions reflected in the most important parts of the organization. I can easily locate myself as an important part of the program of the church. And while people like me gaze at our own portraits on church walls and extol the virtues of the godly men who went before us (my wife calls this "godly man syndrome"), our daughters, who cannot see around us, who sit passively behind us, and who frequently experience the church only at the margins, may slip quietly out the door. And they may not return. If we, the church, lose a generation of daughters, the blame will not lie with the secular world and its lures and attractions. Rather, the responsibility will fall on church insiders—on people like me. For we who manage and direct the church, design its fronts and execute its programs, will have failed to cultivate environments filled with the sort of symbols that could draw our daughters and young women into the center. And the fault will be obvious to everyone, except, perhaps, people like me. Our present generation of girls will not merely sit on the bench as religious spectators—at least not for very long. Ultimately, spectators are strangers. And strangers will not sit and watch us forever. Eventually they will grow weary and leave for places where they can see themselves in sharper focus and where they might move from the outskirts to seats nearer the campfire.

The Nature of Symbols

What is a symbol? Put simply, a symbol is something that stands for something else—something that points to a reality or thing beyond itself. For example, the Christian cross at the front of a church sanctuary is not a testimony to the object itself but rather a signpost pointing us to something else—in this case the death of Jesus (it matters not a bit whether you have a fragment of the "real" cross). If someone hacks up the cross at the front of a church, the faithful are not primarily concerned with the wood itself. Rather, the desecration of a cross is an affront to what it stands for, an offense to a group's understanding of the reality of Christ's death. Without the concrete object (cross) to look at, we would have a hard time understanding and focusing on the more abstract reality of an ancient death and resurrection. Yet a two-thousand-year-old death is the central reality of the collective faith of Christians. The object "cross" draws us into and defines a reality that is otherwise unseen, ideally giving Christianity a coherence and a focus. Likewise, the bread and wine of Communion are, in themselves, ordinary and unimportant objects. They take on importance because they help us locate ourselves in the church universal, linking us symbolically to the congregation of God's people joined together across time and space by participation in Christ's death and resurrection.

The religious image of a dove has very little to do with doves themselves but instead is meant to point to, and to remind us of, the presence of the Holy Spirit in our collective lives. Doves are not the Holy Spirit, and caging one would not bring you closer to God! Rather, the symbol provides a means by which we might understand the movement and reality of God's Spirit. It stands for something it is not. Perhaps the restless, explosive character of doves helps us understand the restless and disruptive character of the Spirit of God, who dwells in us not to reify human-built structures but to change them.

Last, my wedding ring is really immaterial to whether I am married. But my wearing it provides a visible symbol of my bond to my wife—a bond that is somewhat abstract in that it depends wholly on the consciousness both partners have of the union. The ring tells those who observe us something about a more subjective reality that they cannot see.

Symbols perform two primary functions: (1) they point to or reference something beyond themselves—that is, they represent a reality not contained in their substance—and (2) they provide a rallying identity point for a group of people. Thus, they are both inclusive and exclusive. Symbols help a person understand where she belongs and where she doesn't. They function as boundary markers. Perhaps you've seen some of the anti-immigrant sentiment energizing those who promote "English only" in American schools and culture. Such people wish to delineate insiders from outsiders, distinguishing those who belong from those who don't. "They" can get with the program and learn English like "we" did. Furthermore, symbols are both macro (think of an American or Canadian flag) and micro (think of how a minority female college student in a computer science major populated by male students might perceive her "otherness" in all kinds of subtle, nonofficial ways). Symbols tell us what our world means, and they indicate who belongs in it. W. E. B. Du Bois, the first African American to earn a PhD from Harvard, wisely observed that groups who are excluded structurally are also excluded culturally. Structural exclusion produces cultural oppression.[1] This means that within particular groups, those who are not permitted to officially shape the meanings that hold currency in the group (those not permitted into the power structures of the group where important decisions are made) will remain outside those meanings and will be relegated to the parts of the social structure where there are fewer resources and less power. Why? Because they have little (or no) control over the symbols that animate and sustain the group, and that give it its character. To control (and to construct) a group's symbols is to hold the reins of its power. To control symbols is, in effect, to rule.

The Role of Symbols in Maintaining Our Normal

The symbols that structure an environment are frequently invisible to those who control and benefit from them because they become part of the normative order. For example, symbols of male homophily (the meaning of *homophily* is close to the meaning of "birds of a feather")—symbols of male unity, privilege, belonging, exclusivity—can go unnoticed by those who control and derive privilege from them. Elite golfers at the Augusta National Golf Club, which from 1933 until 2012 did not admit women, likely did not significantly notice the monopoly of male symbols and meanings that permeated the club.[2] But undoubtedly Condoleezza Rice and Darla Moore, the first female members added (in 2012), noticed them plenty! And I'm betting that a few things in the symbolic realm had to change when those prominent women teed up for the first time. I'm certain that Rice and Moore could still suggest more than a

1. Allan, *Social Lens*, 206.
2. Wikipedia, s.v. "Augusta National Golf Club."

few remaining symbols that place boundaries around them and "their kind." Likewise, I imagine that female sideline reporters covering the NFL have a keen awareness of their otherness in a world of all but seamless masculine symbols.

Symbols function both to provide comfort for in-group members and to threaten those who transgress their established meanings. The normative order is represented in symbols; it is symbols that hold our worlds together and give them coherence. Accordingly, we act in predictable ways when in the presence of recognizable symbols like a national flag or a cross. Such symbols regulate our actions and place boundaries around our behavior. Because symbols reflect what we've come to see as normal (we frequently conflate the terms *normal* and *natural*), they can be deeply comforting. Symbols tell us what should be, and they help us understand when things have gone wrong or are not as they should be.

Think back to the example of Ruby Bridges. Why in the world would a group of people be so threatened at the prospect of a young girl sitting in a classroom with their children and learning math? How could a six-year-old girl possibly hurt them? Seems crazy. That group of people was responding to a disruption or break in the symbolic order. They (American Whites) had become accustomed to a "normal," or normative, order that supported their view of themselves as more human than, and as categorically different from, the Black people who lived on the margins of their established world. In fact, in the Jim Crow era, Black people were routinely indicted for simply "not knowing their place." Ruby—even more what she stood for—disrupted this normal. She represented an unthinkable breach in reality itself. And a disruption to the normative order is deeply threatening and unsettling. A disruption of this magnitude is a threat in its potential to reorder the symbolic world—a reordering that would undo many things White people took as normal, right, good, and so on. When the symbolic order is at stake, as the presence of young Ruby Bridges in a "normally" White school suggested, people become willing to take extreme action to retain the former patterns. Such action may include hostility toward, threats against, and even acts of violence against the perceived source of the symbolic break. And in November 1960, on an average day, a crowd of rather average American citizens reacted in such an ugly way, all because of the profoundly disorienting presence of a small Black girl walking into a New Orleans public school on a Monday morning.

Sociologist Peter Berger, in a well-known book provocatively titled *The Sacred Canopy*, writes about the process by which groups of people come to take particular ways of life for granted. Catholics, Americans, Muslims, Ku Klux Klan members, Marines, and sports fans all go about their collective lives on the basis of taken-for-granted assumptions about the world and about reality. And all these groups display symbols that represent their frequently unstated assumptions. Just think of what assumptions are represented in the "costumes" worn by Klan members. As various social practices that define a group become encoded in symbols, those symbols mesh together forming what Berger calls "plausibility structures," which establish "our way" as right and inevitable and any other way as inferior and immoral.

For example, when in my sociology classes I emphasize or lend authority to a point I am making by referring to verses in the Bible, I need offer no defense or explanation of why I consider the Bible authoritative or why we might consider what the writers of Scripture have to say on some matter. The Bible is part of a settled, taken-for-granted reality in my college and among the majority of my students, their parents, and their religious communities. In other words, the unquestioned acceptance by "our" community of the Bible as an authoritative text is a very significant part of what gives this religious community its distinctive character. The symbols support the practices, and the practices support the symbols. Everything in the institution supports the plausibility of our customs, habits, and ways of understanding various things. As a professor at my college, to seriously question the authority of Scripture in some public way would be to initiate my severance from the institution! Such a threat to the unquestioned reality on which the institution rests would be intolerable. However, were I to go and teach at a state university, I could not make the same assumptions about the Bible that I do in my present institution, for the state university would be grounded in a different set of symbols and practices that together establish and reinforce the plausibility of that community. Publicly holding to the aforementioned authority of Scripture (the very basis for my employment in the religious institution) might get me terminated in a more secular community with different plausibility structures and related understanding of truth and reality.

The book *The Chosen* by Jewish author Chaim Potok provides a compelling glimpse of how deeply unsettling it can be to challenge the plausibility structures in one's community. In the story, protagonist Danny Saunders, a brilliant young Talmudic scholar with a photographic memory, begins questioning the completeness of reality as it is known in his Hasidic community. He questions whether the Talmud and the Torah can adequately explain all of reality. And he hungers for more. Accordingly, rebel that he is, he begins sneaking off to the library. And gentile libraries are forbidden by the leaders of his traditional community, for libraries pose a grave threat to the world from which Danny comes. All of the knowledge that supports his community's understanding of reality is available in the community, and this circling of the knowledge wagons (by forbidding and threat of sanction) is a way of addressing threat—a way of keeping new ways of understanding reality from entering in. Danny is drawn to psychology, and the ideas and frameworks promoted by secular psychologists offer deeply threatening alternatives to the taken-for-granted reality frameworks maintained in Hasidic Judaism. Can Orthodox Judaism stand in the face of a library?

Do I Look Like These People? Locating Ourselves in the Group

We spend great portions of our lives trying to fit in. Just look at what we wear. It's easy to pick on middle and high school girls for being inordinately fashion conscious, but they're far from the only ones. A couple of summers ago I attended our church denomination's general assembly. When I looked at the male delegates attending the meetings, what uniformity—navy and charcoal suits as far as the eye could see. Every so often someone shook things up with a bow tie, but other than that, fashion conformity was the order of the day. Or look at pictures from a Harley-Davidson motorcycle rally. Bikers pretty much look the same, and they, like middle school girls, spend a great deal of effort in trying to look like bikers look.

We're conformists by nature, and much of this is rooted in the sociological principle that we cannot survive (let alone thrive) apart from a group. We are inherently social beings. And so, as we navigate various social situations, we constantly ask whether we fit, whether we belong, and we generally work hard to conform to the norms of the group. In fact, our need to simultaneously be "like" others yet "distinct" from them is one of the central tensions in human life. This matter of scanning the social environment for clues about whether we will fit, whether we are like others in important ways, is seen over and over again on a variety of social fronts.

When my wife and I adopted our middle daughter from China, we traveled with a group of eleven other couples from various parts of the United States. Since our daughters are all fairly close in age, we've held annual summer reunions for the past eleven years. Each reunion is in a different city—usually where at least one family resides. It has become important for us to attend these each year because they give our daughters (minority girls in predominantly White communities) a chance to be with "sisters" who share a number of important characteristics with them. In effect, for the weekend of the reunion, our girls go from being minorities who look different from almost everyone in their schools, churches, and neighborhoods to being in a racial majority. It's a good time.

Several years ago one host family, who resides in New Jersey, organized the reunion around an outing to Times Square in New York City. While we were there, a number of our families wandered into the enormous American Girl store located on the square. It's hard to even imagine this place with its multiple floors, thousands of dolls, and endless doll outfits and accessories. There are all kinds of dolls—boy dolls, girl dolls, African American dolls, Caucasian dolls, Hispanic dolls, Native American dolls. In 2009 there was even a homeless girl doll. And a new doll with alopecia (no hair) was just introduced into the lineup in 2016. One mother wrote on American Girl's Facebook page, "This may feel to your company to be 'no big deal,' but to little girls who may feel alone and so desperately want to see dolls that reflect their beauty—it means more than you know." All of the dolls come with a historical backstory.

But one variety of doll was, to our group, noticeably absent. We couldn't find any Asian dolls (I think we finally located one!). Think about which dolls nine-year-old African American girls run to. Think about which doll a Mexican girl might choose. If a girl had alopecia, which doll would likely find its way into her home? The great irony in all this was that all of the dolls were made in China! My point is that our girls, though still delighted with the store and the dolls, couldn't readily see themselves in the available merchandise. They aren't White. They aren't Black. They aren't Hispanic. In 2014 Mattel (maker of American Girl dolls) discontinued its only Asian American doll. Google this and you'll see a number of websites hosting petitions by primarily Asian American girls advocating for the introduction of Asian dolls back into the company's lineup. In 2017 American Girl introduced a new Korean American doll and a Hawaiian doll into their collection. Ahh . . . progress![3]

In early 2022, partly in response to the sharp increase in hate crimes against Asian American Pacific Islander communities, American Girl Doll introduced a new Chinese American doll named Corinne Tan, who was honored as the company's "Girl of the Year," the first of Chinese descent to receive that distinction. In a short article for NPR, Rachel Treisman outlines a few of the issues the doll addresses: "In Corinne's books, she's proud to be Chinese American, but is too stunned to respond when a boy at the skating rink tells her she has 'Kung flu.' In another incident, Corinne and her sister hear a man make a racist joke outside their mom's restaurant—and watching her mom confront him gives Corinne 'the words and courage she needs to stand up to her own racist bully.'"[4] Progress indeed!

---

3. Z Yang, the Korean American Girl doll, was released in 2017 but "retired" (discontinued) in 2018 (American Girl Wiki, "Z Yang [doll]"). However, a Hawaiian American Girl doll named Nanea Mitchell is now available (American Girl, "Nanea 1941").

4. Treisman, "American Girl's 1st Chinese American 'Girl of the Year' Doll."

In the scheme of things dolls aren't all that important, but for our group of Chinese girls, the American Girl store was yet another venue where there were few signs that people like them are present, let alone important. Our Chinese daughters just couldn't easily locate themselves in the American Girl store. And although they think of themselves as Americans, there wasn't much evidence in that store to support their legitimacy in American society. The dolls in the store, functioning as symbols pointing out who fits, who is important, and so on, rendered Asian Americans invisible and largely irrelevant to American history and culture.

A few summers ago, our family flew to visit my parents, who live in Ontario, Canada. On the return flight out of Buffalo, New York, our pilot—not the copilot—was a young Asian man, resplendent in his crisp white uniform. As we sat in the waiting area near our gate and watched him walk down the hallway to the jet, I pointed him out to our young son, Alec (who you will recall was adopted from China). I can't remember ever seeing a person of Asian descent pilot a flight I've taken. This young pilot had a friendly, commanding bearing, and he exuded confidence and competence. He greeted passengers as they entered the plane. I was delighted that my son could witness someone who looked like him exercise authority over and pilot our flight. While this may seem insignificant, just think of the odds of having a White man pilot your flight. If you have children who are White, think about how many flights you've taken where they've caught a glimpse of a White pilot through the partially open door of the cockpit. Think about how the presence or absence of racial symbols expands or shrinks the horizons of possibility for a child. When a child sees him- or herself positively reflected, represented in the symbols present in a social environment, they can begin to imagine what they might be and what they might do. "Son, you should become a pilot." Conversely, when there are few symbolic markers suggesting that people like you do things like this, the world shrinks inward, and we set our sights a bit lower.

The 2016 movie *Hidden Figures* provides a compelling example of the power of symbols to define the horizons of possibility.[5] Based on the book by Margot Lee Shetterly, the movie tells the story of Katherine Johnson, Dorothy Vaughan, and Mary Jackson, three impressive Black women who provided vital calculations that put astronaut John Glenn into orbit during the "space race" with the Soviets.[6] The story focuses on the acute disjunction between the coveted abilities of these women (they are extremely gifted mathematicians) and their social position in NASA. The movie provides an illuminating

5. Melfi, *Hidden Figures*.
6. Shetterly, *Hidden Figures*.

glimpse of a symbolic environment that aggressively defends Black inferiority (despite all evidence to the contrary). In the all-White room where Katherine Johnson performs unimaginable mathematical calculations, there is a separate "colored" coffee pot. Instead of using her name, her colleagues refer to her as a "computer." One of the central tensions developed in the movie arises from the dilemma Johnson faces in attempting to balance the organization's demands on her time and abilities with her personal needs. In the NASA building where she works, there is no restroom nearby that she is allowed to use, so she must leave her desk for an extended period several times a day, dash off to another building (sometimes in the rain), use the facility, and dash back. Her supervisor, Al Harrison (played by Kevin Costner), becomes frustrated as he doesn't realize why she is so frequently absent from her desk. When she finally brings the restroom dilemma to his attention, he, in a sweeping symbolic gesture and in front of a large group of people, takes a crowbar and rips the "colored restroom" sign off the wall, proclaiming that people can use any restroom they like, and in Johnson's case, preferably the one closest to her desk! In addition, he decommissions the "colored" coffeepot. Colored coffeepots. Colored restrooms. All-White staff. All-White supervisors.

Once her supervisor reframed the symbols in their world (doubtless many oppressive symbols still remained), she was empowered to locate herself in that group. Katherine Johnson's tenacity and perseverance, amid these oppressive symbols that labeled her a stranger and an outsider, are impressive and inspiring. But the reality is that most people do not thrive in such environments, nor can they develop vision for who they might be when faced with antagonistic symbols or an absence of symbols that give positive meaning to their own presence, value, and belonging. When the symbols in an environment support clear bifurcations—White people over Black people; men over women; rich over poor—those environments tend to impoverish both sides of the division. Would John Glenn have made it into orbit if Katherine Johnson, faced with the presence of soul-crushing symbols in her workplace, had grown discouraged and quit trying? At the end of the movie a formerly antagonistic male colleague is getting her coffee as she works at her desk.

A number of years ago, my church was cultivating a fledgling ministry to Spanish-speaking people.[7] To communicate this to the neighborhoods around us, we parroted the English writing on our church sign with Spanish. Additionally, during our services, we sang songs with alternating verses in Spanish and then English. The intent (and I think effect) was a congregation where

---

7. Chapter 10 of this book provides a fuller account of this ministry to Spanish-speaking people.

Spanish-speaking people could catch a glimpse of themselves in what was happening on the stage, and in so doing, begin to envision themselves as an important part of the congregation.

When we think about achieving diversity and integration—buzzwords in many organizations—we often assume that the main task is persuading minorities to enter. But the presence of minorities in race, gender, and social class does not on its own achieve meaningful integration. Integration happens when people from an array of social locations can see themselves in, and have input into, the symbol systems that govern and give life to the group. In other words, a majority group can't achieve meaningful integration with minorities by simply getting them to "join us." Rather, the more significant undertaking, if meaningful integration is the goal, is for the majority group to step back and examine the symbol world it has constructed around itself. And symbols are everywhere. Every corner of an organization (any organization, but here the church) provides symbolic testimony to who is in charge, who fits, and who matters. From the sign on the street to the cars in the parking lot to the social locations of the people who hold powerful positions in the organizational hierarchy to the gender and race of the theologians whose work informs church orthodoxy, everything provides symbolic clues about who belongs, who decides, and who is the stranger.

In Galatians 3:28–29, Paul instructs his readers that the old hierarchies—Jew/Greek, slave/free, male/female, with their implicit super- and subordination and in-group/stranger implied identities—no longer apply or are suitable identity markers in a kingdom ruled by the risen Christ. Race, social class, and gender, the three primary means by which human identity is established in reference to out-groups (identities that require the continual subordination of out-group members) and that represent controlling interests and power in worldly symbol systems, are dethroned in favor of an in-Christ identity. Our commitment must not be to achieving high or desirable status. On the contrary, the follower of Jesus is called to take the lower place. To live out an in-Christ identity is, consequently, to diminish the role of human hierarchy, especially in the church congregation. The Galatians 3 passage is profound in its radical uncoupling of human identity from its universal in-group/out-group form. The political implications of such an identity transformation are immeasurable.

In effect, Paul is teaching the Galatians that in the kingdom of God, no one must be a stranger, but all must be neighbors and show greater concern for neighborliness and hospitality than for status. Neighbors are roughly equal in power, and for neighborhoods to be successful, people must treat others as they treat themselves. In the new order of the kingdom of God, the boundaries of the old life—the former ways of maintaining identity—are nullified. Additionally, in identifying the three primary social fronts on which strangers are produced and maintained, Paul is pushing the church to remove powerful symbols of divisiveness and worldly identity. These symbols reflect the old ways, and Paul encourages the church to replace them with symbols that are life-giving to all. This will allow those formerly subordinated to locate themselves at the center—a center that is Christ himself. In this new "real and imagined, now and future" kingdom, rather than functioning as an in-group marker, circumcision is of the heart, the weak are strong, slaves are free, women are called "sons of God," and the whole basis for identity shifts away from a concern with protecting position to one of inclusive hospitality. Paul's vision is of a social order where all people can see themselves at the center, where no one is incidental to what is taking place.

The new world of Galatians 3 is an order where the older, exclusive symbols and the reality they imply must fall away. This is a world where the symbols of racial, class-based, and gender-based superiority no longer have monopolistic hold on the meaning systems by which humans understand their lives. Outside of a break with these divisions, the church is just another manifestation of the same divisive worldly identities and status markers. Following Paul's teaching does not mean that we reject all social categories, statuses, and roles. Scriptural references to "every tribe and tongue" (e.g., Dan. 7:14; Rev. 5:9; 7:9) suggest that human categories do not disappear but that, instead, difference is honored and reflected in the group's symbols, and the meaning of the categories themselves is transformed. Diffusion remains, but each facet is valued and embraced in the new reality. The kingdom of God, and the church that is the visible front of that kingdom, should not and must not look anything like Augusta National Golf Club, which identifies a narrow subset of humanity as acceptable, desirable, and fitting. Reflecting the new reality in which we are called to live requires a radical undoing of our deeply entrenched worldly identities. The symbols we display, especially in our churches, provide testimony to whether we really have embraced Paul's vision with enthusiasm and fresh imagination or whether we simply give louder and louder lip service to "identity in Christ alone" while fortifying old divisions that are the very definition of worldliness.

Losing Our Girls to More Compelling Worlds: A Warning to the Church

For the most part, women have always attended church in higher numbers and with greater commitment than men. They still do. But in recent decades, women have been leaving the church at significantly higher rates than their male counterparts. Surprisingly, male church attendance (as a percentage of the US population) has remained steady since the 1970s. Much of the "secular" movement we hear about in the media is a result of *women's* exodus from the church. The data that document this trend come from the Pew Research Center, a fact tank located in Washington, DC. Pew first gathered data for their expansive Religious Landscape Study in 2007, and then again in 2014.[8] In addition, Pew analyzed General Social Survey (GSS) data that have been collected since 1972 by the National Opinion Research Council (NORC). These data are reliable—that is, they are representative of the US national population and among the best data sets we have for measuring the religious tendencies of Americans.

Between 1972 and 1974, the church-attendance gender gap stood at 10 percent, with 36 percent of women and 26 percent of men reporting that they attended weekly church services. It widened to 13 percent in the mid-1980s, when women reported at 38 percent and men at 25 percent. Then the gap began to narrow between the late 1980s and 1990s. By the beginning of the 2010 decade, the gap closed to just 6 points—28 percent for women, and 22 percent for men.[9] This represents an 8 percent drop for women over roughly four decades. It's noteworthy that men's attendance as a proportion of the US population has remained stable over this same period, consistently hovering in the mid- to low twenties.

Various theories offer explanations for this gendered drop in church attendance. One theory explains the decline in women's attendance as stemming from changes in the work women do and their rising status in the workforce. Analyzing Pew data, David McClendon observes, "In the mid-1970s, three-in-ten US women ages 25 to 64 were working full time in the labor force. Today, just over half of women in that age group work full time compared with around 70% of men."[10] The theory is that patterns in the work world exert influence over patterns of church attendance. As women's work patterns (working outside the home, etc.) became more like those of their male counterparts, their religious habits began to mirror the less-robust religious behaviors of males. There are a few caveats to this though. In the late 1970s

8. Pew Research Center, "Religious Landscape Study."
9. McClendon, "Gender Gap in Religious Service Attendance." In fig. 4.1, the data represent three-survey moving averages, which are used to smooth year-to-year variations in attendance patterns. For example, the figures shown for 1973 are an average of surveys conducted in 1972, 1973, and 1974. Data are from the General Social Survey, which has been conducted biennially since 1994. Thus, the data shown for 2012 average data from surveys in 2010, 2012, and 2014.
10. McClendon, "Gender Gap in Religious Service Attendace," para. 5.

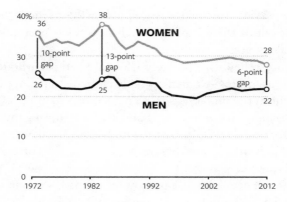

Figure 4.1. US gender gap in religious service attendance (Source: Pew Research Center)

and early '80s, there was a rapid increase of women entering the outside-the-home workforce, but also during this time the church attendance gap actually widened (this was when women's attendance increased to 38 percent). Additionally, McClendon notes that from the mid-1980s through the late 1990s, the number of women entering the workforce increased, and the percentage of them attending religious services continued to decline, but the decline was represented in all kinds of work categories (managerial positions, retail, service workers, etc.), both inside and outside the labor force. In other words, if entering the outside-the-home workforce is the primary culprit in explaining why women's church attendance has been dropping, we're left with explaining why attendance among women in traditional stay-at-home roles also deteriorated.

A second and related theory explaining trends in women's church attendance focuses on the increase in women's formal educational attainment during these decades of religious decline. Seen this way, more education equals less church attendance. McClendon finds this unsatisfactory on its own, because both college-educated women and women with little or no postsecondary education experienced declines in church attendance during these decades.[11]

It is worth noting that in the past two-and-a-half decades, the portion of the American population that does not identify with any organized religion—unaffiliated adults who have been termed religious "nones"—has grown significantly, more than doubling from only 8 percent in 1990 to 21 percent in 2014.[12] This marks a huge, rapid, and alarming decline in the importance of

11. McClendon, "Gender Gap in Religious Service Attendace," para. 8.
12. McClendon, "Gender Gap in Religious Service Attendance," para. 9.

religion in the lives of Americans. And the growth of female "nones" (presumably the result of them leaving church ranks) has been faster than the increase of male nones.

Finally, among religiously affiliated US adults—those who identify with a formal religious group—women's weekly church attendance has dropped from 40 percent in the mid-1980s to 33 percent (in 2012). McClendon observes that attendance patterns among affiliated men during this period were considerably more stable. In fact, in the mid-1990s, 24 percent of affiliated men indicated they attend weekly services, while in the current decade this number has risen to 28 percent.[13]

So men's attendance (both as a percentage of the US population and as a percentage of those who indicate a religious affiliation) has been stable over periods of tremendous change and flux in American culture, while women's attendance has dropped dramatically. How to explain this? I suggest that changes in the symbol worlds women inhabit have been more significant and pervasive than the changes in the symbols that give meaning to the worlds in which men live.

We don't live together in a unified "world." Rather, men and women (and boys and girls) live in worlds that differ based on our social location (and, of course, social location has to do with how one is positioned relative to, and able to control, significant symbols). When, for example, we speak of needing a "women's perspective" (as though a unified "women's perspective" exists) on something, we are seeking to understand how various symbols in a particular environment would be perceived by a woman—someone in a different social location than a man. Furthermore, women live in worlds where the symbols they appropriate and navigate tend to be in tension with one another, whereas men live in worlds that are more symbolically coherent. For example, as women's status has increased and girls and young women are more likely to easily find images of successful and educated working women, there has been a simultaneous increase in the sheer volume of sexualized images of women that they see that tie success to the presentation and eroticization of their bodies and subordination of those bodies to men. The "achievement" images of women thus exist in tension with the "sexy" images of women. There is tremendous pressure to "have it all"—that is, to project a sexualized image of oneself and to acquire the education and singlemindedness that are key factors in occupational success. But when high-school aged young women spend significant time crafting their image, they do not spend that time learning math. This tension—this dualism—is frequently resolved on the "sexy"

13. McClendon, "Gender Gap in Religious Service Attendace," para. 11.

side of the continuum, and "sexiness" easily becomes a submissive posture in environments directed by males, even as it confirms what many males believe about women, their abilities, and their so-called natures.

Women's status and autonomy in the broader society has grown—as evidenced in their increased presence in various fields of employment and in their educational attainment, which has now outpaced that of men. Recent data from the Bureau of Labor Statistics show that women are 8 percent more likely than men to have earned a bachelor's degree[14]—yet their status in the church has been elevated only marginally. And this is not true only for women in conservative churches. Even in liberal/mainline denominations that ordain women, women still occupy the low positions in church-status hierarchies.[15]

Educational attainment and workplace status and position provide a person with increased control over the conditions of life, and increased control over life is a product of the ability to control and navigate the symbols that press in on a person. For example, I am a sociology professor at a small Christian college. I make my living via words, both written and spoken. I direct people (well, students anyway!) more than I am directed by people. Much of this control I have over my life, my work, my students, and so on is a function of my formal education, which, among other things, permitted me to secure my present position.

When we encourage students to "stay in school," it is often with an implicit promise that with a college degree they'll be less accountable to those who direct the world and control its symbols and meaning systems. The dreaded "flipping burgers" careers we showcase to implore our teenagers to stay in school is our plea for them to study symbol systems so that they, in turn, may have a modicum of control over the symbols and thus have a more enriching life. But to be inspired to stay in school, our young people must be able to see themselves doing, being, and delighting in all the things that school has to offer. They must try their hand at manipulating the symbols themselves. Young athletes who only ever sit on the bench and watch the game will eventually opt out and will search for more meaningful fields on which to locate themselves—fields where they can be at the center of the action. And if this is true of school and sports, why would we ever think that our girls will sit in the church pew for their childhood and adolescence, watching others have meaningful contact with religious symbols and rituals, and not opt out for more enchanting worlds? Pew data seem to suggest this exodus is happening, and at an alarming pace. Furthermore, if the symbols structuring life inside

14. Bureau of Labor Statistics, "Women More Likely Than Men to Have Earned a Bachelor's Degree."
15. Chaves, *Ordaining Women*.

the church are radically discontinuous with the symbols that girls and women contend with outside of the church, one or the other environment will be rejected as disingenuous and unimportant.

Several years ago I offered a lecture session titled "Prizes and Consumables: The Super Bowl as a Theology of Women" as part of our denomination's annual General Assembly meetings.[16] The people who attended my session were mostly women (very few men attended). My talk examined the Super Bowl as a sacred festival where women played minor roles, if any, and where any focus on women (think commercials and sideline reporters) centered on the sexual presentation of their bodies. I argued that what we (the people of God) really believe about women is better seen in our posture toward and acceptance of this secular festival than in any of the meticulously argued position papers on gender and women's roles that find their way into venues like the General Assembly.

In the Q&A following my talk, I was surprised at how many women voiced feelings about the ambivalence they experienced as they faced the challenge of reconciling life inside the church with reality beyond its walls. One woman identified herself as a surgeon. She indicated that in her work she held authority over a number of men who worked on her surgical team (male nurses, anesthesiologists, etc.). She explained how difficult it was to hold a high-status, authoritative position in her workplace only to see that status and authority dissolve when she transitioned to church environments, where she received the confusing message that women must not hold authority over men. What did that mean for her? Was the world of the church to be completely discontinuous with the other worlds she inhabited? As she spoke, a murmur of agreement went up from the other women. And her comments raise serious questions that the church must consider. What does it mean for our daughters to see their surgeon mothers lay down scalpels (instruments of authority if ever there were any!) and quietly pick up spatulas when they enter the church? If many of the symbols directed toward women are designed to subordinate them, how will our girls learn to see the church as an organization where they will flourish? What will compel our daughters to willingly and enthusiastically decide that the church is the place to exercise their considerable and diverse talents? And does the church even want their talents? Or will their giftedness be met with implicit threat and ecclesial equivalents of "colored only" signs? One thing seems clear to me. If the church offers our daughters the message "sit here and watch," they will soon leave for more enchanting worlds and more meaningful opportunities. Living within and between incongruent worlds is

16. Vos, "Prizes and Consumables."

difficult at best. If the church fails to embrace our daughters, placing them nearer the center of the new reality described in Galatians 3 and endowing that reality with symbols they can recognize and embrace, they will likely leave for worlds with less dissonance and more welcoming symbols where they can locate themselves and not have to contend with narrow, prescriptive possibilities for their lives.

Stereotype Threat: Seeing Oneself in Negative Symbols

We perform best when in supportive environments. Think about what a roaring, supportive crowd does for a basketball team competing in the state finals. Think about how a college professor feels when her students sit spellbound in anticipation of something interesting. Now think about what it's like to make a presentation to people who appear to think you're not very smart or who are visibly critical of what you're saying. It's hard to be at your best when those around you aren't rooting for or expecting you to do well. An unsupportive social environment can diminish our ability to perform. Imagine doing stand-up comedy for an audience who seems bored or who just doesn't appear to think you're funny.

It is especially difficult to perform when you're in a category of person that is expected to underperform or even fail. Think back to the examples at the beginning of this chapter. Ruby Bridges was not expected to do well. Katherine Johnson (in *Hidden Figures*) worked out complex mathematical calculations in hostile surroundings where she experienced little camaraderie and where few people saw her as the brilliant mathematician she was. And yet they prevailed. But they prevailed in spite of their social surroundings, not because of them. Social psychologists use the phrase "stereotype threat" to explain the self-fulfilling prophecy that can occur when a person or a category of people (Black people, women, overweight people, etc.) expect themselves to perform poorly compared with some other category of people.

In a chapter called "Backwards and in High Heels" in a book titled *Delusions of Gender*, Cordelia Fine explains the results of a compelling experiment that investigated stereotype threat as it applies to gender.[17] In this experiment, City University of New York psychologist Catherine Good and her colleagues put together experimental and control groups composed of more than one hundred smart university students enrolled in an accelerated calculus class designed to funnel people into (or out of) the hard sciences. They gave these students a calculus test with questions drawn from the math portion of the

17. Fine, *Delusions of Gender*, 27–39.

Graduate Record Examination (GRE). To motivate the students, researchers told them that superior performance on the test would earn them extra credit (in reality, they gave all the students the same extra credit).

The researchers set up the test under two conditions. In the stereotype-threat condition, students (both men and women) were told that the test would illuminate what makes some people better at math than others. While this information seems rather innocuous, it can create stereotype threat for women, as they are generally well aware of their own stereotyped inferiority (relative to their male counterparts) in mathematics. Students in the other (nonthreat) condition received an additional piece of information telling them that despite testing thousands and thousands of students, researchers had never identified any gender differences in math ability.

Thus one experimental group was tested under a stereotype threat condition and the other with that threat clearly removed. Placing this in the context of symbols, for one group (women in the stereotype-threat condition), gender functioned as a present, palpable symbol of inferiority. (This is a little like testing the jumping ability of college basketball players and telling the White students that the experimenters are trying to figure out what it is about the musculature of White men that prevents them from jumping as high as Black men.)[18] The men and women in the two groups received similar course grades and were judged to have comparable mathematical ability. Accordingly, if a math test simply measures ability, we would expect the two groups to perform at similar levels. But this was not so. Rather, the researchers found that females performed far better in the nonthreat condition, and they found this was particularly true among Anglo-American participants, who generally show the greatest sex difference in math ability.

In the stereotype-threat condition, men and women scored about the same—all scoring about 19 percent correct on this difficult test. But in the nonthreat group, women scored an average of 30 percent correct, performing better than every other group—men and women—in the experiment. Fine exclaims, "In other words, the standard presentation of a test seemed to suppress women's ability, but when the same test was presented to women as equally hard for men and women, it 'unleashed their mathematics potential.'"[19] These findings are both astonishing and sobering. When stereotype threat is removed, the stereotyped groups not only equal their nonstereotyped peers, but they outperform them by quite a bit. Fine likens women's experience of stereotype threat to track stars running against a stiff headwind. Who knows

18. This is a stereotype with no scientific basis. There is no difference in the musculoskeletal characteristics of White men that distinguishes them from Black men in athletics.
19. Fine, *Delusions of Gender*, 31.

what they could do with the impediment removed? And, of course, these experiments raise all kinds of questions about women's so-called mathematical inferiority. Perhaps women are the superior sex when it comes to math.

Does invoking stereotype threat require elaborate manipulations played out under experimental conditions? What about subtler prompts to stereotype threat? Fine observes that subtle, everyday, frequently unnoticed stereotypes can prompt inferior performance among women.

> Stereotype threat effects have been seen in women who: record their sex at the beginning of a quantitative test (which is standard practice for many tests); are in the minority as they take the test; have just watched women acting in air-headed ways in commercials, or have instructors or peers who hold—consciously or otherwise—sexist attitudes. Indeed, subtle triggers for stereotype threat seem to be more harmful than blatant cues, which suggests the intriguing possibility that stereotype threat may be more of an issue for women now than it was decades ago, when people were more loose-lipped when it came to denigrating female ability.[20]

Consider these findings in the context of girls and young women sitting in church. How often have you heard a subtle, but unmistakably sexist, joke about women from the pulpit? I've heard male pastors joke, "When my wife was working on my sermon . . ." Ha! Ha! This is not uncommon in some places. How often have you heard something like the Super Bowl heralded from that same pulpit as a public good, despite its deplorable and sexist presentation of women? I was once at a service where the congregation had just been introduced to a visiting African missionary pastor who would be giving the sermon that morning. He was introduced as "Dr." X. When he came to the podium, he introduced his wife, who was sitting with the congregation. His main comment about her was, "She keeps me humble." I later learned that each of them held a PhD. The man was introduced with reference to his impressive credentials, but his wife was introduced as his support staff. Our daughters never got to hear that she held a terminal degree. The implicit message was that men are associated with impressive intellect but women are associated with support and humility. I'm fairly certain this pastor meant nothing but goodwill as he said this, but it provided our daughters with yet another subtle nudge toward a less assertive, more subordinate, less credentialed, and less serious approach to and engagement with the church. Who here is smart? Men. Who here is honored? Men. Who here is strong? Men. Who here is wise? Men. If simply acknowledging one's (female) sex as the first

20. Fine, *Delusions of Gender*, 32.

question on a test form invokes stereotype threat and inferior performance, what of church environments that scarcely acknowledge girls and women for their intellects? What of sermons that all but never reference female theologians? What symbols are present? What symbols are absent? How long will our daughters come in the door and quietly sit at the back? Not long, if the Pew data are correct.

CHAPTER FIVE

FROM STRANGER TO NEIGHBOR

Intersex Persons and the Church

by Val Hiebert, Providence University College

The Case of Jackie: Made Stranger to Others and Self

In 1966, a baby was born in New York who confused the attending doctors.[1] They could not determine whether the baby was a boy or a girl. The baby had a rudimentary phallus and fused labio-scrotal folds—in other words, a small penis and a fused vagina. Medical experts were called in, and they ran dozens of tests, did internal examinations of various orifices, and conducted surgery in which the gonads were removed and sent away for further testing. The parents, having had three prior miscarriages and having struggled to conceive again, had prayed for a healthy baby, and they told others that it did not matter whether it was a boy or a girl. Their prayers were answered—the baby was healthy and robust. Still lacking concrete medical answers as to the baby's sex five weeks after birth, they decided to raise the baby as a girl and named the baby Jackie.[2] Later, as an adult, Jackie commented that what

1. Material in this chapter is adapted from Hiebert and Hiebert, "Intersex Persons and the Church," used with permission from the publisher.
2. All personal names in this article have been changed to protect the privacy of the individuals.

her parents had implicitly meant when they prayed was that they wanted a "normal" baby, not just a healthy one.

All cultures across time and history are filled with raw human bodies. Our bodies are objects given by nature but also defined by the cultures created by humans. Bodies are enculturated. The raw facts of nature (in this case our bodies) are given meaning based on how humans use and regulate them—what we sociologists call the "social construction of reality." Despite the historical fact that babies with some combination of male and female genitalia have been present throughout human history (i.e., the "raw" body), most cultures throughout human history have imposed dichotomous norms on physical human sexuality—we must be either male or female. If you do not fit one of these binary categories you are, by default, placed into the "stranger" category. The doctors, the broader medical establishment, the parents, and the broader culture around them all thought that Jackie had to be either clearly male or clearly female. She could not be in between.

Jackie grew up as, in her own words, "a rough and tumble tomboy, a precocious, insecure, tree-climbing, dress-hating show-off."[3] Yearly visits to endocrinologists and urologists, endless medical examinations of her genitals, and her mother's unspoken shame about her "boyish" behavior generated increasing shame in Jackie about herself. She talked of feeling different, like a misfit, an alien, a freak. And though being a tomboy worked well socially when she was a child, it was less acceptable in adolescence. While her friends went through puberty exploring dating, fooling around, and getting hickeys, Jackie's puberty was preoccupied with hormone therapy. She watched in horror from the sidelines, feeling no connection to her own body. All she knew was what the doctors and her parents told her—she was a girl who "wasn't quite finished."[4] That finishing would supposedly come with hormone therapy and a vaginoplasty surgery during her adolescence. However, that left Jackie feeling even more freakish, ever more afraid to let anyone see her body, much less her genital scarring. And all this was enveloped in silence.

Few aspects of human life are more ordered or controlled than sexuality. Western culture has not only traditionally insisted on the binary opposition of heterosexual maleness and femaleness; it has also required medical and religious social institutes to insist on heteronormativity. When bodies and desires deviate from the cultural norms we have laid out for them, they are typically pathologized and stigmatized. Not only did the social and medical world that surrounded Jackie stigmatize and pathologize her; it also taught

3. Hiebert and Hiebert, "Intersex Persons and the Church," 33.
4. Hiebert and Hiebert, "Intersex Persons and the Church," 33.

Jackie to internalize these norms, pathologizing and stigmatizing herself. Her sociocultural world taught her to condemn herself—to view her own body and person as a stranger.

As a young adult, Jackie had a fleeting lesbian relationship and found temporary relief in the reassurance it provided. At least she had some evidence that she was not "nothing," "unfinished," or the freak she feared she was. But the relationship was brief and private. Jackie was too afraid to let anyone really see her, because her genitals were just so unusual, so unlike other women's. Jackie tried to kill herself. Her suicide attempt was not completed, and she was required to spend three months in a community mental health center.

Nature has a way of confronting culture that renders even medical and religious definitions of reality precarious and subject to change. When the raw, undeniable facts of some bodies do not fit the social and moral order into which they are born, something has to give. In Jackie, that "giving" resulted in a suicide attempt. The physical reality of her body could not align itself with the social construction of femaleness that was imposed on it.

A few years later, in the process of a routine check of immunization records for a job application, Jackie obtained her old medical records and learned what her parents and doctors had never wanted her to know. The large clitoris with which she had been born was actually a uniquely formed penis that had been removed as part of the vaginoplasty surgery. Jackie was now fully convinced that she really was a surgically deformed monster.

Shortly after, Jackie met Tracey, fell in love, and came out publicly as lesbian. For a while that felt right to her, but doubts crept in. How could she be lesbian if she was a man with a removed penis? Yet she was not totally a man either—she had been born with some female genitalia as well. Jackie felt like an imposter and a fraud no matter what identity she chose. She was hospitalized a second time for depression.

This was followed by a deeper coming out, this time as an intersex person. She also decided to switch to testosterone instead of estrogen therapy, and she took on a male identity, becoming Jack. Jack married Tracey, and they eventually had two children together through an anonymous sperm donor. The relationship with Tracey brought healing to Jackie/Jack's life, but he remained a deeply restless person who faced bouts of self-doubt, self-loathing, and confusion. He never fully settled into any particular sexual identity because there was no room in the social world for what s/he really was—a combination of male and female. Always the stranger. Jack talks of looking in the mirror every morning and being reminded of how "outward" outward appearances really are. He sees a husband, father, and computer geek who is looking forward to becoming a grandfather, all the while haunted by the question of what the Y chromosome in only some of his cells really means about his sexuality and identity.

Inter-implicated Bodies: The Raw and the Social

The sociology of the body explores the deep inter-implications between the raw body and the culturally controlled body. Synnott summarizes it as follows: "The body social is many things: the prime symbol of the self, but also of the society; it is something we have, yet also what we are; it is both subject and object at the same time; it is individual and personal, as unique as a fingerprint, yet it is also common to all humanity. . . . The body is both an individual creation, physically and phenomenologically, and a cultural product; it is personal, and also state property."[5] Hence we come to understand that "the body is an enormous vessel of meaning of utmost significance to both personhood and society."[6] The full weight of this complex inter-implication comes to bear on intersex people, who must not only control but *eliminate* so much of the uniqueness of their bodies as both male and female, because the definition of sexuality owned by society disallows the presence of intersex people. It is the ultimate act of alter-casting someone as the stranger. It is this deep, tyrannical weight of disavowing that we see at work in Jackie/Jack's life, as the raw and the social continue to clash in her/his world, life, and psyche.

Turner observes that cultural definitions of the body deeply influence personal feelings of desire, pleasure, and pain, and the personal assessments of well-being, relationships, and quality of life.[7] Bodies are representations of the social relations of power. Legal, medical, and religious institutions compete to have their definitions of what constitutes a deviant (i.e., immoral, inappropriate, inadmissible) body win the day. Yet try as they might, intersex people cannot be just anybody they choose. If a person's DNA and hormones are a mixture of both male and female, their bodies impose limitations on self-consciousness. This is true for all of us, each with our own unique DNA and hormone mapping.[8] Instead, binary gender expressions are bodily performances of acquired practices—learning how to manage bodies according to social norms. We "do gender," learning the intricate dance steps guided by the inter-implications of the raw and the social.[9]

5. Synnott, *Body Social*, 4.
6. Waskul and Vannini, *Body/Embodiment*, 3.
7. B. S. Turner, "Sociology of the Body."
8. Merleau-Ponty, *Phenomenology of Perception*.
9. West and Zimmerman, "Doing Gender."

Biological Realities

An intersex person is someone who has physical, gonadal, or chromosomal features that are a combination of male and female. Their sex chromosomes are not XX or XY but a different combination of X and Y chromosomes (e.g., XXY, XYY). The gonads, which develop into testes or ovaries beginning at six weeks, are a unique combination of the two in an intersex fetus. Physically, intersex babies have a wide range of various combinations of external genitalia such as a penis and a vaginal opening, or a scrotum and labia minora and majora.[10] If the combination of both male and female characteristics exists only in the baby's gonads or chromosomes, it will probably not be noticed at birth. Some discover their intersex identity at puberty, others discover it in adulthood in the process of unrelated medical tests, and some are discovered during autopsies, or quite possibly not at all.[11]

We do not know how many persons who live out of bisexual, gay, or lesbian orientations and identities do so without knowing that they were born intersex. There are approximately thirty types of intersex, and only one of them (congenital adrenal hyperplasia) represents a physical medical emergency in a newborn child, because it is related to the failure to produce cortisol, which is the hormone that manages stress. In almost all intersex cases, the newborn's genital tissues are healthy and without disease. They are generally robust, growing babies, just like most of us when we are born.[12]

The rate at which babies are born with both visibly male and female external genitalia, causing medical experts to be called in, is approximately one in every fifteen hundred to two thousand births. If all of these cases are combined, the rate of intersex people is approximately one to two of every one hundred live births, according to a survey of medical literature from 1955 to 2000.[13] We must also consider the likelihood that some never discover that they were born intersex and therefore are not included in these rates. Intersex isn't uncommon; it's just seldom heard of. As a comparison, Down syndrome is present in approximately one of every eight hundred live births in Canada,[14]

10. Creighton, "Surgery for Intersex."

11. Blackless, Charuvastra, Derryck, Fausto-Sterling, Lauzanne, and Lee, "How Sexually Dimorphic Are We?"; Gurney, "Sex and the Surgeon's Knife"; Topp, "Against the Quiet Revolution."

12. For more information on intersex, visit the website of the Intersex Society of North America at www.isna.org.

13. Blackless, Charuvastra, Derryck, Fausto-Sterling, Lauzanne, and Lee, "How Sexually Dimorphic Are We?"; Zeiler and Wickström, "Why Do 'We' Perform Surgery on Newborn Intersexed Children?"

14. Canadian Down Syndrome Society, "What Is Down Syndrome?"

and one in every seven hundred live births in the United States.[15] Therefore, parents are as likely to have a baby who is intersex as a baby with Down syndrome, yet there is much less public awareness about the possibility of having a child with ambiguous genitalia than about the possibility of having a child with Down syndrome.

Sterilizing the *Strange* in the Stranger

These infants—part male, part female—are born into a social world that has no room for their physical sexual ambiguity. Their birth is deemed a psychosocial emergency. Yet despite the lack of threat to their physical health in most cases, the common treatment of intersex conditions recognized at birth in North America in the past sixty years has been to intervene surgically as soon as possible to make the infants either male or female as much as possible. Moreover, out of stated concern for the person's mental health, professional medical literature has unabashedly advocated misrepresentation, concealment of facts, and outright lying.[16] This is a classic example of the medicalization of deviance, in which a person's physical condition, not behavior, is defined as problematic and unacceptable, and the person is stripped of control over their own body. Of course, infants routinely lose personal agency in the parenting process, but in this case even the parents lose agency at the hands of the more powerful medical establishment. The child's body becomes a representation of the social relations of power, the battleground on which institutional power is played out.

Imagine, for a moment, how you as new parents might feel when you are eagerly waiting to hear "It's a boy!" or "It's a girl!" and instead you hear, ". . . it's a . . . baby." Virtually any time a child is born, if their health presents as anything other than "normal," parents are blindsided by the experience. If you have never even heard of the possibility that a child might not be clearly either a boy or a girl, the degree of disorientation deepens significantly. The normal procedure in North America has been that medical experts provide the parents with test results and recommendations, and the parents are then asked to make the decision whether to surgically assign the child as male or female. However, recent research reports that many such parents felt a great deal of pressure from the medical experts to choose surgery, even though they wanted to "wait and see."

15. National Down Syndrome Society, "Down Syndrome Facts."
16. Dewhurst and Grant, "Intersex Problems"; Mazur, "Ambiguous Genitalia"; Natarajan, "Medical Ethics and Truth Telling."

Sex assignment is accomplished by repeated and progressive surgical and hormonal interventions that often last well into adolescence. Parents are strongly counseled by medical specialists not to announce the sex of the baby until a decision has been made and never to reveal the ambiguous nature of their child's genitals. The rationale given for this is that once the sex of the child is selected, it is crucial to the personal and social success of the surgical sex assignment that no one know the baby was actually a combination of male and female. Parents are also strongly encouraged never to tell their child that they were born intersex.[17]

Again, imagine how you might experience this if you were the parent. You've never heard of this biological reality of intersex people, and thus you have no tools with which to make sense out of a baby who is not clearly a boy or a girl. And rather than turning to your family or community to help you process this disorienting circumstance and decision, you are advised by experts to speak to absolutely no one about it . . . for the sake of your child's future. There is nothing you care about more than your child's well-being, yet you are counseled not to confide in anyone who is a part of your and, more importantly, your child's life. The degree of pressure and disorientation is actually almost *un*imaginable.

Recent research interviewing parents of intersex children indicates that, given the highly gendered norms of parenting, they had no idea how to interact with their infant because they could not know whether their child was a boy or a girl. In some cases, a medical specialist declared the sex of their baby only to change their mind a few hours later. In other cases, medical specialists had differing opinions, and the parents were left to decide between two conflicting recommendations. Further research exploring specialized medical procedures and interventions for intersex people reveals that when all the testing is done, genital appearance turns out to be the decisive factor in the final decision, because female genitalia are easier to construct surgically than male genitalia—"it's easier to dig a hole than build a pole."[18]

Because multiple surgeries are necessary to assign maleness—twenty-two in one case[19]—90 percent of such infants are assigned female.[20] Furthermore, medical specialists may conceal necessary information from parents, fearing that parents would feel guilt or shame about their child, or that worried parents would not be able to help their children enact the chosen, surgery-assigned

17. Zeiler and Wickström, "Why Do 'We' Perform Surgery on Newborn Intersexed Children?"
18. Hendricks, "Is It a Boy or a Girl?"
19. Stecker, Horton, Devine, and McCraw, "Hypospadias Cripples."
20. Zeiler and Wickström, "Why Do 'We' Perform Surgery on Newborn Intersexed Children?"

gender identity effectively.[21] Thus intersex children are often left to "manage" their bodies unknowingly contrary to how they were born, and to perform bodily the imposed practice of heteronormativity, what West and Zimmerman term "doing gender"[22] and what Butler terms "gender performativity."[23] One intersex person who has lived the experience says, "We as a culture have relinquished to medicine the authority to police the boundaries of male and female, leaving intersexuals to recover as best they can, alone and silent, from violent normalization."[24] For the sake of our own social comfort, we do violence to others, sterilizing their *strangerness*.

Lived Experience

Intersex adults often report that, as children, they experienced the medical staff and treatment to be focused on righting the "wrongness" of their genitals, in no small part due to the fact that they frequently underwent medical examinations every couple of months. Though unintended, the message the child hears is that their genitals are greatly in need of repair because they are somehow "broken," "unsightly," or "hideous" (terms used by intersex people). It is difficult to grow up in these circumstances without feeling a deepening sense of shame, further reinforced by the silence and secrecy in which they are asked to live (for example, trying to hide being absent from school in order to have surgery by offering a different reason for their absence). What complicates matters much more is that the vast majority of such children have not been told that they were born intersex. Hence, they are left feeling that their genitals are the most important part of who they are, due simply to the sheer amount of attention, time, and energy given to their genitals. Yet they are strongly dissuaded from actually speaking of them. Jim Costich, an intersex person interviewed in the Canadian Broadcasting Corporation documentary *Intersexion*, remarks with both humor and frustration that "people are *not* genitals. People *have* genitals!"[25] Many parents go to their graves never telling their children, and many intersex people never learn that they were born a combination of male and female.

Considerable evidence suggests that there has been a major shortfall in information about long-term outcomes in traditional treatments of intersex.[26]

21. Topp, "Against the Quiet Revolution."
22. West and Zimmerman, "Doing Gender."
23. Butler, *Bodies That Matter*; Butler, *Gender Trouble*.
24. Chase, "Hermaphrodites with Attitude," 135.
25. The film *Intersexion* can be found at the following web address: https://intersexionfilm.com/.
26. Zeiler and Wickström, "Why Do 'We' Perform Surgery on Newborn Intersexed Children?"

Furthermore, many intersex people struggle with, and resist, the sex to which they have been assigned, particularly in puberty, when hormones not in accord with their sex assignment begin to direct their sexual desires.[27] Such was the case with Jackie/Jack, who, though surgically and hormonally assigned as female, felt more like a male.

As research from the past decade continues to unfold, mounting evidence points to patient dissatisfaction with outcomes of medical intervention. A growing consensus maintains that it is impossible to define who needs a clitoral/penal reduction or a vaginoplasty in childhood, because it is not certain that the sex to which the child is assigned will be the one with which they identify as an adult. Rather than being allowed to grow into adulthood to discover the orientation of their gender identity and sexual desires, physical maleness or femaleness is quite literally forced on them via surgeries and hormone therapies. It has become increasingly evident that surgical sex-assignment has been driven more by ideological commitments than by medical research—that is, by the social and ethical desire to impose a binary model on sex rather than allow for the spectrum of sex and gender that exists naturally in human form. The emotional and social lives of intersex people are complex and frequently deeply tormented because they live in social contexts that insist their sexual ambiguity or bisexuality is unnatural and morally wrong, rather than simply being the natural state in which they were born. This perspective and judgment does not originate with the medical community but rather is one they have adopted, becoming a powerful current agent of its enforcement. This exclusively dichotomous perspective is in fact a broader social construction of reality and morality that is not present in all cultures.

Alternative Approaches

A cursory survey of the anthropological record further informs us as we consider how we might respond to all of this. Cross-culturally, we see that there have been, and are, other ways to handle sexual identities than our current North American binary model. The Sambia of Papua New Guinea have a social gender category for a man who, for a time, becomes more like a woman. A *xanith* wears female clothing and has sex with other men, and while some xaniths return to standard male roles later on in life, others do not. Among some Native American groups, a *berdache* is a male who opts to wear female clothing, perform female tasks, and engage in sexual relations

27. Creighton, "Surgery for Intersex"; Topp, "Against the Quiet Revolution."

with either a man or a woman.[28] A more recent term popularized since the 1990s among indigenous populations is a *two-spirited* person, which refers to any LGBTQI+ person and is intended to emphasize the spiritual nature of nonbinary gender identities. In India one can find the *hijras* roaming the large cities, earning a living by begging and offering street performance and dance. They dress and act like women, are born with either male or ambiguous genitalia, and are neither admired nor disrespected—they are simply accepted. Among the peoples of Southeast Asia, a common gender category is the *kathoey*. Usually originally male but dressing and acting as a female, they are a respected third gender that may be either hetero-, homo-, or bisexual.[29] The Bugis people of Indonesia have five gender categories: men, *calabia* (feminine men), *calalai* (masculine women), women, and *bissu* (a perfect combination of male and female that are considered to have special spiritual powers).[30] For the most part, there is no way of knowing how many of the individuals in these various gender categories may have been people who were intersex, either visibly or chromosomally.

Intersex people have also been present throughout human history, including in Western society. Historically, they have been known as hermaphrodites, a term that comes to us from the Greeks. Various discussions of hermaphrodites can be found in the work of Greek and Roman physicians and philosophers, as well as in early Jewish commentaries on the creation of Eve out of Adam, where the first human is posited to have been a hermaphrodite prior to being separated into male and female. No attempts were made to alter natural-born hermaphrodites in the Greco-Roman world, though much discussion was given to how to "manage" them in familial, legal, and religious contexts. European legal history indicates that, prior to the nineteenth century, the individual hermaphrodite him-/herself decided which sex they were and was then required to remain so permanently. Nineteenth-century medical doctors began documenting ever larger numbers of hermaphrodite patients due to the greater willingness of individuals to submit to medical examination. With this intensified attention to sex, gender, and sexual politics in the Victorian era came considerably more obsession with "managing" hermaphrodite conditions socially, medically, and religiously than had been present before. The twentieth century brought a significant historical transition due to the advent of medical/surgical options, which continued into the twenty-first century. Now we are generally no longer socially managing intersex persons; rather, we are attempting to physically

28. Miller, *Cultural Anthropology in a Globalizing World.*
29. Miller, van Esterik, and van Esterik, *Cultural Anthropology.*
30. Paris, *End of Sexual Identity.*

eliminate the biological category of intersex people in society through early medical intervention.[31]

Political Activism

In the past twenty years, intersex people have increasingly been finding each other, forming alliances, and coming out, together resisting current social and medical norms that force them into dichotomous categories of hetero males or females. In 1993, the Intersex Society of North America was formed to "provide peer support to deal with shame, stigma, grief, and rage" and to lobby for respect for "the intersex person's agency regarding his or her own flesh."[32] Other support groups such as Ambiguous Genitalia Support Network and advocacy groups such as Hermaphrodite Education and Listening Post (HELP) advance similar goals. They do not want more intersex people to be violated and harmed either physically or psychologically for the moral, social, or religious comfort of others. They want intersex people to have the choice to wait until the natural course of maturation signals to each person how they identify in terms of gender and sexual orientation. Tragically, their advocacy has been met with resistance from the medical establishment, including the American Academy of Pediatrics, which has remained insistent that medical intervention as early as possible is in the best interests of the person.[33]

An international joint statement compiled by intersex community organizations now calls for "recognition that medicalization and stigmatisation of intersex people result in significant trauma and mental health concerns."[34] Furthermore, "In view of ensuring the bodily integrity and well-being of intersex people, autonomous non-pathologising psycho-social and peer support [should] be available to intersex people throughout their life (as self-required), as well as to parents and/or care providers."[35] Like Down syndrome, intersex is not a disease, disorder, or defect. It is inappropriate and offensive to refer to people with Down syndrome as "afflicted with," "suffering from," or "disabled by" it. Down syndrome itself does not require either treatment or prevention.[36] So too with most intersex conditions. Increasing numbers of medical and psychological researchers now suggest that to label intersex

31. DeFranza, *Sex Difference in Christian Theology*.
32. Chase, "Hermaphrodites with Attitude," 137.
33. Chase, "Hermaphrodites with Attitude," 138.
34. Intersex Campaign for Equality, "Our Mission."
35. Intersex Campaign for Equality, "Our Mission."
36. Canadian Down Syndrome Society, "Down Syndrome Answers."

bodies as problems to be fixed can, in and of itself, bring forth pathology and create psychological illness in a person who would otherwise have none.[37] A public statement made by the Third International Intersex Forum currently stands as the most widely accepted statement by the global intersex community. One of their statements reads, "Intersex people must be empowered to make their own decisions affecting their own bodily integrity, physical autonomy, and self-determination."[38]

There is by now some substantial governmental action on these issues as well. Already in 1999, the Constitutional Court of Colombia passed a law restricting the use of surgery to treat intersex infants. In 2011, Australia instituted a passport in which there are three gender choices available—male, female, and indeterminate. The German Parliament passed a law in 2013 that gives parents the option of leaving the gender designation blank on a child's birth certificate, which frees parents to choose against an immediate surgery in infancy that forces an intersex baby toward full maleness or femaleness.

Religious Roots

According to Berger and Luckmann, religion is the most powerful legitimator of the social construction of reality, because it so effectively grounds meaning in a cognitive and moral ethos that explains and justifies notions of reality.[39] In acting as an agent of social control, the medical establishment takes its orders from culture, which historically has been largely formed by religion. Religion thus functions as the ultimate agent of social control, as demonstrated on multiple fronts of society. On the question of intersex, Western culture has taken its cue from the Christian teaching that God created males and females (Gen. 1:27), interpreting this verse to mean sexual dimorphism, not the two poles of a sexual continuum. This reading appears to be the primary source of Western culture's antipathy toward intersex persons.

For example, Selwyn was born in South Africa with ambiguous genitals and was raised as male, though no surgical sex assignment was performed. In 1987, he was ordained as a Catholic priest in England, after which he went on to teach theology in various university colleges. He only discovered the full nature of his intersex condition at the age of forty, when medical tests revealed that his hormone levels were predominantly female. He was then counseled to take on a female identity and have his penis removed. He took the name Sally

37. Topp, "Against the Quiet Revolution."
38. Intersex Campaign for Equality, "Our Mission."
39. Berger and Luckmann, *Social Construction of Reality*.

and tried to live as a female. Sally did feel that this fit better than trying to live as a male, but she still did not feel entirely comfortable; living as a female was simply less uncomfortable. However, because Sally refused surgery to remove her penis, she was excommunicated, and an academic Christian colleague told her that "an intersexed person does not satisfy the biblical criterion of humanity, and . . . even that [she was] congenitally unbaptizable."[40] In an interview Sally, with eloquent dignity, simply said, "I am a creature of God, and . . . I'm created, and intersexed people are created, no less than anyone else, in the image and likeness of God."[41]

In Matthew 19, Jesus teaches about marriage and divorce, and the disciples conclude, with some surprise, that Jesus is suggesting it is better not to marry (v. 10). Jesus affirms this understanding as correct while recognizing that not everyone can accept this teaching. Jesus then goes on to list three types of eunuchs. First are those who have been so from birth—this is a term of *in-betweenness* roughly equivalent to intersex. The second type are those made into eunuchs by others—individuals who had been castrated by someone else, which was a common practice in ancient Near Eastern culture. These eunuchs, who could not threaten or disrupt generational hereditary patterns of inheritance by impregnating a man's wife or daughter, were ideally suited to serve as household managers for the wealthy as a result. The third type are those who had made themselves eunuchs for the sake of the kingdom. These were men who were not literally castrated but who were celibate in order to focus on the work of the kingdom—functional eunuchs. Jesus includes himself in this final category. The first two categories of eunuchs were highly stigmatized in ancient Near Eastern culture, yet Jesus aligns himself with despised eunuchs, *and* he aligns service to the kingdom of God with eunuchs, adding, "Let anyone accept this who can" (v. 12).

These verses invite us to consider the possibility that Jesus did not exclusively assume a binary model of human sexuality. Jesus aligned himself with a sexual identity other than clearly male or clearly female in ancient Near Eastern culture, presumably because all eunuchs remain whole persons. Irrespective of our own degree of (dis)comfort with this, Jesus frequently made countercultural choices, and this situation is no exception. Megan DeFranza "hope[s] that by (re)educating ourselves on the phenomena of intersex we will be better able to read the Scriptures afresh, recover the full humanity of intersex persons and their place in the community of faith, and attend to the lessons they can teach us about the complexity of sex difference so that we

---

40. DeFranza, *Sex Difference in Christian Theology*, 16.

41. Sally Gross, speaking in J. Wentzel van Huyssteen, *The Third Sex*, broadcast SABC (South Africa), November 2003, cited in DeFranza, *Sex Difference in Christian Theology*, 16.

can advance our exploration of the theological significance of sex, gender, and sexuality."[42] We must "de-stranger" them.

Western culture is now becoming increasingly informed about the presence of intersex people as they actively seek social and medical reform, as well as the reality that biologically, human sex is not a binary opposition. If the Christian church, as each of us experiences it, continues to ignore these biological realities and persists in being the ultimate agent of the social control of bodies, it will continue to be an oppressor of intersex people, rather than the messengers of grace God has called Christians to be, even as the medical community and popular culture at large may come to liberate them. The Christian community must come to accept that intersex bodies are temples of the Holy Spirit within them too (1 Cor. 6:19).

From Stranger to Neighbor

The biological reality of intersex people significantly muddies traditional Christian moral, ethical, and theological categories and conclusions, not least because the LGBTQI+ person in front of you or me may indeed have been born that way. But complexity, and "seeing through a glass darkly," does not absolve us from authentic engagement. The second of the greatest commandments, "like unto the first," remains unmuddied, and intersex persons remain our neighbors regardless of our (in)ability to satisfactorily categorize them theologically. And it is a harmful oversimplification of a complex biological and social reality to pathologize the body of a person who is intersex as a simple solution to our ethical and theological conundrum, by suggesting that they are a de- or malformed person and not what God intended. We inflict greater wounds when we do so. We turn them, our neighbor, into a stranger. In talking about eunuchs, Jesus does not dismiss biological in-betweenness as a product of the fall to be overcome. Rather, he teaches his disciples that they can learn from eunuchs and instructs them that they should in some way model their lives after eunuchs, who do not fit neatly into a male-female dichotomy. We must do the same, not only welcoming the stranger but learning from the stranger and in the process becoming neighbors.

Socially, we have gained increased sensitivity regarding the negative psychosocial impacts of pathological labeling in understanding and interacting with persons with Down syndrome, the partially abled, and those with other types of cognitive and behavioral challenges. We would be wise to learn from this regarding the way that we think and talk about intersex people. Some

---

42. DeFranza, *Sex Difference in Christian Theology*, 9.

theologians suggest that bodily differences, perceived by some as impairments, may persist in the next life.[43] In this light, it is how communities perceive bodies that will be healed, not the actual bodies of persons, to the point that identities of difference that now divide and diminish communal life will no longer do so. In other words, it is not the stranger who will be changed but those who constructed them as a stranger. Again, we would be wise to learn from this in the way we theologize about intersex people.

What does the Christian community have to say *to*, and *for*, the intersex person? Can we anticipate heaven on earth, as we are called to do, by changing ourselves into a more hospitable and safe community? The current, usually dominant, discourse surrounding issues of LGBTQI+ Christians in the evangelical church primarily functions to alienate *all* LGBTQI+ people (some of whom are intersex), Christian and otherwise. The inadequately informed nature of the public Christian discourse on these issues, and the often too-easy applications of the biblical text, results in the practice of socially distancing ourselves from all LGBTQI+ people. And it seems the most intense judgment is reserved for those LGBTQI+ persons who dare to claim they are Christians. Whether Christian or otherwise, they are our neighbors who we are called to love and live with in community, yet the message we send often sounds otherwise. Families who have intersex members are frequently isolated, silenced, and alienated—alone within the church. We usually do not even know they are there—but there they are. I've spoken with some of them, and their stories are heart-wrenching—they are often rendered nameless, faceless, and invisible. Let us not presume to pronounce, categorically, what God thinks about an intersex state or an intersex child or a nonhetero orientation before we have at the very least heard their stories and become aware of the most basic facts about the biological and psychosocial realities they face.

When the search for biblical and theological truth is divorced from basic kindness (not to be confused with politeness) and love (the great, overarching commandment), we have lost our way in a most painful fashion. When "truth" serves to create boundaries around community that construct strangers rather than creating practices of welcome and hospitality that produce neighbors, we wield truth as a weapon. History is our witness to the tragically misguided nature and consequences of such practices. But to even have the opportunity to hear their stories, both the tone and content of the still-predominant Christian discourse surrounding homosexuality and all LGBTQI+ persons, Christian or otherwise, must change. Or they will continue to remain our unknown, unwelcomed, unwanted neighbor, the stranger who we have shamed

---

43. Cornwall, "Kenosis of Unambiguous Sex in the Body of Christ"; Eiesland, *Disabled God*.

into silence, who we have left standing at the doorstep, alone. The Christian command to love our neighbors as ourselves calls us to a more careful attention to persons as they are found in the real world rather than in the ideal world of philosophical and theological systems.[44] Let us instead practice the profound hospitality and the generous, life-giving love of neighbor that both the Old and New Testaments require of us.

44. DeFranza, *Sex Difference in Christian Theology*.

CHAPTER SIX

STRANGERS AT THE BORDERS

Immigrants and the Heart of the Gospel Message

In *Just Hospitality: God's Welcome in a World of Difference*, the late theologian Letty Russell suggests that the Christian doctrine of election has become deformed. She argues that election is often taught and promoted as a boundary marker that separates the faithful from the unregenerate—"God chose *us*, pursues *us*, loves *us*, and gives *us* eternal life." This way of thinking depicts election as a divine sorting into "we" the people of God and "they" the enemies of God. We and they. Insiders and outsiders. Friends and strangers. Sound familiar? But such an understanding, she contends, fails to ask the important question: Elect to what? Are God's people elected simply to wait, enjoying the things of this world, while God winnows out the riffraff? Are we to huddle in our churches and gated Christian communities with the other favored elect while God, in an ultimate sense, pushes the strangers (apparently outside his mercy) further from us and further from the rewards that accompany our favored status? Russell thinks not. She suggests that we think of election less as a noun and more as a verb. The people of God are elected to the this-worldly task of making neighbors of strangers.[1] Seen thus, the call on God's people is to seek out and draw others into God's resources, protection, love, and comfort, to the end of discipling them that they may, in

---

1. Russell, *Just Hospitality*, 38–41.

turn, do these things for others—a divine "pay it forward." The goal of such election is unity, not division.

Another theologian, Bryan Stone, echoes this sentiment, writing that we are *the people of God for the world* and that evangelism itself is an act of joining with different others, many of whom are not like-minded, that we may share a common "Christian" story.[2] Likewise, missionary theologian Lesslie Newbigin writes that the purpose of election in the Bible has been consistently misunderstood:

> It is election, not simply to privilege but to responsibility. God's people have constantly forgotten that fact both under the old covenant and under the new and have therefore brought the whole idea of divine election into disrepute. . . . The end [of God's plan and purpose in election] is the healing of all things in Christ, and the means therefore involve each of us from the very beginning inescapably in a relationship with our neighbour. Salvation comes to each of us not, so to say, straight down from heaven through the skylight, but through a door that is opened by our neighbour.[3]

Theologies like those evidenced in Russell's, Stone's, and Newbigin's work stand in contrast with otherworldly ones that tempt the faithful to view their relationship to God in ethnocentric, self-serving ways that keep strangers behind barriers, both existential and material.

Our earlier examination of social identity theory demonstrated how people identify as group members, establishing their collective identities in the contrast with relevant out-groups. Rooting identity in out-group contrasts poses a serious problem for humans in general and for the people of God in particular. It is so natural, so human, to locate and construct identity behind the boundaries drawn between us and "inferior" others. Identity pursued via downward social comparison forms the basis for much, if not all, conflict, and it prevents groups from finding common ground, forging alliances, and minimizing differences. Remember the Danireans, Pireneans, and Wallonians from chapter 2? Although these groups were fictional, people disliked them simply because they sounded different—unlike "us."

For the people of God this normal process of identity formation and maintenance is especially problematic. We are called to consider others better than ourselves, make disciples of every nation, give to anyone in need, and root our collective identity in Christ Jesus, "who, though he was in the form of God, did not regard equality with God as something to be exploited, but

2. Stone, *Evangelism after Christendom*.
3. Newbigin and Weston, *Lesslie Newbigin*, 50.

emptied himself, taking the form of a slave, being born in human likeness" (Phil. 2:3–7). Emulating Jesus and bearing witness to him requires adopting a similar posture toward others and a similar understanding of self. This turn-the-other-cheek, love-your-enemies, and the-last-will-be-first Jesus inverts the social basis for human identity. The Jesus described in the Bible flips our identities upside down. If anyone could legitimately denigrate an out-group, it would be Jesus. But he didn't.

Scripture shows Jesus privileging marginalized out-group members, irrespective of their nationalities or social standing. Jesus's human identity never depended on dominating those of humble stature. Rather, Jesus consistently drew the marginalized and disdained into his wealth, identity, and person. Remember Zacchaeus, the woman with the issue of blood, lepers, the gentiles, the demon possessed, the unclean—and you and me. His posture is one of invitation and welcome. By these examples, and in other ways, Jesus calls us to dispense with normal and worldly identity formation as people who are a new creation. Jesus, in characteristically counterintuitive fashion, calls the people of God to fresh understanding of what it means to be a person among persons. When someone strikes you, offer the other cheek. When someone asks you to walk a mile, walk two. When your neighbor has no coat, offer yours. If your enemy is hurt because one of your friends has taken off his ear, heal him—perhaps he will no longer be an enemy. Of what credit is it if you love only those who love you?

Followers of Jesus are, against worldly wisdom, to show little concern for their lives or futures. Entering into the identity of Jesus offers freedom from the "nightmare of scarcity"—from the need to protect, reserve, and hoard for ourselves—thus empowering us to engage with the needs of others as we enter into the abundance of divine generosity.[4] Evidence of Christ in us is most clearly seen when we, at cost, meet the needs of others, as the hands and feet of Jesus. Serving strangers is the essence of Jesus's gospel. Jesus most frequently comes to us in the form of a stranger, and in the parable of the sheep and the goats Jesus explains that failing to assist the least of these is a failure to enter into his identity (Matt. 25). Furthermore, the word *gospel* means good news, and good news isn't primarily for people who already have it—the well-hydrated don't need the good news that water has been found! Good news is for the strangers of God who desperately need it, lest they perish. If we, the people of God, raise our hands against strangers, denigrate them with our speech, or in other ways neglect them, we make ourselves inaccessible to them in the interest of protecting our claim on the things of this world. If

4. Brueggemann, *Journey to the Common Good*.

we allow them to perish, physically or spiritually, then we reject the gospel message we claim to herald. Jesus came for strangers. Keep out the stranger and you just might keep out Jesus!

This chapter is about immigrants as strangers, and about how the people of God are to care for migrants and others with no claims to land. Part of the chapter will help familiarize the reader with important features of national immigration debates that are frequently hidden from view and lost or negated in political rhetoric. Other parts will examine various ways that sociologists and others have understood the intricate relationships between migrants, borders, and citizens, with the goal of promoting and realizing social justice for the poor. In these efforts to better understand the Christian responsibility to the world's disenfranchised, I adopt Tisha Rajendra's idea that the people of God can understand themselves either as the people of Egypt or as the people of the Sinai covenant.[5] I conclude with a reminder that Christians are called to show hospitality to others—a practice as relevant and necessary in our present relationship with the migrants at our borders as it has been for the people of God in any time or place. To offer ourselves to the poor and landless—to strangers—though not without risk, is to invite the blessing of the God of the poor who stand at our borders and knock.

(Don't) Build That Wall

The relationship between immigrants and those with claims to land is in large measure about fear and identity. Over the past year or so, I have noticed some of the ways that immigrants are depicted by Christian people on social media platforms. As I searched through Facebook looking for posts about immigrants, I found the following—and all were posted by sincere and likable Christian people whose lives resonate with compassion and kindness:

"If you build it, they won't come."

"For those of you who support the migrant invasion coming our way please post your home address. They'll need a place to live."

"We've all survived [government] shutdowns. Build the wall."

These are just the kinder ones.

Recently one of my Christian Facebook friends enthusiastically reposted the following sentiment from [then] President Trump: "If Illegal Immigrants

5. Rajendra, *Migrants and Citizens*.

are unhappy with the conditions in the quickly built or refitted detentions centers, just tell them not to come. All problems solved!" Trump said on Twitter.[6] All problems solved? Really? Out of sight, out of mind?

Absent from these maxims is a sense of mourning for the poor and desperate men, women, and children who lack the basic resources needed to maintain human dignity. Missing is the Christian sentiment of hospitality, of "come share in our wealth . . . it's not really ours anyway." Present, but shrouded in sarcasm, is the fear of not having enough, of needing to hoard and conserve for ourselves, of holding a superior position. When Christians publicly express a "keep away from us" sentiment, will those in great need who stand at our borders with their hungry children see Jesus in us? Are we treating them as we would wish to be treated were our circumstances reversed? Will we be known as the hands and feet of Jesus? Will the needy and marginalized say, "Oh good, it's the Christians . . . things will be okay." Or will our embodiment of the good news of Jesus Christ be seen as a sham—just another disappointment for people struggling for basic human dignity? Are "they" someone else's responsibility? Are we not the people of God "for the world"? How should we think about our relationship to *Christian* migrants who stand in need at our borders? Will we watch as they die? Will we applaud when their children are restrained in cages? Will we revel as we "kick ass" around the world and put "illegals" in their place? People die when national boundaries are militarized. How should Christians react to the use of violence to restrain the poor? How is an oppositional posture consistent with the embodied witness of the people of God?

I think that very little of the Facebook sentiments shared above derives from actual fear of scarcity or victimization. Some of the richest people in the United States (I write as an American) lead the charge in the effort to build walls and restrain migrants. Rather, a fundamental identity-need animates this hostility. If, as social identity theories suggest, we define ourselves as group members in contrast with relevant out-groups—we are who we are not—then much of the anti-immigrant sentiment we hear is part of an effort to create and maintain out-groups. Pretty normal. Our oppositional stances function as identity markers. But it is precisely this basis for identity that Jesus calls us to abandon, saying, "Regard others as better than yourselves" (Phil. 2:3). "Give to those in need" (Luke 12:33 CEB). "Do not worry about your life, what you will eat or what you will drink, or about your body, what you will wear" (Matt. 6:25). "Consider the lilies . . . , they neither toil nor spin" (Matt. 6:28). And so on.

6. Brice, "Trump Says Immigrants 'Unhappy' with Detention Centers Should Stay Home."

Christian identity is inseparable from the person of Jesus. Being one with Jesus eliminates the need to fortify our identities by denigrating out-groups. If we are in Christ, out-groups become those we serve and to whom we minister. The people of God *should* erect walls and maintain boundaries—but not between ourselves and others. God calls us to be separate but not to separate ourselves. Rather, as we adopt a posture that is in, yet not of, the world, boundaries shift from keeping others out to restraining the evil that lives in our hearts. God desires that we be present with and accessible to those who are not like-minded, those who are not like us. Bridges to people; walls before worldliness.

Shocking a Stranger: Two Kinds of Distance

Years ago, my wife and I attended a fundraising banquet hosted by Bethany Christian Services, the adoption agency that facilitated our three adoptions. During the program, they made a plea asking attendees to consider adopting a child or in some other way supporting adoption. Noting that the number of Christian families who adopt remains small in the face of overwhelming need (there are some 140 million orphans worldwide), they offered an example to help narrow the distance between "us" and faraway orphans. They asked us to imagine that a ship transporting parentless children from faraway places had come down the Tennessee River and into Chattanooga. As it entered the city's waterway, something catastrophic happened, and the vessel began to sink. Though there were life jackets and other equipment on board, there was still a real danger that children would drown. They needed help. Even if they made it to shore, they would be cold, shivering, and in need of food, shelter, and comfort. The banquet hall we were sitting in was quite close to the location in the example, and our host asked whether we would abandon the food on our plates, head out to our vehicles, and rush over to save these children. Had this scenario been real, I feel confident that all attendees would have answered with their feet as they rushed out the door. After all, we were at the banquet because we cared about orphans. Furthermore, I feel certain that people who rescued a distressed child would offer to host him or her in their homes, provide medical care, bring comfort, and help ensure the child's well-being even after the immediate crisis had passed. Many would undoubtedly take steps toward adopting a child they had assisted.

Bethany Christian Services told this story to illustrate some of the things that deter people from adopting a child in need. When children are strangers, separated from and unknown to us, two kinds of distance keep us from meeting their needs. The first is physical distance. A host of research in social psychology shows that a greater physical distance between people makes it more likely easier to ignore the others' need and even do them harm. For example, in the obedience experiments conducted by Stanley Milgram in 1963, experimenters instructed study participants to deliver a reinforcement shock to "learners" when they gave incorrect answers in a task involving memory.[7] Although the shock apparatus delivered no shocks at all—it was just a clever ruse—participants really believed they were administering a punishment. They thought the shocks were real, and they thought the shocks were severe enough to cause serious damage and even death. Among other things, Milgram found that the closer the study participant was to the learner/victim (who was really one of the experimenters), the less likely he or she was to continue administering shocks that might harm them. When separated by a wall that permitted them to hear but not see the learners, a high percentage of study participants administered apparent shocks to the point that the unseen learner's screams turned to silence. Many of them kept shocking well beyond the point of learner nonresponse, even when the shock lever they were depressing read "Severe Danger, XXX, Death." In one variation, Milgram had participants sit in the presence of learners, in a position where they had to push the learner's hand down to have them feel the shock. Under these conditions, participants were far less likely to do things they believed were harming the learner. These findings demonstrated how comparatively easy it is to disregard the needs of those far from you, especially when you don't see the effects of your action or neglect. Bring them closer and sensitivity to their needs increases.

The second kind of distance that comes between people is what sociologists call "social distance." You can think of this as the social space between people, which may or may not be augmented by physical distance. Think about a person of modest means from a lower social class who gets on a subway car and has no option but to sit next to a person with all the trappings of the upper middle class (new, fashionable clothes; mannerisms; an expensive-looking briefcase). The person of modest means may feel discomfort and sense little common ground with the person of more upscale trappings. He may have little idea of what to say to this person and may feel relief when his well-dressed seatmate leaves the train. The interesting thing is that the middle-class person may have had equal feelings of discomfort at being around the poorer person. None of this has much to do with what each person is like as an individual. Rather, these feelings of discomfort are produced by a lack of familiarity

7. Milgram, *Obedience to Authority*.

with the perceived world of the other—and this unfamiliarity or perception of difference is likely to push the other further into the category of stranger.

Another example is the way that men and women sometimes have vastly different perceptions of a workplace they share. Men and women may work side by side (little physical distance), but due to the gendered character of many organizations, wherein males are more easily seen as leaders and have greater access to rewards, their social distance may be pronounced. When male bosses take male subordinates out for lunch during the workday—something gender scholars call "homophily"—but seldom offer the same to female subordinates, they may, perhaps unwittingly, increase the social distance between men and women in the organization. Race can function in a similar way. Recently, I heard a report from a Black male sociology major at the college where I teach, in which he described how Black people experienced our organization very differently from White people. I came away from his presentation with a sense of the social distance between races. Social distance can be much more difficult to overcome than physical distance.

The Mythical and Dangerous Immigrants

At this point we move from fictional stories about orphans on a boat to an actual account of immigrants on one. A 2011 issue of Canadian magazine *The Walrus* features an article by Rachel Giese titled "How Immigration Helps to Lower Crime Rates." The article begins with an account of a Thai cargo ship entering Canadian waters off the coast of British Columbia in 2010. On board were 492 Sri Lankan Tamils, including men, women, and children. The Canadian authorities, who had received intelligence that the MV *Sun Sea* was smuggling refugees from Sri Lanka, had been monitoring the vessel for months as it made its journey. Giese observes that Canada has been a popular destination for Sri Lankans who were fleeing the devastation of a twenty-six-year civil war and a 2004 tsunami and that there were (in 2011) approximately twenty thousand Sri Lankans living in Canada.[8]

A few days before the *Sun Sea* arrived on the Canadian coast, Giese explains, public safety minister Vic Toews expressed concerns for national security in a speech he gave to the Economic Club of Canada. In his speech, he speculated about whether members of the Tamil Tigers, banned in Canada as a terrorist group, were aboard the ship and poised to infiltrate and set up operations.[9] Giese writes, "That the point person was Toews, and not Jason

8. Giese, "How Immigration Helps to Lower Crime Rates."
9. Giese, "How Immigration Helps to Lower Crime Rates."

Kenney, the minister of citizenship, immigration, and multiculturalism, was telling. It framed the *Sun Sea* situation as a potential danger to the public, and prompted a swift response."[10]

Upon arrival, the passengers of the *Sun Sea* were sent to a detention facility, where many of them remained for more than a year. By mid-May of 2012, most of them had been released, and Canadian authorities were processing their refugee claims. Two passengers found to have ties to the Tamil Tigers were deported back to Sri Lanka. But out of the hundreds aboard the *Sun Sea*, only a handful were ever charged with being part of a human smuggling operation, and by July 2017, of those passengers suspected of having ulterior motives, there were seven acquittals and only one conviction.[11] Just one. Canadian authorities later learned that one of the passengers deported back to Sri Lanka was brutally physically and psychologically tortured while detained in a Sri Lankan prison.[12] This man eventually died after being struck on the road in a hit-and-run.

As the *Sun Sea* incident unfolded, Giese reports, the public was unsympathetic to the plight of the Sri Lankan refugees. Public animosity was further fueled by various pundits who proclaimed the refugees both dangerous and opportunistic. For example, Giese writes that "in a column for the *Sun* chain of newspapers, conservative author Ezra Levant referred to the refugees as 'gatecrashers' who were exploiting the country's largesse. 'Taxpaying, law-abiding Canadian citizens don't even get free dental care, in case you'd forgotten,' he wrote."[13] Oh no, not their largesse! (*Largesse* is a fancy literary term for generosity—clearly not the writer's central concern.) Additionally, Giese notes, an Angus Reid poll showed that 46 percent of Canadians thought that immigration was having a negative effect on the country. She wryly notes the irony in this, given that no one outside of Canada's aboriginal people can legitimately claim to be from Canada! And all this in a country that is "particularly supportive of diversity" and internationally recognized as "one of the best nations in the world at integrating immigrants, scoring high marks for educational and job opportunities, as well as for anti-discrimination and equality policies."[14]

One thing that integration and support for diversity fail to achieve is an out-group. If social identity theory is correct, *nations*, just like individuals,

10. Giese, "How Immigration Helps to Lower Crime Rates."
11. Quan, "Years after Two Ships Brought 568 Migrants to Canada, Seven Acquittals and One Conviction."
12. Woodward, "Canada Deported Man to Torture in Sri Lanka."
13. Giese, "How Immigration Helps to Lower Crime Rates."
14. Giese, "How Immigration Helps to Lower Crime Rates."

families, sports teams, colleges, and Chevy dealerships, work out their identities by establishing and maintaining out-groups that offer them the opportunity for downward social comparison. And immigrants are such convenient out-groups. They often represent a different racial group, speak a different language, have what seem to be puzzling cultural customs, and perhaps even practice a religion that seems strange or questionable. While Jesus calls the people of God to consider others better than themselves and to give freely to those in need, we, the people of God, can easily prioritize our national identity over our Christian duty to let another person take our coat and to walk an extra mile with them. This can lead us to join the chant to "build that wall." Insiders and outsiders. We're better than you. We and they. The same old story.

While identity-needs drive the denigration of immigrants as national out-groups, fear is what keeps the animus alive. In 2015, then candidate Donald Trump announced his presidential campaign at Trump Tower, offering a nationalist tough-on-immigration platform and proclaiming these now well-known sentiments: "The US has become a dumping ground for everybody else's problems. Thank you. It's true, and these [the people he is addressing] are the best and the finest. When Mexico sends its people, they're not sending their best. They're not sending you. They're not sending you. They're sending people that have lots of problems, and they're bringing those problems with us. They're bringing drugs. They're bringing crime. They're rapists. And some, I assume, are good people."[15]

Notice the "we and they" language. They're not like we are. They're people with problems. They're bringing drugs . . . crime . . . rape. This is the language of fear, and it can hold considerable weight with in-group members as they work to establish positive identities and address their anxieties. But are charges like the ones Trump and Canada's Vic Toews leveled against asylum-seeking migrants accurate? Do they truthfully reflect the people who stand at "our" national borders and knock? Mostly not.

In early April 2018, in a speech in West Virginia, President Trump brought up his 2015 speech, again referring to Mexican migrants as rapists. Here are his words: "And remember my opening remarks at Trump Tower, when I opened. Everybody said, 'Oh, he was so tough,' and I used the word 'rape.' And yesterday, it came out where, this journey coming up, women are raped at levels that nobody has ever seen before. They don't want to mention that." However, according to Z. Byron Wolf in a CNN article, "The President did not provide a scintilla of evidence to back up his claim. And what's truly

---

15. Wolf, "Trump Basically Called Mexicans Rapists Again."

troubling is that Trump continues to generalize such allegations against a large group of people."[16]

In her analysis of the *Sun Sea* situation, Giese examines the general claim (frequently made by politicians with nationalist agendas) that immigrants are dangerous, opportunistic, and bent toward criminality. She begins with a reminder that unsubstantiated claims and nationalist positions against asylum-seeking migrants are not benign. Strong and wealthy nations should pause to consider what sometimes happens when they turn away migrants. Giese offers two sobering stories from Canada's past. First: In 1914 a Japanese freighter carrying four hundred Sikhs and Indians landed in Vancouver, where it was denied permission to enter Canada. The vessel returned to India, and after disembarking, twenty passengers were killed. Second: In 1939 a ship called the MS *St. Louis*, carrying more than nine hundred Jews, was denied entry by Canada, the US, and Cuba. "Back in Europe, nearly a third of those passengers [about 254] would die in the Holocaust."[17] These tragic events were later chronicled in a book titled *Voyage of the Damned*,[18] which was also adapted into a feature film. In a brief account Amy Tikkanen writes, "In 2017 the ill-fated voyage received new attention through a Twitter account that listed the passengers who had died during the war. The account was created the day before U.S. Pres. Donald Trump signed an executive order that suspended immigration from certain Muslim countries. The following year Canadian Prime Minister Justin Trudeau formally apologized for his country's failure to grant asylum to the Jews on board the St. Louis."[19] Prior to the Canadian apology, in 2012 the US State Department had apologized for their role in the incident.

As you ponder the gravity of abandoning the migrant, consider figure 6.1, a photograph of the MS *St. Louis*, and look into the hopeful eyes of the children standing on the ship's deck before being turned away, many of them to their deaths. Look closely, and imagine Jesus standing among these destitute people on their doomed quest for help. Turning away those without claims to land is not without consequence. To turn away from the stranger is to forsake the ways of God. We can be "Egypt" or we can be the people of the Sinai covenant, but we cannot be both.[20]

16. Wolf, "Trump Basically Called Mexicans Rapists Again."
17. Giese, "How Immigration Helps to Lower Crime Rates."
18. Thomas and Witts, *Voyage of the Damned*.
19. Tikkanen, "MS *St. Louis* German Ocean Liner."
20. I have placed "Egypt" in quotation marks to remind the reader of the importance to both contemporary theology and to the contemporary study of geopolitics (not to mention to sociology) of maintaining distance between Egypt as a national state in the twenty-first century and "Egypt" as a symbol in the Old Testament of an oppressive force in the story

Figure 6.1. June 17, 1939: Some of the more than nine hundred Jewish refugees aboard Hamburg–America liner MS *St. Louis* on arrival at Antwerp (Source: Keystone/Getty Images)

Are They Dangerous?

Much of life is spent negotiating risk. A while ago our family flew back from Ontario where we had been visiting my parents. While we might have crashed, we thought the risks inherent in hurtling across the friendly skies at thirty-five thousand feet in a pressurized aluminum tube were acceptable. Commercial plane crashes are quite rare. Automobile accidents are not. While I was growing up, my dad had a pithy saying that he employed as a rationale for his reticence to let me drive the family car with my friends safely belted in: "One boy is a boy; two boys is half a boy; three boys is no boy at all." He was willing to shoulder the risk of my driving myself but not the risk that increased in proportion to the peer pressure reverberating through the vehicle. Now that I have a teenage daughter who recently obtained her driver's license, I embrace my father's wisdom! Teenage driving aside, if you want a scare,

---

of the liberation of the faithful people of God, also known in the Old Testament as "Israel." Our thoughts and feelings about contemporary nations in the Middle East should be carefully guarded from our sense of the symbolic meaning of the names of those nations as they appear within the narrative of the Old Testament, difficult as that may be.

read about how risky it is to have stairs in your home. The National Safety Council reports that nearly forty thousand deaths occur in the United States each year from people falling, either at home or at work.[21] This is why I live in a one-story ranch—stairs are just too risky!

Barry Glassner debunks some of our fears in a fascinating book titled *The Culture of Fear: Why Americans Are Afraid of the Wrong Things*. Great title! Glassner begins by examining the 1996 road-rage epidemic. ABC's *20/20* featured a story on it. Glassner replays the highlights of that story, covered by reporter Tom Jarriel, with details so frightening I can barely reprint them!

> A seemingly innocuous beep of the car horn can lead, Jarriel said, to "anger so explosive it pushes people over the edge: fist fights, even shootings, between perfect strangers." Out in the real world people honk their horns all the time without getting socked or shot, but in the fluid logic of Jarriel's narrative, stark imagery and atypical anecdotes eclipsed reality. "It happens without warning to ordinary people," Jarriel said, and to prove the point, he interviewed a man who was shot in the face after cutting someone off on a highway.[22]

A year later, Oprah Winfrey revisited the road-rage epidemic, further sensationalizing the horror of it. As Glassner recaps,

> First she transmuted familiar occurrences into a huge new danger. "We've all been there. It starts out with the tap of the horn, an angry gesture, a dirty look . . . ," she declared. Then she proceeded to recount a few actual incidents in which the outcome was a shooting or fistfight. That expressions of annoyance almost never intensify to a shooting or fight was beside the point. "This is a show that affects so many people," she said, and then cleverly produced an impressive but ultimately meaningless number. "This woman's biggest offense was pulling out of her driveway . . . countless millions of you have done that," she said in the course of introducing someone who had been attacked by another driver.[23]

In 1998 the *Los Angeles Times* declared that "road rage has become an exploding phenomenon across the country" and depicted the Pacific Northwest as a region particularly "plagued by a rise in road rage."[24] This all sounds very scary—the sort of thing that might make a person like me keep his teenage daughter home, friends in the car or not. Scary until you read that "only after

21. National Safety Council, "Make Fall Safety a Top Priority."
22. Glassner, *Culture of Fear*, 4.
23. Glassner, *Culture of Fear*, 4.
24. Glassner, *Culture of Fear*, 4.

wading through twenty-two paragraphs of alarming first-person accounts and warnings from authorities did the reader learn that a grand total of five drivers and passengers had died in road rage incidents in the region over the previous five years."[25] Five? Just five?! That's one per year. By my estimation (using today's data), you're approximately 40,000 percent more likely to die from tripping or falling down the stairs than you are from road rage. Some epidemic. Some plague. If there were just ten road rage deaths identified in the five years following the 1998 *Los Angeles Times* piece, the commercial news might report a 50 percent increase in road rage! Talk about fake news! Glassner goes on to divulge all kinds of alarmist and baseless statistics that will make you think twice about honking your horn or extending a particular finger during your morning commute. But it's all hype—flame and fizz.

In thinking about immigrants, we "citizens" easily succumb to sensationalism with a similar logic. Read a few Facebook posts from build-the-wall sympathizers, and you'll see what I mean. Hearing a story about an immigrant who shot and raped his way across the border (perhaps from a government official who suggests this is typical), we begin to think that all, or at least many, migrants arrive with dangerous and nefarious purposes. But what if just five migrants in five years are identified as gun-toting rapists? That would make "their" rate of this particular pathology substantially lower than that of our own citizens. The point here is that jumping to conclusions about some phenomenon can lead us in a seriously wrong direction if we fail to consider the broader context and veracity of the claim. The outcomes of these leaps in logic are seldom without consequence, especially when aimed at a group of people framed as an out-group. Glassner explains that the focus on road rage as a national epidemic served to obscure the "primary instrument of murder on the nation's roadways," which is the illegal carry of loaded weapons and drunk driving.[26] He writes, "By the mid-1990s groups like MADD [Mothers Against Drunk Driving] were finding it difficult to be heard in the media over the noise about road rage and other trendy issues. In the years that followed, the fatality rate stopped declining. Polls taken on the Eastern Seaboard during the late 1990s found people more concerned about road rage than drunk driving."[27] Trumped-up and inaccurate fears are not benign. Glassner wryly states, "I do not contend, as did President Roosevelt in 1933, that 'the only thing we have to fear is fear itself.' My point is that we often fear the wrong things."[28]

25. Glassner, *Culture of Fear*, 4.
26. Glassner, *Culture of Fear*, 7.
27. Glassner, *Culture of Fear*, 9.
28. Glassner, *Culture of Fear*, xvii.

In the remainder of her article "How Immigration Helps to Lower Crime Rates," Giese debates whether immigrants are as dangerous as those who politicize their alleged criminality suggest. The short answer is no. The longer answer is "not by a long shot." Giese persuasively demonstrates that not only are immigrants less likely than their (American or Canadian) hosts to commit a crime, but their very presence in a school or community seems to temper and reduce the criminality of the citizens they settle among.

Properly understanding how immigrants affect a country's crime rate necessitates understanding national crime trends. Crime in the US has been trending downward for quite some time. Giese writes about how in the 1990s criminologists and sociologists began looking for connections between dropping crime rates and the immigrant influx. Some studies found that cities with the highest increase in immigrants also had the largest decrease in violent crime—not what most would expect. Harvard University sociologist Robert Sampson, one of the first to "connect the dots," looked at the violent acts committed by men and women over an eight-year period in 180 different neighborhoods in Chicago—a city with a fair amount of diversity and a sizable population of Hispanic immigrants. He and his colleagues found that Mexican Americans were a lot less likely to commit violent acts than were White people or African Americans.

> When all variables were accounted for it became clear that this was in large part because a quarter of the subjects were born outside the US and more than half lived in communities where the majority of residents were also of Mexican heritage. Overall, first generation immigrants of any background were 45 percent less likely to commit violent acts than third generation Americans, and living in a neighbourhood with a large concentration of immigrants of any nationality was associated with lower levels of violence. In a nutshell, immigration protected these Chicago communities against violent behaviour.[29]

Sampson's findings are not consistent with American attitudes about crime or immigrants. Although six in ten Americans think violent crime is on the rise, the rate in the US has been falling dramatically over the past quarter century. Using FBI data, the Pew Research Center reports that in the US, violent crime fell 49 percent from 1993 to 2019. Bureau of Justice Statistics (BJS) data indicate that it fell 74 percent during the same period. Likewise, FBI data document a 55 percent drop in the property crime rate between 1993 and 2017, with BJS data placing the reduction at 71 percent for the same interval.[30]

29. Quoted in Giese, "How Immigration Helps to Lower Crime Rates."
30. Gramlich, "What the Data Says (and Doesn't Say)."

Additionally, since 1965, the presence of immigrants in the US has more than quadrupled, and the immigrant share of the US population currently stands at 13.7 percent, nearly triple the share (4.8 percent) in 1970.[31] "However, today's immigrant share remains below the record 14.8% share in 1890, when 9.2 million immigrants lived in the US."[32]

Interestingly, as immigrant numbers and share of the US population approached record highs, crime did not go up but fell consistently and dramatically. A rigorous study published in the journal *Criminology* that examined data on undocumented immigrants and crime, gathered from all fifty states from 1990 to 2015, states, "Our findings suggest that undocumented immigration over this period is generally associated with decreasing violent crime. . . . Indeed, of the 57 point estimates reported throughout our analysis (including in the online supporting information), not one shows a positive association between undocumented immigration and violent crime."[33] The authors conclude, "At a minimum, the results of our study call into question claims that undocumented immigration increases violent crime. If anything, the data suggest the opposite."[34]

Next, Giese describes a university study that offers compelling evidence that immigration lowers crime. In 1976, John Hagan, a professor at both the University of Toronto and Northwestern University in Chicago, surveyed 835 teenagers in an area just west of Toronto. He asked them about their families, attitudes toward school, what they did with their friends, what kind of trouble they got into, whether they smoked pot, whether they had ever "borrowed" a car and taken it on a "joy ride," among other things. At the time, Hagan's interest was in juvenile delinquency, not immigration. However, Giese explains, the region in which he conducted the 1976 study was about to undergo significant changes in its demographic makeup. When Hagan returned in 1999, with University of Toronto colleagues Ronit Dinovitzer and Ron Levi, to repeat the study, the city had become a "global edge city." It now had "a high proportion of visible minorities, mainly South Asian, black, Filipino, and Chinese. Of Dinovitzer and Levi's 900 respondents, a full 66 percent were from immigrant, non-European backgrounds (up from 10 percent in the original group)."[35] The influx of immigrants in the twenty-two-year interval between the two studies afforded the perfect opportunity to examine the relationship between immigration and crime.

31. Budiman, "Key Findings about U.S. Immigrants."
32. Budiman, "Key Findings about U.S. Immigrants."
33. Light and Miller, "Does Undocumented Immigration Increase Violent Crime?," 394.
34. Light and Miller, "Does Undocumented Immigration Increase Violent Crime?," 396.
35. Giese, "How Immigration Helps to Lower Crime Rates."

This second (1999) phase of the study revealed patterns many would not expect. For example, "The overall rate of what they called 'youthful illegalities'—drinking, taking drugs, petty theft, vandalism, fighting, and so on—was significantly lower in the immigrant-rich 1999 cohort, and in both groups immigrant kids were less likely than their peers to engage in delinquent behavior."[36] Another noteworthy finding was that lower crime rates were not associated with immigrants from a particular nationality—say, European immigrants. Dinovitzer and Levi's study found that "it didn't matter whether a teenager's family was from India or Trinidad or China. Specific cultural values were not at play; nor could behaviour be chalked up to a given ethnic group's parenting style (sorry Tiger Moms)."[37] Regarding the model-minority hypothesis (the racialized idea that, say, Asian immigrants are "good" while others are "bad"), Dinovitzer asserts, "They want to focus on the good Korean kids, or some other group. Our study unequivocally shows there's no difference between these immigrant groups."[38]

Giese concludes her article with several compelling glimpses into immigrant communities residing in an area near Toronto, probing the various ways that they adjust to the dominant culture around them and the strategies they use to create safe and successful living spaces. Her stories are heartwarming and human, and, for me anyway, they serve to diminish the fear that increases distance between "we" and "they."

Giese leaves us with a final observation from the Dinovitzer, Hagan, and Levi study. In addition to probing the deviant behavior of teens in the study, researchers asked teens about their habits, values, and so on. For example, they asked respondents things like whether they talked to their mothers about their feelings and whether they liked to take chances. Their conclusions: "What ultimately set the first generation kids apart were three important protective factors against delinquency: strong family bonds, commitment to education, and aversion to risk. What's more, these three qualities acted in a kind of feedback loop: the kids who regularly did their homework were also the kids who admired and confided in their parents, and were also the kids who shied away from troublemaking behaviour."[39] In short, immigrant kids seemed to manifest the very qualities we hope for in our own (native-born) children—qualities such as respect for parents and authority, appreciation for educational opportunities, and finding value in and holding onto their faith, language, and culture.

36. Giese, "How Immigration Helps to Lower Crime Rates."
37. Giese, "How Immigration Helps to Lower Crime Rates."
38. Giese, "How Immigration Helps to Lower Crime Rates."
39. Giese, "How Immigration Helps to Lower Crime Rates."

Lamentably, this "recent immigrant" effect does not last. The longer an immigrant population assimilates into the host culture, the more they tend to behave like their hosts. Accordingly, second-generation immigrant youth engage in more violent and criminal behavior than first, and third-generation youth more than second. New immigrants commit less crime and even lower it in the host communities they inhabit . . . until they succumb to our influence . . . until they become like us. Perhaps we have something to learn from them.

Moral Panics and Folk Devils: How to Make a Stranger

At age fifty-three, I am no longer suspicious of people with tattoos, afraid of people with HIV or AIDS, worried about my children learning math from a gay teacher in their public school, or alarmed about backmasking on LPs (records). Furthermore, I'm not even mildly concerned when my seatmate on a flight from Atlanta to Toronto appears to be someone of Middle Eastern descent. I'm much more concerned that he or she might talk a lot, as I like to sleep on flights. As hinted at earlier, I'm considerably more afraid of stairs than of Middle Easterners—stairs have claimed more victims in their relentless reign of terror! All these things—tattoos, AIDS, gay teachers, backmasking (hidden messages by shady rock stars that could be revealed by reversing a record on a turntable), and Middle Eastern seatmates, at one time or another, registered a threat in the public consciousness. And before these nightmares kept us awake, we (I write as a White man in the American South) were afraid of Black people. Google "Jim Crow laws" and marvel at the exaggerated fear many White people had of simply bumping into a Black person on the street.[40] Lynchings were frequently based on outrageous and unsupported charges of rape that were later found to be nothing more than perceived insubordination. In exposing them for what they were, Ida B. Wells wrote that many American lynchings functioned as a tactic to keep Black people terrorized and in their place as they acquired wealth, property, and social status.[41] Why? All these things—from the quirky backmasking to the much more serious way that White American society framed Black people as subhuman—raise the possibility of changes to the existing social order. They all suggest a reordering of "we" and "they," and perhaps a change in our position in the social hierarchy. All of them serve as threats to a group's identity.

Many of the phobias just reviewed have faded into the background as our society has changed, redefined their meanings, and moved on to other things.

40. Smithsonian National Museum of American History, "Separate Is Not Equal."
41. Wells-Barnett, Bay, and Gates, *Light of Truth*.

At present, many of the Christian college students I teach, both male and female, proudly display tattoos. The unmarked student is now the one who stands out—"What, no Greek inscription on your ankle? Are you ashamed of your faith?!" The church my family attends participates in a ministry to people with HIV/AIDS that works to restore their dignity, in part by encouraging us to "touch" these suffering people as Jesus touched and dignified the lepers of his day. On this issue we've made progress—we're no longer afraid of simple contact, and we move tentatively toward, rather than away from, "them." If we're honest, the lessons our children learn from Netflix and YouTube are more morally corrupting than yesterday's backmasking, and the moral threat raised by the frequently unnoticed yet omnipresent heteroerotic agenda (just look at the tabloids in your grocery store, the cosmetic surgery billboards on your street, the eroticized cheerleaders and violent men we all but worship in the NFL, and Victoria's Secret stores that beckon in most malls) is more sinister and invasive than the perceived threat of a gay teacher or two. Things change. Many of yesterday's threats are, today, just part of the social fabric. I still draw the line at Wallonians!

Recall the features of social identity theory outlined in the early chapters of this book. Personal identity is a function of group membership. Group identity is established and maintained in downward comparison with relevant out-groups. In fact, out-groups are themselves frequently social constructions (when we don't have one handy, we make one). As group members interact and fall into patterns, they develop a distinctive "culture" or set of shared meanings. When other groups begin to cross important group boundaries (national, religious, social class, racial, etc.), offering alternatives to the dominant group's narrative, they register as threats. For example, the Canadian province of Quebec is embroiled in debates about whether teachers and other authority figures in public (government) service can wear religious symbols on the job. With anti-Muslim sentiment on the rise in Quebec, much of the issue centers on whether Muslim women who teach in public schools may wear the hijab as they work.[42] There are all sorts of unquestioned Catholic religious symbols in the same environments, but the focus, critics of proposed legislation contend, is on keeping Muslims in line. The hijab is a visible symbol of difference and change, and it is often taken as a challenge to in-group values. Likewise, perhaps you will recall just how threatening interracial marriage was to American White society. It blurred the lines between in-group and out-group. The underlying mechanism driving groups to stand against other groups is the same whether it concerns women wearing a hijab, Black people

42. Montpetit, "As Fight over Quebec's Religious Symbols."

gaining status in a White-dominant society, or immigrants crossing national borders.

Perceived threats to the normative social order are frightening and disorienting to established groups, and under certain conditions they can coalesce in what sociologists call a "moral panic." This term was first used in a late 1960s study by criminologist Jock Young that focused on "the sudden and escalating public reaction to drug abuse, during a period of increased law enforcement and arrests in Britain."[43] The expression "moral panic," according to sociologist and criminologist Samantha Hauptman, "marries two terms where *moral* refers to a righteous or just social order and *panic* is denoted as a crisis or sudden change, causing turmoil or distress in society."[44] Basically, people in a society come to think of their way of doing things, their way of living, their culture and customs as the right way, or even as God's way. When something threatens a group's ways or meanings—immigration, gay people gaining equal rights, or controversial ideas taught in public schools (say, evolution)—especially when the group sees it as an imminent threat to their way of life, the resulting crisis isn't seen as simply a rational problem to be solved but as an assault on the basic moral elements in the society. In effect, if this is allowed, our society will be ruined, unrecognizable, or gone.

Moral panics are religious in character. When a threat is seen as having the potential to change core social values and norms, the group views it as a violation of what counts as sacred in that society. For example, "illegal immigrants" are frequently seen as a threat to "American values." We and they. Hard-working, law-abiding citizens versus largesse-exploiting law breakers. American values are general in character—it's hard to name them with accuracy—but they are regarded by many citizens with something approaching religious reverence. This past Fourth of July I saw a Facebook post of a painting that offered a patriotic rendering of the (Caucasian) hands of Jesus coming out of the clouds, flanked by a rainbow (which I'm pretty sure wasn't intended as a hat tip to the LGBTQI+ community), hovering protectively over the American flag, the head of a bald eagle, and an American city skyline. Renderings of this sort align the ways of God with "our" ways. Sociologists call this "civil religion"—the worship of the society, which is really just self-worship. The painting gave the sense that we Americans are God's people and that America's core values are God's core values—God is on our side (see the social identity theory in that?!). My point is that whether a given group associates with the God of the Bible or simply with some set of core ideals

43. Quoted in Hauptman, *Criminalization of Immigration*, 3 (italics added).
44. Hauptman, *Criminalization of Immigration*, 3.

and cultural expressions, out-groups that threaten to end or significantly modify the way of life emanating from those values can provoke a moral panic. Hauptman summarizes: "Thus, moral panics are a reaction to 'symptoms or signs of struggle over rival discourses and regulatory practices' and what is considered unacceptable to a society as a whole, potentially leading to the elevation of the level of suspicion against anyone or anything associated as a threat. In moral panics, threats must therefore include some incarnation of *folk devils*."[45]

A folk devil provides an out-group focus for people in a moral panic and as such offers a way of rallying in-group identity. If a group believes their way of life is being threatened, they can give expression to their fears by singling out the deviants, or category of deviants, responsible. Accordingly, these "perpetrators" become regarded as the enemy of the society. And, recalling chapter 3 of this book, folk devils function as scapegoats—eradicating them helps a group atone for its sins. Throughout American history, Native Americans, Black people, Middle Easterners, Muslims, Jewish people, Japanese Americans, gay people, drug users, cults, heavy metal music, and, of course, immigrants have all functioned as folk devils. Folk devils come to be regarded as the enemy, and citizens feel and are encouraged to feel justified in directing outrage, anger, hostility, punishment, and exclusion their way. In effect, to take a stand against Muslims, crack addicts, or immigrants becomes a posture of righteousness that is valued within the group. Furthermore, once a folk devil is identified, it actually becomes part of the moral panic and serves to intensify it—creating panic where none need exist.

Several factors augment moral panics and aid in identifying and turning group sentiment against folk devils. One is the "moral entrepreneur," who functions to "expose" and amplify latent social concerns and who ensures that the threat posed by a particular folk devil remains a constant presence in the group's consciousness. Moral entrepreneurs generally have a stake in controlling, maintaining, and directing moral panics. Watch the way politicians employ "I" language as they raise concerns, suggest that "our" way of life is at risk, and hail themselves as, perhaps, the only solution. "I will take care of this threat to our way of life." In cultivating moral panics, politicians identify threats, designate and develop folk devils, and disseminate alarmist statistics and exaggerated claims about the so-called crisis.

Think back to Donald Trump's 2015 presidential candidacy announcement in which he characterized Mexican immigrants as drug peddlers and rapists, contrasting them with the "good people" of the United States. Acting as

45. Hauptman, *Criminalization of Immigration*, 13.

moral entrepreneur, with vested political interests in enhancing moral panic as a means of maintaining power, then candidate Trump voiced these and other claims against migrants. Among these are blanket statements that immigrants "take American jobs" (they do, but only from high school dropouts and prior immigrants, both groups that would be helped by vocational training and other educational opportunities) and that requiring police to apprehend undocumented immigrants will reduce crime. In an article by the Brookings Institution, Vanda Felbab-Brown writes, "Forcing local police to apprehend undocumented migrants doesn't reduce crime either. Fearing the police, they stop reporting crimes and criminality escalates. When people reject the fairness and legitimacy of law enforcement, homicides and other crimes increase."[46] Regarding immigrants and gangs, she writes, "Creating a boogeyman out of Central American gangs in the United States also wastefully diverts resources. In Central America, the gangs are highly violent, extort and control local communities, and forcibly recruit children, even as they also provide them with identity, belonging, and economic resources. But in the United States, the maras are no more violent than gangs composed of native-born Americans and only 13 percent of homicides in the United States are gang-related."[47]

When the powerful wage misinformation campaigns against the powerless, it frequently results in the stereotyping of the subordinated group. This can have devastating effects on how the very humanity of the targeted group is perceived. "The act of stereotyping also allows the general public to place the folk devil in a "despised category . . . [which] permits the conventional member of a society to feel justified in strong, even savage condemnation. . . . Unambiguous hostility toward him or her should not only be expected—it is demanded."[48] Think back to the Ruby Bridges story and remember how the disdain and savage anger—acts of terror—directed against young Ruby as she simply walked into a school were regarded by many of the White onlookers as praiseworthy actions. And these were the adults! Strong adults screaming at a vulnerable child. We and they.

Folk devils are distortions of the truth—politicized distortions that aid the strong in exploiting the weak. Like most devils, they must be exposed and discredited. Credible evidence against the supposed danger immigrants pose to "us" is overwhelming—"they" are not criminals, sinister in purpose, or exploitive. They are not rapists or thieves. In the end, the folk devil and moral panic rhetoric we direct against immigrants, both legal and undocumented, predisposes "us" to close our hands to the very people God has sent

46. Felbab-Brown, "Order from Chaos."
47. Felbab-Brown, "Order from Chaos."
48. Hauptman, *Criminalization of Immigration*, 38.

us. When the poor show up on the doorstep of the people of God, how is that a bad thing? Who knows, "they" might even want to worship with us in our churches—in our sanctuaries. Think of what happens if we simply shift our language from "illegal immigrants" to "brothers and sisters." According to Pew Research Center, most unauthorized immigrants come from Latin America and the Caribbean, and the overwhelming majority, an estimated 83 percent, are Christian. This is slightly higher than the percentage of Christians found in the US population as a whole. If we think about "them" as brothers and sisters, friends and neighbors, and if we give at least some thought to the mass of compelling evidence that suggests that "they" are not the threat we've been led to believe, maybe we can regard them with more compassion. Maybe we can meet their outstretched arms with our open hands. Maybe we can dispense with the "we" and "they" divisions that Jesus came to destroy.

In a compelling new book titled *Refuge Reimagined: Biblical Kinship in Global Politics*, Mark Glanville and Luke Glanville summarily dismantle the argument that the stranger in Deuteronomy 10 "is a person who has been given the *legal authority* to reside within a community, and who on that basis has the right to benefit from the protections prescribed in Deuteronomy." Consider: "First, the stranger in Deuteronomy is most certainly *not* a person who had 'followed legal procedures to obtain a recognized standing as a resident alien.' Rather, we have shown that the stranger is simply someone who is vulnerable and seeking a home. It is the Israelite's responsibility to offer the stranger a home, not the stranger's responsibility to adhere to legal procedures for immigration according to Deuteronomy."[49] All they must be is vulnerable and in need of help.

If the poor immigrants who huddle at our borders in dirty clothes with malnourished children and little hope, or who hide in our cities hoping our police won't arrest and deport them, aren't the "least of these," and if the doomed Jews on the MS *St. Louis* weren't, and if the Sri Lankan Tamils huddling on the MV *Sun Sea* weren't . . . then who is? God have mercy on us if we turn our hands against the vulnerable ones who should find protection among the people of God. Shall we worship in our sanctuaries while denying sanctuary to our brothers and sisters?

Whose Neighbor? What Relationship? Whose Responsibility?

"Who is my neighbor?" is an increasingly complex question in a global society growing smaller and arguably less neighborly by the day. Technological

49. Glanville and Glanville, *Refuge Reimagined*, 45.

"advances" bring us close to people who previous generations would never have met, raising new questions about what it means to be neighborly. Just recently I engaged in a WeChat communique with our adopted (Chinese) daughter's foster mother, who lives in northern China. She and her family cared for our daughter for the first year of her life. Is she our neighbor? As I write, I sit in a Starbucks sipping coffee purportedly from central Africa. Who grew it? Who picked it? Are they my neighbors? Pondering this, I spill coffee on my shirt—something bought at some discount clothing store like T. J. Maxx. The tag inside sources it in Bangladesh. Are the people who wove its cloth and sewed its seams my neighbors? And finally, my office is in a building that was built mostly by Spanish-speaking people with brownish faces—from Central America, I presume. Are they my neighbors? Did my connection to them end when they vacated the finished building? Do I have any responsibility to them? Come to think of it, most of the material goods I enjoy come to me via materially poor others whose labor makes such articles possible. But who are they to me?

In a thoughtful and convicting book titled *Migrants and Citizens: Justice and Responsibility in the Ethics of Immigration*, Loyola University professor of theological ethics Tisha Rajendra calls us to examine the narratives we sustain about the migrants who would live among us.[50] Are the stories we tell accurate? Are they complete? Does our discourse about "we and they" adequately reflect the historical realities that shaped the relationship? Do our proclamations about those who would cross our borders do justice to the social complexities of a global society? Are borders, citizenship, rights, and justice really simple and binary we-and-they matters, or do our dualisms replace complex narratives with simpler ones? In the end, Rajendra explains, immigration, and the myriad debates that surround it, hinges on cultivating right relationships. She writes, "I mean to show that the responsibilities that ancient Israel had to the resident aliens in their midst were rooted in a conception of justice as right relationship—with God, with the resident aliens, and with one another."[51] In her book Rajendra identifies and illuminates the complex contexts surrounding our relationships with others. This is helpful. We, the people of God, need to move beyond simplistic universal proclamations about justice to careful thinking about who has responsibility to distribute the mercy that God requires of people. Standing up for universal human rights is a good thing, but it's also quite meaningless if no one actually attends to

50. Material from Rajendra in this section is derived primarily from Vos, "Who Is My Neighbor?," 27–35, used with permission of the publisher.
51. Rajendra, *Migrants and Citizens*, 10.

such rights. "Be well-fed and clothed" means little to people if they're being pushed back to the impoverished side of the wall.

In formulating her theory, Rajendra takes as a starting point the legal materials about resident aliens described in the Hebrew Bible and moves to an "account of justice that is rooted in the relationship between God and Israel and the complex of historical relationships among God, Israel, and the various strangers in the biblical narratives."[52] Not only are the Israelites to care for the marginal ones among them—indigent people with no claim to their land—but they are even commanded to love them (Deut. 10:19). To abuse, neglect, or show indifference to the suffering of the *ger* (Hebrew for "stranger") is a rejection of who God is and how God is. To neglect the stranger is to step away from being the people of God. And, Rajendra observes, "The Hebrew Bible's relational perspective on justice is also reflected in the new covenant of Jesus Christ, which changes relationships between members of the community and strangers."[53]

The Sinai covenant, Rajendra explains, is addressed to a people with membership, belonging, and a claim to the land they inhabit. The Pentateuch, she notes, is unique among various ancient Near Eastern texts in the way it includes strangers in its legal requirements. In relating to strangers, as in all things, God's people are to be like God. Accordingly, the new land they've come into must not become a means by which they assume a "this is ours—hands off" practice such as they were subject to in the old land they just left. In Egypt, the Israelites labored and were oppressed without being able to consume and benefit from the fruits of their toil. In Egypt they sat by the fleshpots of their masters, living in poverty amid plenty. Thus, as God's people, when the Israelites come into a land of their own, they are explicitly commanded to remember that they were strangers (*gerim*) in Egypt and that their new and improved situation is because of God's goodness, not something of their own making. After all, God "gave" them the land they now inhabit. It's a gift, not a right. Rajendra concludes, "Israel is to be the anti-Egypt, because God is the anti-pharaoh."[54]

In considering the strangers around and among us, the people of God must continually decide whether to be an Egypt or a Sinai. Indeed, relationships that honor and reflect the Sinai covenant look profoundly different from those in Egypt. Has God brought the Israelites out of Egypt merely to become a new Egypt? Old and New Testament Scriptures constantly associate care for the

52. Rajendra, *Migrants and Citizens*, 93.
53. Rajendra, *Migrants and Citizens*, 94.
54. Rajendra, *Migrants and Citizens*, 105.

stranger with the blessing of God, while abuse of the stranger kindles God's wrath. The Egyptian army, in hot pursuit of the *gerim* they had exploited for their labor, ends up at the bottom of the Red Sea. Furthermore, for the people of God, protecting national wealth is never identified in Scripture as an overriding concern. The only prosperity that matters is that which comes from the generous and open hand of God. Our hand, in turn, should be like God's—open, generous, merciful.

Rajendra includes a number of migrant stories in her analysis. For example, she offers the compelling story of Mario Castro, who migrated from Guatemala to the United States without his family, partly because he needed critical medical treatment that his home country could not provide. When US Immigration and Customs Enforcement (a title that reduces to the inhospitable acronym "ICE") apprehended him, they sent him across the border to Mexico, another country where he held no citizenship, thus placing him between social systems and depriving him of meaningful citizenship. Who then should help him? Rajendra explains that "while documents like the UN Convention on the Rights of Migrants are quite insistent that migrants are endowed with rights by virtue of their very humanity, few UN statements or academic books discuss who has the duty to protect the rights of migrants and why."[55] Lamentably, the website for ICE, as of my writing, appears to boast about its effectiveness at simply getting rid of undocumented people who have crossed into the United States without helping them.[56] "Who is merciful? Not us!"

Rajendra writes, "I do wish to suggest, however, that the relationships between citizens and migrants that initiated and sustain migration systems must be at the heart of the Christian ethics of migration. Indeed, the central question of the book [*Migrants and Citizens*] is: 'What responsibilities do citizens have to migrants?' Responding to that question involves accurately understanding the relationships between different groups of citizens and migrants."[57] I recently heard several political radio ads that promoted their candidates in part with the promise that they would vote against the main-tenance of sanctuary cities, where "illegal immigrants" take up residence. I live in the American South, in a city that in recent years was voted the most Bible-minded city in America, whatever that means. It is curious that political rhetoric and action against sanctuary for poor migrants holds currency in, arguably, the epicenter of Christian America. For me, the feel and tone of these ads, and of similar sentiments I sometimes see promoted on Facebook ("Click

---

55. Rajendra, *Migrants and Citizens*, 12.
56. U.S. Immigration and Customs Enforcement, "Keeping America Safe."
57. Rajendra, *Migrants and Citizens*, 52.

'Like' if you think illegal immigrants make too many demands"), root them more in Egypt than in Sinai. They are predicated, I believe, on the assumption that no significant prior relationship exists between migrants and the United States. "They" see what "we" have, and they want a slice of the American dream—like a stranger entering your house, asking "What's for dinner?" and then demanding you make it gluten free. But prior relationship does exist, even if it is not immediately apparent, and meaningful justice requires that we unearth complex and difficult structural and relational histories. There really is no simple "we and they." Using the case of a nanny as an example, Rajendra explains:

> When Lourdes is employed as a nanny, the relationship between her and the couple employing her is not only a relationship among three individuals. The relationship between these individuals is shaped by the numerous relationships of social position between undocumented domestic workers and upper-middle-class, double-income suburbanites, between Latinas and whites, and between citizens and migrants. In other words, the fact that Lourdes's wages fall far below a living wage is not simply the result of her employers not paying her enough: the interaction between Lourdes and her employers is, to a certain extent, conditioned by the relationship between undocumented migrants and citizens in Los Angeles. It is characteristic of the relationship between these two groups that citizens tend to underpay migrants, taking advantage of the cheap labor that they offer.[58]

Rajendra's book clearly illuminates how specific past relationships have influenced present ones and why Christians especially should be careful about disparaging sanctuary cities or oversimplifying migrants as "free riders." Of guest-worker programs, Rajendra explains that wealthy host countries like to think they are just hiring workers. But you cannot get "workers" without getting "people." Extracting an individual's labor while ignoring his or her person, family, identity, or future creates migration ripples that continue across time and must be addressed if relational justice is the standard. Accordingly, host countries who invited and benefited from guest labor bear responsibility for the full humanity and context of those whose labor they enjoyed. After all, how should one treat a "guest"? And shouldn't extended-stay "guests" become friends over time? Or do we Christians just capitulate to secular paradigms for which economic legitimations are sufficient?

Rajendra's treatment of colonial migration is equally illuminating. For example, she reminds us that "British immigration was a direct consequence

58. Rajendra, *Migrants and Citizens*, 57.

of British colonialism."[59] The British colonized others, recruited their work, and then later resented and resisted the implications those relationships had for British culture: "British colonialism and the subsequent migrations it engendered changed British society, which today is rife with reminders of colonialism, not only in the presence of these migrants and their descendants, but in British food and culture."[60] Her point? Present relationships between migrants and host cultures derive from past relationships. Working to identify and understand the particular histories that have shaped present migrant-host relationships, though frequently obscure and therefore difficult, is necessary to meet the requirements of justice as "right relationships."

Finally, we must also account for the influence of foreign investment on contemporary migration patterns if we wish to properly understand the relationship between host countries and migrants. The activities "we" engage in abroad influence contemporary migration patterns and require that we take responsibility for their aftermath. For example, as I write, Harley-Davidson has been moving some of their manufacturing to Thailand. How will a new factory influence the lives of native people who will build "our" motorcycles? Seen one way, it appears benevolent. Now "they" have an income source that they didn't have before. But is this the whole story, and does American responsibility end with providing Thai factory workers with low-wage jobs for a time? What happens when the factory closes and unemployed workers want to migrate to the US to make a better life for themselves? Rajendra details some of the implications of US investment in Mexico, writing, "Migration systems initiated by both private companies and government guest-worker programs had been in place for decades, and this history forms the context of US investment in Mexico."[61] She explains that international treaties such as the General Agreements on Tariffs and Trade (GATT) and the North American Free Trade Agreement (NAFTA) encourage countries to build factories through the elimination of import tariffs. Whatever the benefits such agreements bring, "the creation of these factories often disrupts traditional work structures by drawing people from traditional work in agriculture or crafts into work in factories. Not only does the creation of factories draw people from traditional work, whose infrastructure collapses in the absence of workers, but the promise of factory work draws new people into the work force, particularly women. . . . In Mexico this process was exacerbated by the elimination of government grain subsidies to Mexico's farmers, which

59. Rajendra, *Migrants and Citizens*, 64.
60. Rajendra, *Migrants and Citizens*, 66.
61. Rajendra, *Migrants and Citizens*, 68.

made it difficult for them to compete with an influx of cheap grain from the United States."[62]

When "we" profit from the labor of poor people in other countries, and when our activity in their communities dismantles traditional ways of making a living, we—like it or not—have cultivated responsibility toward them. We can pretend the relationship is one-sided when "they" cross the border—legally or otherwise. We can develop self-serving narratives that tell half-truths at best. But to do so is to sit by our heavily guarded fleshpots under a sign that reads "Welcome to Egypt—keep out."

Migrants and Citizens clearly communicates just how central the practice of respect, care, and love for the stranger is in the Hebrew Bible. One could argue that it is this care and concern for the stranger, this diminishing of otherness, that makes the Pentateuch truly unique among other ancient texts. In making this argument, Rajendra draws insight from Walter Brueggemann's work on the relationship between Torah, memory, land, and *gerim*. She writes,

> While God gives the land to the Israelites as his chosen people, living as God's chosen people requires what could be called a preferential option for the non-Israelite. Walter Brueggemann addresses this irony in his exploration of land as both gift and temptation in the Hebrew Bible [see Brueggemann, *Land*]. As Israel goes from being a wandering band of former slaves in the wilderness to a settled nation with a land of their own, they face the temptation to forget the covenant. Having land represents satiety, comfort, and power, and the satiated, comfortable, and powerful are prey to "the seduction of imagining it was always so, and that Israel made it so" [see Brueggemann, *Land*, 52]. . . . The power that comes with land tempts Israel to forget that they were once powerless strangers in need of God's protection.[63]

This centrality of care and concern for the stranger finds expression in the New Testament in the way Jesus himself presents as a stranger who ministers to those who have become strangers to God. Jesus continually befriends strangers, takes responsibility for them, nurtures relationship with them, and provides for them:

> Matthew 25 explicitly links the image of Jesus as a stranger with the moral imperative of hospitality: "I was a stranger and you welcomed me." Like the Hebrew Bible materials that place the *gēr* in the most-vulnerable triad, the Gospels identify the stranger as one of the "least of these" who reveal the face of Christ. . . . The hungry, the thirsty, the stranger, the naked, the sick, the prisoner

62. Rajendra, *Migrants and Citizens*, 69.
63. Rajendra, *Migrants and Citizens*, 108.

. . . all represent Christ, and by caring for the "least of these," the Christian community cares for Christ. The stranger cannot literally be a stranger, for the stranger is the literal personification of Jesus.[64]

And, of course, the logic of evangelism rests on making neighbors of strangers. Obvious conclusion: to neglect or oppress the strangers among us is to forsake what it should mean to be the people of God, followers of Jesus's way of being in the world. When Christians oppose strangers by blocking them from fellowship and resources, it raises questions about whether the gospel really is "good news" or just another dead end for the "least of these." So, who is my neighbor in this complex world we share? Neighbors are those with whom we are in relationship. And in a world of instant electronic communication, multinational corporations, guest-worker programs, factories in foreign lands, imports, and exports, neighbors are everywhere, near and far.

The narratives we so frequently hear, and tell ourselves, are hidden by structural sin. Life as we experience it is taken as a given, and we fail to see the marginalized ones who weave our cloth, make our shoes, and so on. Rajendra writes, "Simply by eating dinner, citizens participate in the structures of sin that take advantage of undocumented migrants. This participation does not require any ill will. In fact, opting out of this participation would require almost superhuman amounts of attention, time, and money simply because these structures have become so much a part of the way citizens live their lives. . . . Responsibilities to undocumented migrants come from this unwitting participation in labor markets that benefit from the labor of these migrants."[65]

We the people of God are called to lift the veil of the legitimated order we take for granted in order to actually see the migrant worker, separated from her family, picking the apple we put in our child's lunch. To wonder how good coffee with origins in Africa made it to our cups. To resist folk-devil narratives about immigrant ranks being full of rapists, criminals, and drug peddlers. To learn to see structural sin and to recognize how we benefit from it, even when its origins were beyond our control. And to take responsibility for our part in it. Relationships bind people, and justice is right relationship. To be people of justice, we must expose hidden narratives, retell them truthfully, and serve as vocal opponents of false, self-serving, and incomplete stories. For in seeking out and telling the truth about marginal strangers who press in on our worlds, and then engaging them in right relationship, we just might

64. Rajendra, *Migrants and Citizens*, 110–11.
65. Rajendra, *Migrants and Citizens*, 130.

embrace the Jesus who stands among them, just beyond the barbed wire, along our border walls.

Postscript

This chapter leaves quite a few questions unanswered. The reader may leave with the impression that immigration is a simple matter requiring only simple solutions—just love the stranger and all will be well in God's world. But it's not simple. Understanding and addressing global migration by proposing and enacting humane solutions to the immeasurably complex issues framing the relationships between those with and those without land is well beyond the expertise of this writer. The myriad books offering a wide array of perspectives and approaches stand in testimony to the lack of consensus on this issue. Nonetheless, in the midst of all the complexity, in the absence of clear pathways that resolve the issues of immigration, perhaps there is some merit in beginning with the simple things.

As part of the Christian sociology conference discussed in chapter 1, we visited several Amish homes to listen, learn, and glean wisdom from a group of Christians who live by a very different socio-theological ethic than that of most Western Christians. While we visited in one older couple's home, we noticed that several adults with intellectual disabilities had taken up residence there. They weren't blood relatives of their hosts. When we asked about this, our hosts offered the following: "We take in who God sends us. When someone with need comes to us, we open our door." There was no expiration date on their hospitality. There was no sense that our new Amish friends were trying to understand or solve the world's problems. They simply had a tacit understanding that the people of God have no higher calling or more important task than to show hospitality and to offer mercy to the ones God sends. Breathtakingly simple. There were no words about whether their guests had a right to be there, no attempts to get them to move on, and certainly no unkind words or concern with their own rights. Just simple service, done in the name of God, for those in need. I have; you need; come on in. Maybe this ethic is a place to start.

When I was a child, my mother used to play Raffi records in our home. Raffi Cavoukian, of Armenian descent, was born in Egypt, and with his family immigrated to Ontario, Canada, in 1958. Raffi is well known for his children's music and child advocacy. He employs a simple, guitar-based folk style. My childhood was saturated with his catchy melodies and positive, child-friendly music. One of his best-known songs—a hit in the world of six-year-olds—is titled "The Sharing Song." The following two lines from the chorus capture its central message:

> 'Cause if I share it with you
> You'll have some too[66]

Absolute simplicity. The essence of biblical theology in a children's song. What if this sentiment reflected how we approached the poor immigrant who with her children stands hopeful at "our" borders? What if approaching migrants could one day raise their weary eyes to the horizon at their journey's end, look our way, and in exhaustion fall to their knees saying, "Oh good, it's the Christians. Things will be okay."

What if . . .

---

66. Cavoukian and Whiteley, *Singable Songs for the Very Young.*

CHAPTER SEVEN

STRANGERS BEHIND BARS

Examining the System of Mass Incarceration

by Scott Monsma, Northwestern College

[Jesus] said to him, "You shall love the Lord your God with all your heart, and with all your soul, and with all your mind." This is the greatest and first commandment. And a second is like it: "You shall love your neighbor as yourself." On these two commandments hang all the law and the prophets.

Matthew 22:37–40

Come, you that are blessed by my Father, inherit the kingdom prepared for you from the foundation of the world. . . . I was a stranger and you welcomed me, . . . I was in prison and you visited me.

Matthew 25:34–36

One morning in September, while skimming through Facebook posts, I noticed numerous reposts of a Bernie Sanders tweet claiming, "We have a criminal justice system which is racist, broken, and must be fundamentally reformed."[1] Sanders's tweet referenced another tweet pointing out the considerable disparity

1. Sanders (@BernieSanders), "We have a criminal justice system . . ."

between the prison sentences given to Felicity Huffman and Tanya McDowell. Huffman, a White actress, was sentenced to fourteen days in prison plus a $30,000 fine and community service for working to fraudulently increase her daughter's SAT scores. In contrast, McDowell, an African American woman, received a five-year sentence for using a false address to enroll her five-year-old son in a school district where she did not reside. McDowell claimed to be homeless at that time and unaware that she was committing a crime.[2] At face value, the facts presented in the tweet seem to support Sanders's claim, demonstrating disparities in the way the criminal justice system treats individuals depending on their social class and racial/ethnic identity.

As is often the case, the facts of the matter are more complicated.[3] The comparison of Huffman and McDowell breaks down when additional details omitted from the original tweet are considered. Huffman's shorter sentence took into account that this was her first criminal charge. In contrast, McDowell had a prior criminal record for robbery and possession of a weapon in a vehicle.[4] At the time of McDowell's trial for education fraud, she was also tried and sentenced for selling drugs to an undercover police officer.[5] These additional details help to explain the large disparity in sentencing outcomes, and might, should logic and facts actually matter on social media, challenge the integrity of using this particular comparison to critique the criminal justice system.

However, even if we acknowledge that the contrast between Huffman and McDowell is problematic, the frequent reposting of Sanders's commentary still points to larger, more important questions. We might ask whether the indignation generated by the comparison of Huffman and McDowell reflects concerns about how the intersections of race and class affect the likelihood of arrest, conviction, and incarceration. We might ask whether McDowell's five-year prison sentence is connected to the five-decades-long "war on drugs" in the United States. Furthermore, we might consider the relevance of using prior convictions to determine sentencing outcomes and examine how convictions can label and stigmatize those who have been previously incarcerated. Does it feel like justice to reference her prior drug convictions when McDowell broke a different law, knowing the difference a school could make in the life of her child?[6] Finally, we

2. Perkins, "Felicity Huffman Sentencing Compared to Bridgeport Mom Tanya McDowell."
3. Palma, "Did Tanya McDowell Get 5 Years for Sending Her Son to a Better School while Felicity Huffman Got 14 Days?"
4. "Comparison of Tanya McDowell and Felicity Huffman Sentences Misleading."
5. Tepfer, "Tanya McDowell Sentenced to 5 Years in Prison."
6. To provide some insight into the educational inequality issues facing Tanya McDowell's son, readers might consider listening to the podcasts by Nikole Hannah-Jones, "The Problem We All Live with—Part One," and Shankar Vedantam, "Zipcode Destiny."

might step back and ask if incarceration for any length of time is the appropriate response to either Huffman's or McDowell's crimes.

Acknowledging the important differences between Huffman's and McDowell's cases, the questions raised in the previous paragraph suggest we should
not ignore the larger context. Crime and punishment are not just about individuals, not just about these two women. Instead, we need to consider the
socially constructed boundaries and norms governing group membership. We
need to examine why boundaries are created and whether such boundaries
are selectively enforced. We also need to consider the consequences for those
judged to be violators of the boundaries. In line with the focus of this entire
book, we can question whether the criminal justice system is a communal
form of stranger-making.

First, I will consider several sociological theories that highlight the community's role in creating strangers. Then I will focus on the United States
and look at how these theories find reinforcement in US crime and incarceration rates before discussing current literature that critically examines the US
criminal justice system. And finally, as we consider the communal creation of
strangers, the US criminal justice system, and patterns of incarceration, I will
suggest a few ways that those of us who seek to follow Jesus might respond.

You Made Me a Stranger, Theoretically Speaking

Any discussion of crime and the criminal justice system recognizes that groups
require social norms and boundaries in order to function. These norms reflect
acceptable ways of thinking and acting as part of the group and, by extension,
define what is not acceptable for members of the community. Such norms are
inherently necessary for humans to function collectively and to avoid chaos
or what sociologists call "anomie." As an example, consider the ubiquitous
red octagonal stop signs found throughout the US. In any of the contiguous
forty-eight states where I have driven, I know the meaning of stop signs, and
I appreciate how the signs provide guidance to safely navigate intersections.
However, when I moved to a small town of six thousand people in rural Iowa,
I discovered that most of the four-way intersections in town are not marked
with any type of sign. I do not know whether the lack of stop signs is a reflection that the community is too cheap to pay for the signage or whether this is
to enable folks to reduce a time-consuming one-mile commute across town!
Either way, the lack of signage at intersections can lead to an adrenaline rush
and a bit of chaos when several vehicles try to negotiate the intersection at
the same time. While a simple example, stop signs point to how social norms

and boundaries make life within a community possible and remind us of the chaos we experience in their absence.

The work of sociologist Émile Durkheim can help us connect the critical importance of social norms and boundaries to the role of the larger community in producing strangers. As Durkheim studied issues of deviance and crime, he made a provocative claim: "Crime is normal because it is completely impossible for any society entirely free of it to exist."[7] As a theorist working from a functionalist perspective, he contends that if something exists in all known societies, then it must serve a useful purpose. Just as kinship systems exist because of the need for socializing children and organizing inheritance, and economic systems are essential for the communal organization of allocation, production, and distribution of goods, crime will exist in all societies if it serves a useful purpose. This claim moves the focus away from individual offenders to the role of the larger community in the creation and persistence of crime and, by extension, the role of the community in creating strangers. Furthermore, as Durkheim claims, if crime is functional, then we cannot expect that any normal society will ever be free of deviant or criminal activity.

To understand the social functions tied to crime, Durkheim proposes that we consider the larger concept of deviance, recognizing that crime is just one form or subset of deviance. He asserts that deviance occurs in every community, partly because group members have been socialized in slightly different contexts and will not have identical views on the importance of conforming to particular social norms. In other words, group members are not like-minded clones, and deviance is not the result of a bad batch. However, the function of deviance (or crime) is not linked to the diverse views about norms and boundaries; the function is tied to the community response to violations of the social norms. When deviance occurs and the community responds and attempts to correct the deviant action, it clarifies norms for members of the community and strengthens group boundaries. In contrast, if the community fails to respond to deviance, it indicates to members of the group that those norms and boundaries are unimportant and can be ignored, potentially weakening the group or substantially altering what it means to belong. Thus, the functional explanation for deviance and crime focuses on how the collective response to deviance plays an essential role in affirming what it means to belong to a particular community. Oddly, Durkheim is suggesting that communities *need* to create strangers in order to define what it means to belong within the community. You can't have insiders if you don't have outsiders.

7. Durkheim, *Rules of Sociological Method*, 99.

Durkheim's assertion that crime serves an essential function, and that no society can eliminate deviance, may appear to legitimate the status quo. Accordingly, it might be all too easy to look at the punishments delivered to Huffman and McDowell and conclude that their sentences were inherently necessary. Their sentences could serve the function of reinforcing social norms and group boundaries. However, Durkheim's work offers additional refinements to the functionalist perspective and provides a more critical analysis of the link between deviance (and crime) and the role of stranger-making in strengthening or challenging group boundaries.

Although not a focus for Durkheim, implicit in his thinking is the understanding that social norms and boundaries vary from group to group and from society to society. As Berger and Luckmann suggest in *The Social Construction of Reality*, we cannot take norms and boundaries for granted because norms and boundaries are relative to a particular culture.[8] They point out that humans are not born preprogrammed with social norms governing our participation in the community.[9] Rather, over time, human communities develop patterned ways of thinking and acting in response to challenges in the environment that, in contrast to most other animals, enable humans to inhabit and thrive in a wide variety of environments. For example, stop signs and other traffic norms reflect the social construction of reality in response to the rise of automotive transportation. No doubt the social norms governing interactions between vehicles pulled by horses or cows were utterly insufficient to ensure the safety of cars on the road, necessitating the creation of new norms to govern the flow of traffic. Thus traffic norms are not shared across all cultures. While visiting places like Taiwan or Oman, I have noted differences in road signs and traffic norms. Some of these differences may seem trivial, such as camel-crossing signs in Oman. Some of these differences are more important, such as the norms shaping interactions in three-lane roundabouts with heavy traffic (as an outsider, I found such interactions much more stressful and riskier than negotiating unmarked intersections in my rural town).

Calling attention to the social construction of norms and boundaries means paying attention to how the community defines their social world and how they understand who is normal and who is a stranger. It also leads us to pay attention to how issues of social power and influence can shape boundaries and the process by which a person or a group is labeled as a stranger. While Durkheim does not focus on the issue, implicit in his discussion is the idea that deviance or crime is a process that depends on the response of the community.

8. Berger and Luckmann, *Social Construction of Reality*, 3.
9. Berger and Luckmann, *Social Construction of Reality*, 47.

Writing from the perspective of labeling theory, sociologist Howard Becker points out the critical importance of this process when he writes, "Social groups create deviance by the making of rules whose infractions constitute deviance and by applying those rules to particular people and labeling them as outsiders. From this point of view deviance is not a quality of the act the person commits, but rather a consequence of the application by others of rules and sanctions to an 'offender.' The deviant is one to whom the label has successfully been applied; deviant behavior is behavior that people so label."[10] Becker echoes Berger and Luckmann's contention that group boundaries are socially constructed. More importantly, he argues that deviance is not a particular act but rather the outcome of a labeling process. By focusing on the process, labeling theory recognizes that not all norm-breaking may be labeled as deviant. Just as important, he implies that a person could be labeled as deviant even if they have not violated any social norms.

Becker is critical of the labeling process. He points out that the application of the deviant label varies over time, varies by perpetrator of the act, and varies by who is applying the label. Becker notes,

> Rules tend to be applied more to some persons than others. Studies of juvenile delinquency make the point clearly. Boys from middle-class areas do not get as far in the legal process when they are apprehended as do boys from slum areas. The middle-class boy is less likely when picked up by the police to be taken to the station; less likely when taken to the station to be booked; and it is extremely unlikely that he will be convicted and sentenced. This variation occurs even though the original infraction of the rule is the same in the two cases.[11]

Becker makes the critical points that social power influences the social construction of norms and that social power plays a critical role in whom the community decides to label as strangers.

Labeling theory problematizes how, and to whom, a deviant label may be applied. Labeling theory also calls attention to the consequences of the label. Once a person or group is labeled deviant, that label can function as a "master status," a primary social status that profoundly shapes interactions with that individual or group.[12] The label also has the potential to propel the individual or group into further deviance, or what labeling theorists call "secondary deviance." For example, we easily recognize how the label of "felon" becomes a master status. It is not just that a person has committed a

10. Becker, "Relativism," 41.
11. Becker, "Relativism," 41–42.
12. Becker, "Relativism," 43.

felony (an act), but once labeled as a deviant (a status), it can be difficult to obtain employment and reach financial stability. Up against these problems, and blocked from the "normal" ways of, say, acquiring necessary resources, the individual may engage in further deviant or criminal activity.

This brief review of sociological theory provides several key ideas to consider as we turn our focus to the US criminal justice and prison system. First, Durkheim contends that deviance and crime are functional, that the community response to deviance is essential to reinforce social norms and group boundaries. Second, Berger and Luckmann call attention to how all norms and boundaries are the result of the social construction of reality. Finally, Becker problematizes both issues by calling attention to the labeling process, asserting that the labeling itself determines who is deviant or criminal, challenging the way social power shapes who is labeled by the community and observing the consequences of labeling in terms of the creation of a master status and the potential for secondary deviance.

Counting Strangers: US Crime, Arrest, and Incarceration Data

It can be tempting to treat crime and incarceration data as simple facts, as objective counts of the number of crimes, criminals, and prisoners. However, what is or is not considered a crime is a product of the social construction of reality. For example, the criteria for what counts as rape has changed over time. To count as rape, there had to be evidence of force, and it was limited to specific actions a male perpetrator took when victimizing a woman. Now the definition and subsequent counting of rape is not limited to an act committed by a specific sex, nor is it an action requiring force. Labeling theory is also relevant to our examination of the data. Arrest, conviction, and incarceration do not reflect a simple counting of crimes and recording of those punished for the crimes. The numbers reflect the process by which agents of social control and the larger criminal justice system label individuals. Therefore, in reviewing data, we must keep in mind how crime is socially constructed and the role social power plays in establishing which individuals or groups are labeled as criminals.

The most frequently cited data on US crime rates come from the Uniform Crime Reports (UCR) compiled by the FBI. Each year, the FBI collects data on eight index crimes to measure the overall crime rate in the US. These include four types of crimes considered violent crimes (murder, rape, robbery, and aggravated assault) and four types considered property crimes (burglary, larceny/theft, motor vehicle theft, and arson). Data on other types of offenses,

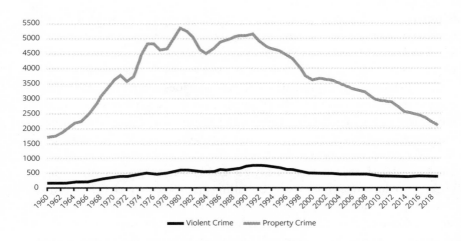

Figure 7.1. US crime rates per 100,000 people: 1960–2019 (Source: The Disaster Center [FBI UCR Index])

such as prostitution, drug abuse violations, and driving under the influence, are collected but not included in the list of index crimes.

UCR data do not provide a perfect measure of crime. The UCR relies heavily on law enforcement agencies' voluntary reporting of arrest data and of crimes reported to their agency, and not all agencies report each year. Additionally, not all crimes result in an arrest or a report to a law enforcement agency. The likelihood of being arrested for a crime, or of a crime being reported, can vary significantly between jurisdictions and between types of crimes. For example, murder is much more likely to result in an arrest or a report than is rape. Likewise, motor vehicle theft is substantially more likely to result in an arrest or a report than is larceny/ theft. UCR data are also limited because of the FBI's practice of recording only the most serious offense when an individual commits several crimes at the same time. These issues suggest that in any given year the number of crimes or the crime rate (crimes per 100,000 people) varies from the actual number and type of crimes committed during that year. Still, if we make the reasonable assumption that the problems with data reporting are consistent from year to year, UCR data can be useful for examining trends in the crime rates across years, and they may offer a sense of how overall crime rates are fluctuating.

Using UCR data to examine trends, we observe a large increase in the crime rate after 1960, with crime peaking in the early '80s (see fig. 7.1). After declining for a few years, the rate rose until it peaked again, at a slightly lower

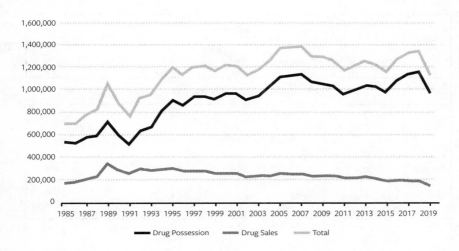

Figure 7.2. Drug arrests: 1985–2019 (Source: FBI Crime Data Explorer)

level, in the early '90s. Since the '90s, different from what many assume, the overall crime rate has steadily declined.[13]

As most crimes listed in the UCR index are property crimes, the scale of difference between property and violent crimes makes the changes in the violent crime rate less obvious. Nevertheless, we can still observe that the peak in the violent crime rate occurred in the early '90s and that the violent crime rate has been declining since that point.

In contrast to the general patterns in the index crime rate, arrests for drug-related offenses have not decreased since the 1980s (see fig. 7.2). Instead, drug-related arrests increased steadily after the early '80s and peaked in 2006. However, after a period of decline, the drug arrest rate began to rise again in 2015.[14] Susan Stellin concludes, "Drugs have been the top reason people have been arrested in the United States for at least the past 10 years."[15]

In 1985, arrests for possession made up 76.3 percent of all drug arrests.[16] In 2018 arrests for possession composed 86.4 percent of all arrests, with most of the arrests for possession involving small quantities.[17]

13. Disaster Center, "United States Crime Rates 1960–2019."
14. Federal Bureau of Investigation Crime Data Explorer, "Arrests Offense Counts in the United States."
15. Stellin, "Is the 'War on Drugs' Over?"
16. Federal Bureau of Investigation Crime Data Explorer, "Arrests Offense Counts in the United States."
17. Stellin, "Is the 'War on Drugs' Over?"

		White	African American	Hispanic/ Latino	Asian
Percent of U.S. Population		76.4%	12.5%	18.3%	5.7%
	Total Crimes	**Percentage of Arrests by Offense**			
Violent Crimes	Murder	9,468	44.2%	53.1%	15.4%	1.3%
	Rape	18,063	67.5%	28.7%	21.0%	1.7%
	Robbery	73,764	43.6%	54.3%	17.2%	0.9%
	Aggravated Assault	302,941	62.1%	33.5%	20.2%	1.6%
Property Crimes	Burglary	154,970	67.5%	29.8%	16.1%	1.1%
	Larceny-Theft	740,546	67.7%	29.1%	10.7%	1.2%
	Motor Vehicle Theft	70,617	66.0%	30.3%	20.6%	1.4%
	Arson	7,086	71.3%	25.2%	15.1%	1.6%
Drug Abuse		1,262,660	70.4%	27.1%	16.0%	1.1%
Driving under the Influence		755,726	81.7%	14.0%	18.6%	1.9%

Figure 7.3. Arrests by offense and race/ethnicity, 2017 (Source: FBI UCR)

These data give us a sense of the changing crime rates in the US. However, to address questions raised earlier in this chapter, we also need to examine how the possibility of an arrest varies with racial/ethnic identity. Figure 7.3 documents arrest rates for the eight index crimes, plus arrests for drug abuse or driving under the influence. Instead of just presenting the total number of offenses for each type of crime and for each racial/ethnic identity, the table presents the percentage of those arrested for an offense identified with a particular racial/ethnic identity.[18] This allows for a direct comparison between the percentage of arrests and the percentage each group composes in the US. This calculation provides a window into whether members of a specific racial/ethnic identity are over- or underrepresented in national arrest rates.

18. Federal Bureau of Investigation, "Arrests by Race/Ethnicity, 2017." Because those who are Hispanic/Latino may be of any race, the sum of the percentages in each row will be larger than 100 percent.

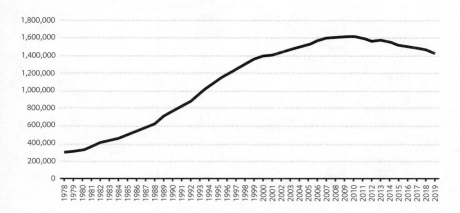

Figure 7.4. US state and federal prison populations (Source: Bureau of Justice Statistics: National Prisoner Statistics Program)

For example, White people compose about 76.4 percent of the population. If all factors were equal and racial/ethnic identity was irrelevant, we would expect White people to account for about 76.4 percent of all arrests in each category. Instead, arrest data show that for all crimes, other than driving under the influence, White arrest rates are lower than we might expect. Similarly, Asian American arrest rates are lower than we might expect. Hispanic/Latino arrests rates are slightly higher than we might expect in some cases, such as for motor vehicle thefts, and lower than we might expect in other cases, such as murder. In contrast with other racial/ethnic groupings, African American arrest rates are significantly higher than expected, given the percentage of the population identifying as African American. Without exploring explanations at this point, we can observe how arrest data document that African Americans are more likely to be arrested and labeled as potential criminals than are any of the other racial/ethnic groups.

Crime report and arrest data provide a window into the initial encounter between law enforcement and individuals who may (or may not) have engaged in criminal activity. In contrast, incarceration data provides insight into one way that individuals are formally labeled as criminals and removed from the population for a length of time. As such, incarceration not only reflects the formal application of a label, but it also demonstrates, through physical separation from the larger community, that these individuals are now strangers.

One striking aspect of the US criminal justice system, and the prison system in particular, is seen in the rapid rise in incarceration rates since the late 1970s. From roughly 300,000 prisoners in federal and state prisons in 1978, the number of prisoners has grown significantly, peaking at over 1.6 million

United States	639
Spain	122
United Kingdom	114
Canada	107
Italy	90
France	87
Ireland	74
Germany	69
Sweden	68
Iceland	33

Figure 7.5. Incarceration rates by country

(Rate is number incarcerated per 100,000 population;
source: World Population Review)

incarcerated individuals in 2019. Similarly, local jail populations have grown dramatically, from 184,000 incarcerated individuals in 1980 to 740,000 in 2016, leading to an estimated total of over 2.16 million individuals incarcerated in in the United States in 2016 (see fig. 7.4).[19]

Comparing incarceration numbers to the crime rates discussed earlier, we see that the rapid rise in the prison population occurs at around the same time as the crime rates start to decline.[20] While it is tempting to link the decline in crime rates to the rise of incarceration rates, this rise is likely linked to other factors, some of which will be explored later in this chapter.

The massive growth in incarceration rates in the US also stands in stark contrast to other similar Western democracies and much of the rest of the world. According to World Population Review, approximately 25 percent of the world's prison population is in the United States.[21] The table in figure 7.5 provides a sense of the contrast between the US and Western European nations, documenting the disparity in incarceration rates (prisoners per 100,000 in the population) between the United States and these countries.[22]

In terms of incarceration, the US is an outlier among these nations, with an incarceration rate five times higher than Spain, the next closest country. However, the US is an outlier not just among this set of nations but among *all* nations. World Population Review lists the incarceration rates for 206

19. Kaeble and Cowhig, "Correctional Populations in the United States, 2016."
20. Carson, "Prisoners under the Jurisdiction of State or Federal Correctional Authorities."
21. World Population Review, "Incarceration Rates by Country, 2021."
22. World Population Review, "Incarceration Rates by Country, 2021."

Age Group	Male				Female			
	White	Black	Hispanic	Other	White	Black	Hispanic	Other
Total	385	2,203	979	1,176	48	83	63	109
18–19	58	720	188	222	6	20	12	11
20–24	347	2,772	1,105	1,133	49	116	78	118
25–29	707	4,158	1,957	2,091	120	186	150	239
30–34	891	4,496	2,156	2,404	156	199	178	276
35–39	958	4,832	2,181	2,687	148	187	164	270
40–44	821	4,334	1,877	2,348	110	151	114	201
45–49	696	3,553	1,500	2,023	83	128	82	144
50–54	561	2,970	1,210	1,697	54	110	64	123
55–59	418	2,227	972	1,318	32	68	42	83
60–64	254	1,404	705	895	14	32	20	48
65 or older	101	485	317	362	4	9	6	15

Figure 7.6. Federal and state imprisonment rates by age and sex, 2019 (Source: Bureau of Justice Statistics)

nations. From these data, the average incarceration rate among nations is 172.1 prisoners per 100,000 in the population.[23] Few other nations even come close to the incarceration rate evidenced in the US. The US appears to be unique in the world in relying on incarceration as a response to crime, and for some this is a source of national pride.

Incarceration data show dramatic growth in the United States prison population since the 1980s, demonstrating that the US relies on incarceration more than any other nation. If we examine incarceration rates for a single year, we also observe that the probability of incarceration varies markedly by age, race, and sex. Figure 7.6 documents the difference in incarceration rates for each group, with the incarceration rate taking into account the size of each corresponding age, sex, and racial/ethnic grouping.[24]

The incarceration rates in figure 7.6 document that the likelihood of being incarcerated varies significantly by racial/ethnic identity. Overall, a Black male is five times more likely, and a Hispanic male approximately two-and-a-half times more likely, to be imprisoned than a White male. It is also evident that

23. World Population Review, "Incarceration Rates by Country, 2021."
24. Carson, "Imprisonment Rates of Sentenced State and Federal Prisoners."

an offender's sex has a large effect on incarceration rates, with men far more likely to be incarcerated than women.[25] But even though the incarceration rates for women are smaller, racial/ethnic identity still is a factor, with Black women more than twice as likely, and Hispanic women more than 1.3 times as likely, to be incarcerated than White women. Finally, the incarceration data reflect a link between age and crime, with younger members of the population more likely to engage in crime, more likely to be arrested, and more likely to be incarcerated. However, we should not overlook the fact that African American and Hispanic people, even after reaching age sixty-five, continue to be incarcerated at far higher rates than White people.

The crime report, arrest, and incarceration data we have reviewed provide additional context for thinking about the convictions and sentencing of Huffman and McDowell. These data indicate that concerns about the differential treatment of racial/ethnic groups have a basis in the differences in arrest and incarceration rates. The data show that, even as overall crime rates have fallen, arrest rates for drug possession (even for minor amounts) have increased. Moreover, as crime rates have fallen in the US, the US has dramatically increased the number of individuals incarcerated, to the point of becoming a global outlier on this measure. Even if we continue to acknowledge the differences between Huffman's case and McDowell's case, the data suggest that furor over their treatment reflects an awareness of the disparities in the larger US criminal justice system.

Making Strangers: The War on Drugs

Durkheim's functionalist theory suggests there is a need for groups to establish norms and boundaries for acceptable behavior. We might recognize how some norms and boundaries are beneficial to the community, serving to protect individuals and the larger community from harm. Certainly, this is the justification used to support the regulation or prohibition of particular drugs. In the 1980s, the need to safeguard communities was used to encourage us to "Just Say No" to drugs, and to justify increasing enforcement and stiff penalties to address the sale and use of illegal drugs. I also remember how the news at that time often featured stories about the emerging crack cocaine epidemic, the highly addictive and deadly properties of crack, and the tragic situation of pregnant women giving birth to "crack babies." While many of

25. This chapter does not focus on how sex and gender connect to crime and incarceration. For readers interested in exploring this issue, start with Chesney-Lind and Pasko's *Female Offender*.

these stories later turned out to be inaccurate, such as the hysteria over "crack babies," they reflected concerns about the threat drugs posed to communities.[26]

Even if we acknowledge there may be value in laws regulating drugs and drug use, we should not ignore how views about *which* drugs are harmful, and which are beneficial, is the result of a social construction.[27] This is obvious in current debates over the legalization of marijuana and in the efforts in several states to pass legislation legalizing its medical or recreational use. We see a similar social shift in the passing of the Eighteenth Amendment to the US Constitution banning the manufacture, transportation, or sale of alcohol, something later repealed in 1933. Even the debates about smoking and nicotine reflect shifting social beliefs about the danger of smoking. Some have raised concern not just about the health risks to smokers but about the effects of second- and thirdhand smoke on nonsmokers.[28] These concerns have led to increased regulation and taxation on tobacco products in an effort to reduce their use.

Considering how the social construction of reality shapes our views about the harm or benefits of drugs, we might wonder why crack cocaine was so feared in the 1980s, but the same fear and moral panic was not applied to regular (powder) cocaine. What might lead the larger society to tolerate or embrace the use of some drugs and fear (or demonize) the use of other drugs? That question leads us to consider the relevance of labeling theory for understanding the war on drugs.

Sociologist Craig Reinarman, in his article "The Social Construction of Drug Scares," argues that drug scares, antidrug campaigns, and moral panics about drugs are not a recent historical phenomenon. Rather, the US has a "history of antidrug crusades and a history of repressive drug laws."[29] Relevant to labeling theory, he highlights how each drug scare and antidrug campaign is tied to a powerful group that feels threatened by some other group. Consider the following:

- The temperance movement, which worked toward passage of the Eighteenth Amendment, was composed of "native-born, middle-class, non-urban Protestants who felt threatened by working-class, Catholic

26. Winerip, "Revisiting the 'Crack Babies' Epidemic That Was Not."
27. The writing of this chapter was enhanced through the regular consumption of a legal stimulant, purchased from a local barista or an internet supplier (https://duluthcoffeecompany .com/). While most would consider caffeine beneficial and mostly harmless, overuse or overdosing can have serious health consequences or even lead to death.
28. Hays, "What Is Thirdhand Smoke?"
29. Reinarman, "Social Constrution of Drug Scares," 159.

immigrants who were filling up US cities during industrialization."[30] The push to ban the manufacture and sale of alcohol was not just about the dangers of consuming alcohol; it was also about the danger of moral corruption and moral decay that came from working-class individuals stopping at a local bar or saloon on the way home. The temperance movement was linked to class conflict, moral boundaries, and making strangers of immigrants.[31]

- In 1875, prior to the temperance movement, laws targeting opium dens were passed in San Francisco. Opiates had been widely available and were used in legally available products before this point. But difficult economic times, anti-Chinese rhetoric and sentiments, and concerns about White people intermixing with Chinese immigrants resulted in laws targeted at opium dens.[32] And in the early twentieth century, a nationwide panic over opiates began "when the addict population began to shift from predominately white, middle-class women to young, working-class males, African Americans in particular."[33]

- During the Great Depression, fear of Mexican Americans was part of the motivation for the passing of federal legislation and the criminalization of marijuana in 1937.[34] Like other drug scares, the push to criminalize marijuana was not just about the purported, and often highly inaccurate discussion of, effects of the drug; it was also about the "moral decay" and class-based threat of those who used it.[35]

- The drug scare around crack cocaine in the 1980s was not linked to rising rates of cocaine use, as usage of cocaine had been rising for at least a decade before this. Instead, the drug scare began "in 1986 when freebase cocaine was renamed 'crack' (or 'rock') and sold in precooked, inexpensive units. . . . Once politicians and the media linked this new form of cocaine use to inner-city, minority poor, a new drug scare was underway."[36]

30. Reinarman, "Social Construction of Drug Scares," 160.
31. For several years I attended a church near Pittsburgh, Pennsylvania. Some elderly women in the congregation were still members of the Women's Christian Temperance Union, and they would annually distribute flyers lamenting the overturning of prohibition and linking the elimination of prohibition to both moral decay and the rise of social evils in the US.
32. Reinarman, "Social Construction of Drug Scares," 161.
33. Reinarman, "Social Construction of Drug Scares," 162.
34. Reinarman, "Social Construction of Drug Scares," 162.
35. I recommend watching the trailer to the movie *Reefer Madness* as an example of the distorted and inaccurate propaganda from that time: https://www.youtube.com/watch?v=yX tumnTN6zg.
36. Reinarman, "Social Constrution of Drug Scares," 163.

Reinarman summarizes the role of labeling and class conflict in the making of drug scares and states: "Drug scares are never about drugs per se, because drugs are inanimate objects without social consequence until they are ingested by humans. Rather, drug scares are about the use of a drug by particular groups of people who are, typically, already perceived by powerful groups as some kind of threat. . . . In each case, politico-moral entrepreneurs were able to construct a 'drug problem' by linking a substance to a group of users perceived by the powerful as disreputable, dangerous, or otherwise threatening."[37] The result of the drug scares and the labeling process was an increase in the severity of drug laws and penalties, even if increased criminalization of these drugs did not reduce drug use or associated problems.[38]

Reinarman provides compelling evidence that recurring drug scares are linked to class conflict and reflect the outcome of the labeling process in the US. In the late 1970s these drug scares morphed into something new, an all-out "war on drugs." The start of this rhetorical and policy shift can be traced to John Ehrlichman, an adviser to Richard Nixon. In an interview for *Harper's Magazine*, the interviewer claims Ehrlichman started the "war on drugs" rhetoric to help Nixon win and keep the presidency:

> The Nixon campaign in 1968, and the Nixon White House after that, had two enemies: the antiwar left and black people. You understand what I'm saying? We knew we couldn't make it illegal to be either against the war or blacks, but by getting the public to associate the hippies with marijuana and blacks with heroin, and then criminalizing both heavily, we could disrupt those communities. We could arrest their leaders, raid their homes, break up their meetings, and vilify them night after night on the evening news. Did we know we were lying about the drugs? Of course we did.[39]

The rhetoric of the war on drugs did not stop with the ignominious end of the Nixon presidency; instead, the rhetoric continued under President Reagan, who elevated it and officially announced a war on drugs in 1982.[40]

The rise of crack cocaine use in the 1980s contributed to the escalation of the efforts by Reagan and his administration to sell this "war" to the public, and in 1986 both *Newsweek* and *Time* declared that crack use was the most important story of the year.[41] Michelle Alexander in her book *The New Jim Crow* writes that within a year,

37. Reinarman, "Social Constrution of Drug Scares," 164–65.
38. Reinarman, "Social Constrution of Drug Scares," 163.
39. Baum, "Legalize It All."
40. Alexander, *New Jim Crow*, 49.
41. Alexander, *New Jim Crow*, 51.

with the media frenzy at full throttle, the house passed legislation that allocated $2 billion to the antidrug crusade, required the participation of the military in narcotics control efforts, allowed the death penalty for some drug related crimes, and authorized the admission of some illegally obtained evidence in drug trials. Later that month, the Senate proposed even tougher antidrug legislation, and shortly thereafter the president signed the Anti-Drug Abuse Act of 1986 into law. Among other harsh penalties, the legislation included mandatory minimum sentences for the distribution of cocaine, including far more severe punishments for the distribution of crack—associated with blacks—than powder cocaine, associated with whites.[42]

Moreover, as Reagan's presidency drew to a close in 1988, Congress revised US drug policy, ramping up the severity of the consequences for offenders, including eviction from public housing and new mandatory minimum sentences, even for first-time offenders.

The war on drugs did not end with Regan's term in office; it continued under George H. W. Bush and in some form under each successive president. This all-out war on drugs has affected individuals in several troubling ways. For example, efforts to quickly identify drug users have led to the widespread use of inaccurate roadside tests for drugs, frequent arrests, and the pressure to plea bargain to felony drug charges, even though there is a good chance the roadside test produced a false-positive result.[43] Just recently, an individual was accused of using meth or ecstasy when officers tested a container of his daughter's ashes and the test returned a false positive.[44] In addition, drug forfeiture laws allow law enforcement agencies to seize cash or property that they suspect is linked to a drug crime, even before a guilty plea or verdict is obtained. Those who have their assets seized have the burden of trying to prove their innocence in order to reclaim their property. A report from the Institute for Justice, based on federal, state, and local data, suggests that over $68 billion has been confiscated through forfeiture laws.[45] Finally, as demonstrated by drug arrest data, even as the crime rate began declining in the 1980s, arrests for drug-related charges started increasing, with the majority arrested for possession and not for drug sales or manufacturing. With increased enforcement, increased penalties for drug possession, and mandatory minimums for drug crimes, the war on drugs has contributed to the rapid rise in prison populations, with slightly more than 46 percent of the federal prison

42. Alexander, *New Jim Crow*, 52.
43. Gabrielson and Sanders, "Busted."
44. Salcedo, "Police Told a Man a Container in His Car Tested Positive for Drugs."
45. Knepper, McDonald, Sanchez, and Pohl, "Abuse of Civil Asset Forfeiture."

population behind bars for drug offenses.[46] Combined prisoner data from all federal, state, and local jails indicate that about one in five US prisoners was incarcerated for a drug offense.[47]

A great deal more has been written about US drug policy and the social construction of reality that shapes drug laws and punishments. However, it seems clear that drug scares, and more importantly the war on drugs, are not ultimately about drugs or drug policy. Instead, the war on drugs, which contributes to the US system of mass incarceration, is about intergroup conflict, frequently using drug policy to target groups that appear to threaten the way of life of others. It is about using drug policies to turn individuals and groups into strangers and to exclude them from the larger community.

We can also contrast the stigmatizing of groups during drug scares, and the five-decades-long war on drugs, with the more recent discussions of opioid overuse (often called an "opioid epidemic"). Proposed solutions have focused more on expanding *treatment* instead of turning to incarceration. The difference in rhetoric, treatment, and enforcement may be linked to the fact that opioid addiction has significantly affected the White population.[48] Apparently, in the US, we are willing to treat as a disease, fund treatment, and reduce criminal penalties when the affected group holds a much greater degree of social power.

Making Strangers: The Criminal Justice System and Racial/Ethnic Identity

In Sanders's tweet, he made a claim that the criminal justice system is racist. For those who view the criminal justice system as simply functioning to reinforce important social boundaries and protect the larger community, the comparison of Huffman and McDowell does not provide sufficient evidence to support Sanders's claim. In fact, no single story, however emotionally compelling, would be adequate to demonstrate systemic problems. Instead, to address Sanders's claim, we should start by recognizing that racial/ethnic identity is not based in any biological reality; it is a social construction.[49] Then we can work to identify more persuasive evidence that shows how labeling individuals based on racial/ethnic identity has relevance for understanding the criminal justice system.

Michelle Alexander, in her critically important work *The New Jim Crow*, makes a compelling argument that racial discrimination is one major characteristic of the current US criminal justice system. She starts by proposing

46. Federal Bureau of Prisons, "Inmate Statistics."
47. Sawyer and Wagner, "Mass Incarceration."
48. Hansen and Netherland, "Is the Prescription Opioid Epidemic a White Problem?"
49. Diamond, "Race without Color."

that in the US, different institutionalized systems have intentionally created a caste system based on race, and as one system was overturned, a new one emerged in its place. She claims that when the first system of legalized slavery was overturned, a new system emerged—the Jim Crow system.[50] Later, the civil rights movement worked to overturn the Jim Crow system, culminating in the passage of the 1964 Civil Rights Act.[51] But after the passage of civil rights legislation, Alexander claims, a new system emerged that utilized mass incarceration to reinforce a racial caste system. Consider:

> In the era of colorblindness, it is no longer socially permissible to use race, explicitly, as a justification for discrimination, exclusion, and social contempt. So we don't. Rather than rely on race, we use our criminal justice system to label people of color "criminals" and then engage in all the practices we supposedly left behind. Today it is perfectly legal to discriminate against criminals in nearly all the ways that it was once legal to discriminate against African Americans. Once you're labeled a felon, the old forms of discrimination—employment discrimination, housing discrimination, denial of the right to vote, denial of educational opportunity, denial of food stamps and other public benefits, and exclusion from jury service—are suddenly legal. As a criminal, you have scarcely more rights, and arguably less respect, than a black man living in Alabama at the height of Jim Crow. We have not ended racial caste in America, we have merely redesigned it.[52]

Alexander supplies substantial evidence to support these claims, and several points connect directly to the ideas in this chapter.

Alexander notes that as the civil rights movement grew in strength and influence, Southern governors increasingly turned to the rhetoric of "law-and-order."[53] This allowed governors and conservatives to oppose civil rights through linking the civil rights movement to increasing crime rates. At first, the link between race and the law-and-order rhetoric was explicit. Alexander states, "Early on, little effort was made to disguise the racial motivation behind the law and order rhetoric and the harsh criminal justice legislation proposed in Congress. The most ardent opponents of civil rights legislation and desegregation were the most active on the emerging crime issue."[54] After the passage of the Civil Rights Act, the law-and-order rhetoric would continue, albeit as a racialized dog-whistle, a concept that captures how the focus on law and order became coded language for talking about race.

50. Alexander, *New Jim Crow*, 35.
51. Alexander, *New Jim Crow*, 38.
52. Alexander, *New Jim Crow*, 2.
53. Alexander, *New Jim Crow*, 40.
54. Alexander, *New Jim Crow*, 42.

Law-and-order rhetoric caught on and became a central feature of the 1968 Nixon presidential campaign. In an effort to win, Nixon developed the Southern Strategy to appeal to working-class and poor voters in the South and to swing those Southern states to vote Republican. Alexander writes, "Some conservative political strategists admitted that appeal to racial fears and antagonisms was central to this strategy, though it had to be done surreptitiously. H.R. Haldeman, one of Nixon's key advisors, recalls that Nixon himself deliberately pursued a southern, racial strategy. 'He [Nixon] emphasized that you have to face the fact that the whole problem is really the blacks. The key is to devise a system that recognizes this while not appearing to.'"[55] Thus Nixon's Southern Strategy, facilitated by H. R. Ehrlichman's "war on drugs" approach (discussed earlier in this chapter), illustrates how the shifting rhetoric on race shaped the current system of mass incarceration.

Even though Nixon's presidency was cut short by the Watergate scandal, Alexander argues that the use of coded language to inflame racial tensions grew under Reagan, a candidate whose campaign rhetoric included the use of coded racialized rhetoric: "To great effect, Reagan echoed white frustration in race-neutral terms through implicit racial appeals. His 'color blind' rhetoric on crime, welfare, taxes, and state's rights was clearly understood by white (and black) voters as having a racial dimension, though claims to that effect were impossible to prove. The absence of explicitly racist rhetoric afforded the racial nature of his coded appeals a certain plausible deniability."[56] After winning the election, Reagan's coded appeals were put into practice with his declaration of a war on drugs, which shifted federal crime enforcement efforts from white-collar crime to focus more on drug crimes. Federal budgets for the FBI, Drug Enforcement Administration, and Department of Defense were substantially increased, and the administration launched a media campaign to sell this war on drugs to the public.[57] The rising rates of crack cocaine use in inner-city neighborhoods were central to this campaign and fed a media frenzy and moral panic. This war on drugs proved popular with White voters, "particularly whites who remained resentful of black progress, civil rights enforcement, and affirmative action."[58]

As previously discussed, the Anti-Drug Abuse Act and the later revision of that act dramatically escalated enforcement and punitive legal actions against those who manufacture, sell, or use drugs. However, the evidence strongly suggests that enforcement has been particularly harsh against the

55. Alexander, *New Jim Crow*, 43–44.
56. Alexander, *New Jim Crow*, 47–48.
57. Alexander, *New Jim Crow*, 49.
58. Alexander, *New Jim Crow*, 53.

African American community, a fact that should not be surprising in light of the racialized use of law-and-order rhetoric. Alexander supports this point, writing,

> Human Rights Watch reported in 2000 that in seven states, African Americans constitute 80 to 90 percent of all drug offenders sent to prison. In at least fifteen states, blacks are admitted to prison on drug charges at a rate from twenty to fifty-seven times greater than that of white men. In fact, nationwide, the incarceration for African American drug offenders dwarfs the rate for whites. When the War on Drugs gained full steam in the mid-1980s, prison admissions for African Americans skyrocketed, nearly quadrupling in three years, and then increasing steadily until it reached in 2000 a level *more than twenty-six* times the level in 1983.[59]

Critics might look at these disparities and assume that differences in arrests and drug charges reflect differences in the use of drugs among racial/ethnic groups. However, based on self-report studies, more Whites report use of illegal drugs (53.8 percent) than do African Americans (47.6 percent) or Hispanic/Latinos (38.9 percent).[60] Rather than usage rates, a number of factors shape the likelihood of a drug arrest, with some studies suggesting that the racial/ethnic composition of a neighborhood is a predictor of arrest rates. Other studies find that in areas where manufacturing is declining, arrest rates for African Americans increase while arrests of White people do not.[61] Even though the legal system is purportedly race-neutral in the application of the law, Alexander's arguments, combined with the data on arrests and incarceration reviewed earlier in the chapter, provide strong evidence that the criminal justice system continues to be shaped by the racist legacy of the law-and-order rhetoric. Racial/ethnic identity continues to play a role in the way that the criminal justice system creates strangers.

Strangers for Life

So far, we have explored two intertwined ways in which the criminal justice system makes individuals into strangers and incarcerates many of these individuals at rates higher than any other nation. However, we should not ignore that the criminal justice system can keep individuals "imprisoned" even after they have finished serving any formal period of incarceration. The reality is,

59. Alexander, *New Jim Crow*, 96.
60. Shelden and Vasiliev, *Controlling the Dangerous Classes*, 88.
61. Shelden and Vasiliev, *Controlling the Dangerous Classes*, 89.

after serving out a sentence and being released from prison, those with felony convictions find it challenging to find housing, since they are legally barred from public housing, and many landlords will not rent to those with a criminal conviction. Those with a criminal record find it difficult to obtain a job, not only because applications ask about past criminal convictions but because it is legal to discriminate based on those past convictions. Such persons may also be shackled with fees and charges from their time in incarceration or for supervision related to their probation and parole. Finally, the majority of states do not allow people to vote while serving time, many do not allow the formerly incarcerated to vote while on parole, and some do not allow them to vote for a number of years after their release or to ever vote again.[62] Alexander says, "For many it seems inconceivable that, for a minor offense, you can be subjected to discrimination, scorn, and exclusion for the rest of your life."[63]

Given the lifelong impact of a criminal record, perhaps it is not surprising that recidivism rates remain high, reflecting labeling theory and the concept of secondary deviance. As Bacote and Perrin observe, "Within three years of release, 67 percent of ex-convicts will be re-arrested and in five years that number will rise to 77 percent. Rather than helping to reform criminals, prison seems to do more to increase recidivism rates than reduce them."[64] The recidivism rates reflect that the criminal justice system, having turned offenders into strangers, makes it difficult for the majority to escape that label and its consequences.[65]

Reimagining Criminal Justice and Stranger-Making

Durkheim is correct that communities need boundaries to function and to protect individuals or the larger community from harm. For example, we need traffic laws (such as stop signs) and enforcement of traffic regulations to provide a measure of safety as we commute. Yet, Durkheim's ideas must be balanced with attention to the social construction of reality and labeling theory. The arrest and incarceration data reviewed in this chapter, the brief examination of the rationale for the war on drugs, and the discussion of the disproportionate impacts on racial/ethnic groups indicate that our socially constructed boundaries have been enforced in ways benefiting some groups while targeting and harming others. This intergroup conflict has led

62. Alexander, *New Jim Crow*, 152.
63. Alexander, *New Jim Crow*, 158.
64. Bacote and Perrin, "Redemptive Rehabilitation," 5.
65. For a compelling, in-depth examination of life after incarceration, I highly recommend Reuben Miller's text *Halfway Home*.

to millions of individuals living behind bars or in other ways being turned into long-term strangers.

In the Gospel of Matthew, when asked to identify the greatest commandment, Jesus responds that it is to love God with all our heart, soul, and mind (Matt. 22:36–38). And the second commandment is like the first: to love our neighbor as we love ourselves (22:39). Later, when Jesus discusses the judging of the nations, he indicates that his followers are those who live out the commandments and love their neighbors as they love themselves by feeding the hungry, welcoming the stranger, and visiting the prisoner (25:34–36). As we wrestle with what it means to live out these commandments in relationship to the criminal justice system, we must avoid the temptation to assume that individual actions are enough. I cannot imagine that it is sufficient to visit individual prisoners while ignoring a larger system of unjust stranger-making, characterized by racial/ethnic disparities, high rates of incarceration, and the lifelong consequences of a criminal conviction.

In their article "Redemptive Rehabilitation," Bacote and Perrin make the case that Christians should support approaches that move away from a focus on retribution to focus on rehabilitation, as this aligns with a call to love our neighbors. One such approach would be a focus on restorative justice, which seeks to bring about reconciliation and restoration between offenders and the community.[66] The authors write, "Through adopting a posture of charity and love towards those who have broken the laws of the community, Christians can find ways in which they can help redeem the incarcerated and offer them hope in being restored to live a free, healthy life. Restorative Justice can provide a remedy after crime and give a sense of closure and possible reconciliation for both perpetrators and victims."[67] Additionally, they suggest that Christians should support individualized therapeutic approaches that help orient individuals to proper ways of living, and therapeutic communities where offenders can be rehabilitated and learn to live in community with others. However, they caution that rehabilitation can only do so much for individuals, and "if the real world has no place for them, then any hope of redemptive restoration is ultimately fruitless."[68] For rehabilitation to be effective, the community must also address employment barriers, voting rights, and other barriers to full reintegration into the community.

Just as importantly, Bacote and Perrin note that rehabilitation of offenders is not sufficient to address all the problems with the criminal justice system.

66. For a compelling example, see the first of three stories of the neighbor, under the heading "Apology Accepted," in chap. 10 of this book.
67. Bacote and Perrin, "Redemptive Rehabilitation," 22.
68. Bacote and Perrin, "Redemptive Rehabilitation," 23.

In line with other concerns discussed in this chapter, they argue that "the problems of over-incarceration and the racial disparity in American prisons show how deeply the criminal justice system needs reform."[69] Working with individuals is not enough if there are systemic problems with the criminal justice system.

Only a few problems with the criminal justice system have been discussed in this chapter, and to address any systemic problems it will take multiple partial solutions. But as a start, I suggest that loving our neighbor, seeking justice, and reforming our stranger-making could include

- Stopping the overreliance on incarceration as a response to crime. Lengthy or mandatory punitive prison sentences may appease a sense of collective outrage. Yet the evidence suggests this strategy is not effective in reducing crime and recidivism.[70] As a global outlier in terms of incarceration, it is time for the US to examine how other, similar nations address crime and maintain dramatically lower incarceration rates.

- Ending the war on drugs and not incarcerating drug offenders. The majority of those incarcerated for drug crimes are users, not those who manufacture and sell drugs. Incarceration for possession and drug use does little to address the problem of addiction. Moreover, the harsh penalties for drug use have disproportionately affected communities of color. Instead, we should shift spending to focus on addiction treatment and community support (similar to some of the recent efforts to address opioid addiction).

- Letting criminal records expire. Frost, Clear, and Monteiro argue,

> Criminal Justice is one of the few realms where transgressions—even the most minor of transgressions—can be held against a person for life. It can no longer be argued that these records must remain accessible for decades because they continue to be relevant. Research has demonstrated that with each year that passes, a prior record becomes less determinative of future criminal conduct. After approximately seven years, a person with a prior criminal record is virtually indistinguishable from a person without one.[71]

- Recognizing and addressing how the system disproportionately affects communities of color. We should acknowledge that political actors used

69. Bacote and Perrin, "Redemptive Rehabilitation," 23.
70. Frost, Clear, and Monteiro, "Ending Mass Incarceration," 31.
71. Frost, Clear, and Monteiro, "Ending Mass Incarceration," 34.

(and continue to use) the rhetoric of law and order to shape a criminal justice system that polices Black people, Indigenous people, and other people of color in ways that it does not police the White community. And we need to address the laws, policies, and differential enforcement of laws that have turned mass incarceration into, as Michelle Alexander asserts, the new Jim Crow.

What about That Tweet?

At the start of this chapter, I shared Sanders's tweet about the different sentences given to Felicity Huffman and Tanya McDowell. That comparison by itself did not support Sanders's claim that the criminal justice system was racist and broken. But as I conclude, we can return to the larger questions I raised when thinking about that tweet. First, even if race did not directly play a role in the sentences given to either woman, the evidence in this chapter supports the contention that racial/ethnic identity is shaping the criminal justice system. Second, McDowell's longer sentence was connected to the racialized war on drugs and the way we hold a person's prior convictions against them for the rest of their life. Her life might be very different if we allowed crime records to expire and if we changed how we address drug issues. And finally, we could acknowledge that the incarcerations of Huffman and McDowell reflect a system based more on retribution than on rehabilitation or reconciliation. Is it justice, and is it truly beneficial to the larger community, to declare them strangers and place them behind bars? Can we not find other ways, for these women or for others, to provide a path toward restorative justice and to help strangers become neighbors?

CHAPTER EIGHT

COMPETING IN CEDAR

Nike, Superstar Athletes, and the Unseen Strangers Who Make Our Shoes

Woe to him who builds his house by unrighteousness,
    and his upper rooms by injustice;
who makes his neighbors work for nothing,
    and does not give them their wages;
who says, "I will build myself a spacious house
    with large upper rooms,"
and who cuts out windows for it,
    paneling it with cedar,
    and painting it with vermilion.
Are you a king
    because you compete in cedar?
Did not your father eat and drink
    and do justice and righteousness?
    Then it was well with him.
He judged the cause of the poor and needy;
    then it was well.
Is not this to know me?
    says the LORD.
But your eyes and heart
    are only on your dishonest gain,

> for shedding innocent blood,
>   and for practicing oppression and violence.
>   Jeremiah 22:13–17

Though the word is never mentioned, with a little imagination you will see the theme of the stranger nestled between phrases in the Jeremiah passage above.[1] The prophet does, however, mention neighbors. Only they're not really neighbors. Those harnessed to work for nothing are not neighbors—they are strangers and possibly slaves. They do not share in the abundance. The passage anticipates that those paneling the spacious house of the wannabe king would be barred from entrance before the second coat of vermilion was dry and the sconces installed. No, the activities of this self-appointed monarch do not correspond with the things the Lord loves: righteousness, justice, right judgment, and compassionate care for those in need. Rather, his self-aggrandizement and the social distance he maintains between would-be neighbors is associated with oppression, violence, and the shedding of innocent blood. It is worth noting that any religious beliefs this castle-builder may hold are merely incidental to "knowing" the Lord. They're not even mentioned. On the contrary, knowledge of God is manifest in how a person treats those marginalized by the social system, those who fall outside its protections, those living on the outer bank of the moat, or those without a passcode to the gated community—themes reiterated in Matthew 25. Acting like a "lord" may lead one to forget *the* Lord.

We the people of God (and perhaps especially evangelicals) routinely employ the religious language of "relationship." "Do you have a *relationship* with God? Do you *know* the Lord?" Or are you a stranger to God? This ancient passage pointedly underscores the point that relationship with God—knowing and being known by God—emerges as a person (or a community) cares for the vulnerable in their orbits. To know the Lord, proclaims the prophet, is to *do* justice. And doing justice requires that God's people draw near to strangers, sharing with and embracing them as neighbors and friends. When you build a magnificent house with exploited labor, force those who built it off your property, put a moat or a wall around it, plan your next business venture, and live in upper rooms away from the riffraff (the higher up you are, the less you can see the poor), you have shown contempt for justice. You may make it into the next issue of *Architectural Digest*, but you will not know God. Know strangers, know God; no strangers, no God.

1. Material in this chapter is adapted from Vos, "Competing in Cedar," used with permission from the publisher.

Perhaps the rich man in the passage is not a king, but he is a pretty shrewd businessman. Good thing we're not like him! Or are we? Do *we*, too, compete in cedar?

Strangers in Unseen Worlds

One of the touchy things about being a sociologist is that we are, paraphrasing the words of Peter Berger, the professional muckrakers of society. Berger also calls us professional Peeping Toms. In *Invitation to Sociology*, he writes, "It can be said that the first wisdom of sociology is this—things are not what they seem. . . . Social reality turns out to have many layers of meaning. The discovery of each new layer changes the perception of the whole."[2] Sociologists take great pleasure in dissecting the social world, exposing the underbelly of our "normal" practices and drawing attention to the complexities and hidden inner workings of our lives. In 2013, then Canadian Prime Minister Stephen Harper, in response to questions about the arrests of two men accused of plotting an attack on a Canadian passenger train, said, "I think, though, this is not a time to commit sociology, if I can use an expression. These things are serious threats, global terrorist attacks, people who have agendas of violence that are deep and abiding threats to all the values our society stands for."[3] Sociologists laughed, and the phrase "commit sociology," which was not an expression before, quickly became one! I've even seen this wisdom printed on a T-shirt! In effect, Harper was saying, "Don't overcomplicate this obvious 'terrorism' with context, nuance, and an exploration of root causes. It's annoying. Let's just get on with things."

In a way, we sociologists are in the business of unclothing society. Show us some social practice, and we'll tell you what's wrong with it (or die trying!). It's a perverse profession. I'm pretty sure that I've ruined Disney, fast food, cruises, big sport, Walmart, and possibly even church for more than a few of my students. But isn't critique of our "normal" akin to the admonitions of Jeremiah and the other prophetic voices we encounter in Scripture?

As duly noted, sociologists are pretty good at identifying and illuminating what is wrong with the world(s) we inhabit. Lamentably, we are less adept at offering reliable and feasible fixes to these problems. The sheer complexity of the world around us, the innumerable variables that must be identified and considered, the weight and lingering effects of history, and the subjectivity of

2. Berger, *Invitation to Sociology*, 23. See p. 19 for a reference to professional Peeping Toms and p. 46 for the reference to professional muckrakers.
3. Fitzpatrick, "Harper on Terror Arrests."

human beings combine in ways that resist our efforts to prescribe solutions. Additionally, the kinds of problems we deal with do not lend themselves to easy fixes. Although sociologists have made significant contributions to our understanding of racism, sexism, and problems inherent in class structure (there are numerous good books on each of these topics), these matters are complex and multilayered, and their effects continue to plague us. Furthermore, the solution to one problem often germinates the seeds of a new one—sociological whack-a-mole. We may not always know how to fix things, but we can offer important insights into context, unseen factors, and the unanticipated consequences of purposive social action.[4] Peter Berger was right; social phenomena are rarely simple and frequently not what they seem.

Amid the unfathomable complexity of human problems—problems that resist sociological solutions—the biblical prophets offer remarkably simple courses of action. In response to problems of race, gender, and social class (all problems of the stranger), the prophets simply tell us to do what God loves, which boils down to the oft-cited wisdom offered in Micah 6:8:

> He has told you, O mortal, what is good;
>   and what does the LORD require of you
> but to do justice, and to love kindness,
>   and to walk humbly with your God?

Justice, kindness, and humility are qualities that tend to emerge as we make strangers into neighbors and when we consider others better than ourselves. All of these virtues, however, remain dormant if we oppress or neglect strangers. If we are the people of God "for the world," it follows that God does not intend us to practice the Micah 6:8 virtues only among ourselves as a means to in-group solidarity. We are fond of John 3:16, "For God so loved the world . . ."—it's an evangelical staple for bumper stickers, highway billboards, and heartfelt postings on social media. What if we focused on and applied it this way: "For God so loved the strangers . . ."? Are strangers not included in the meaning of John 3:16? Is not the gospel of Jesus Christ a message about a God who suffers for, lives among, and embraces those who were strangers? As Paul writes in Ephesians 2:13, "But now in Christ Jesus you who once were far off have been brought near by the blood of Christ." From far to near. Be like Jesus; love the strangers.

Some strangers are easy to see. When someone outside familiar social circles comes into your church, sits at the back, and leaves before the final

---

4. Merton, "Unanticipated Consequences."

"amen" resolves, they're a stranger. Follow them out, shake their hand, learn their needs, and invite them back. Pretty clear. But what about strangers who aren't so visible—the strangers half-a-world away? What about the social systems we participate in that "use" faraway strangers to increase "our" wealth and comfort? What about global capitalism, metanational corporations, and the poor workers who make clothes, consumer electronics, and other goods for Western markets? Who are those people to us? What are their lives like? Should they be included among the "least of these" to whom God has called us as agents of mercy?

Most social contexts described in the Bible, such as the scenario depicted in the Jeremiah passage, are far simpler than the contexts structuring our lives in modernity. In our world, the routine mouse click of an Amazon purchase establishes us as participants in multiple and overlapping social systems, complete with global financial markets and world politics that elude our understanding. Postindustrial society is substantially more complex than the relatively simple rich man / laborer example supplied by Jeremiah. How do we navigate such complexities as the people of God "for the world"? What are our responsibilities to those we cannot see? Are "we" the rich man of Jeremiah 22? Are "they" the "neighbors" who work for (next to) nothing? Are the prophets speaking to . . . us?

Structures and Strangers: The Alienating Effects of Economic Systems

When sociologists offer critiques of global capitalism, they make people nervous. For one thing, it makes people wonder if we're some kind of socialists or communists. For another, critiques of capitalism question the foundation on which our (wealthy) Western lives are situated. Most everything we have and do draws on global economic systems, including the food we eat, clothes we wear, vehicles we drive, steel we import, sports we watch, iPhones we tweet on, energy we consume, waste we export, church buildings we worship in, and so on. Insinuate that capitalism as we experience it depends on exploitable labor—on an endless supply of disenfranchised strangers—and you've poked a hornet's nest. It seems downright un-American—or in Canadian terms, exactly what you'd expect from those who "commit sociology"!

Sociological theory texts often begin with the work of Karl Marx. Marx is, of course, a controversial figure. Try to land a teaching position at a Christian college while professing Marxism and you're out of luck. However, although you may see communist or postcommunist countries as visible signs of the failure of Marxism—and your critique would be correct in many respects—to outright dismiss Marx is to miss important wisdom he has to impart. Marx's primary value lies, in my opinion, not in his economic model of communism but in his trenchant analysis and critique of capitalism. Arguably, we're uncomfortable with Marx not because we really fear a plunge into communism but because his work requires that we take a pretty critical look at how it is that we can walk into a Walmart and buy a pair of hiking books on sale for $12.[5] Who made them? Under what conditions? For what pay or benefits? We'd rather not think about it. Despite some of the problems we legitimately associate with Marx's ideology, his work offers prophetic insight that can help us examine ourselves and better understand the ways in which the social systems we support may undermine our efforts to live out a Micah 6:8 ethic.

Marx viewed society through a structural lens. He looked at the social problems of his day—poverty, stratification, abysmal conditions for workers—and understood them as an effect of the structures of society. For Marx, the idea that social problems could be eradicated at the individual level had serious shortcomings. For example, recall the Ruby Bridges story from chapter 4. Young Ruby required a police escort to safely enter school. As she walked in amid armed guard, she stood as a symbol that challenged a fundamental structure—she challenged the way racial "pieces" were arranged in her society. To speak of someone "knowing her place" is to refer to a structural arrangement. In this way, you can think of race relations as a kind of pattern that is continually acted out and reinforced, even by those who bear no conscious ill will toward "the other" race. Over time, people come to think of various structural arrangements as normal, and this makes them resistant to change— these pieces belong here and those pieces belong there. If you think about it, because of people like Ruby Bridges challenging and dismantling the widely accepted racial structures of the Jim Crow era, most White Americans now assume that schools are integrated and are not surprised when they see African American students walk into a public school. They say you can't legislate morality, but it seems that you can legislate new structural arrangements. Sometimes fairly successfully.

What would have happened had the angry White people present for young Ruby's iconic walk into William Frantz Elementary School simply been exhorted to "search their hearts" and extend welcome, without the required (and enforced) structural change? Probably nothing new, and we'd be locked in the same segregated gridlock today. "We" Christians sometimes like to think that problems and injustice will recede as our hearts are renewed. Maybe. But the evidence is against this. In a book titled *Divided by Faith: Evangelical Religion*

---

5. A couple years ago, I did this—bought hiking boots at Walmart for $12.

and the Problem of Race in America, sociologists Michael Emerson and Christian Smith found that a high percentage of evangelical Christians invoked some version of the "miracle motif" when asked their ideas about resolving racial problems in the United States.[6] The miracle motif is the idea that as more people become Christians and "hearts are changed," problems will simply evaporate. Such a solution requires little of the dominant group. Emerson and Smith also found that many White evangelicals opposed modifying structural arrangements present in their lives for the sake of racial reconciliation. Thus, the expectation was that "I" can go to my racially segregated church, live in a gated community where I have little contact with people of a different race, and perhaps attend a private school where there are few minority students, but as long as I am "bearing witness" and people are "getting saved," racial problems will dissipate. One other approach to addressing racial inequity given by White evangelicals went something like this: "God will intervene in his good and perfect timing—who are we to rush things?"

When Emerson and Smith asked African Americans about solutions to racial problems in the United States, they heard quite a bit about the structural problems that deter racial strangers from becoming neighbors and friends.

Structural approaches to understanding the social world stand in contrast to individual or social psychological approaches. When Marx looked at the dehumanizing work environments ensnaring nineteenth-century factory workers, as well as a host of other social problems, he did not recommend sermons or seminars telling people to "be their best selves" as remedy. He offered no "be honest," "work hard," "love yourself," "your day will come," or inspirational rags-to-riches stories. Marx was convinced that not only did such approaches not work; they functioned to keep present arrangements intact by supporting the privileged class in society. "God wants you to work hard and obey your earthly masters" translated to "Support the present system. . . . Don't challenge it." For Marx the only effective solution to social problems—and especially problems inherent in the world of work—lay in collapsing the two-class (workers vs. owners) system. Break apart the unjust structure, and you can begin to build something more just and equitable.

The concept of alienation occupies a central position in Marx's sociology. For Marx, people were alienated (aliens are strangers) from one another, from the world around them, from their work, and even from themselves (their own human natures), because of the way that social systems governed their existence. Marx believed that the two-class structure, through which the owner (upper) class dictated the life chances of the lower class, kept people

6. Emerson and Smith, *Divided by Faith,* 117–31.

from what they could truly become if freed from such constraints. The class structure alienated workers from each other and the world around them, and led them to internalize these arrangements as normal. He referred to the worker's acceptance of exploitive arrangements in the world of work as "ideology" or "false consciousness," and he directed much of his intellectual energies to helping the working class acknowledge and challenge the arrangements they took for granted.[7] While Marx's analysis falls short in several respects, it can help us see two things that often remain hidden: First, social structures produce alienation in ways that can function independently of an individual's will or consciousness. Second, social structures can hide injustice and inequality in ways that reinforce those things as normal.

With these ideas in mind, let's explore one rather "normal" part of our Western lives that obscures injustice while we "panel in cedar." Let's turn our attention to the faraway strangers who make our shoes, the structures that constrain their lives, and their masters—the Nike corporation.

Just Do It—Make Our Shoes

A number of years ago, at the annual Christian sociology conference I attend, our small group watched the documentary *No Logo*, which explains branding, how multinational corporations work, and how rich (core) countries procure labor from poor (peripheral) ones.[8] That film deeply affected me. I returned home from the conference feeling disturbed, discouraged, and greatly overwhelmed by the magnitude of the problems in society. How to live in a world such as this—a world where my comfort and wealth comes, in no small measure, from the exploited labor of faraway strangers. *No Logo* features a segment on the Nike corporation that serves, to the present day, as a model of metanational exploitation—of the superrich taking from the very poor while disguising the transaction as virtue. Nike is the center of the hegemonic model of sport in this country and in other countries.[9] "Just Do

7. Marx, *Capital*; Marx and Engels, *Communist Manifesto*.
8. Jhally, *No Logo*. This documentary is based on the best-selling book by Naomi Klein by the same name.
9. *Hegemony*, as used here, is a term that explains how powerful individuals, institutions, or entities cultivate public support by influencing what people perceive as desirable and by associating themselves with the satisfaction of those desires. In effect, companies like Nike exert hegemonic control over average citizens, through the manipulation of cultural channels (for example, mass media) that encourage people to internalize norms and values that serve the interests of powerful elites. Because control is exerted not through violence but through pleasurable experiences like those found in the consumer culture, the populace assents to the dominant models being promoted—lending support to things that may not be in their best

It" and the Nike swoosh are some of the most widely recognized corporate symbols on the planet. For many they symbolize excellence in sport and in life, and they represent overcoming obstacles, perseverance in the face of adversity, and pushing oneself to new heights. Moreover, Nike is exceptionally good at cultivating an image identifying the company and its products with these so-called virtues. Their short promotional video "Nike Better World" is one good example.[10] Just don't believe everything you see and hear!

I'm interested in how Nike—with one of the most dubious human rights records in modern corporate history—manages to promote itself as virtuous and excellent. We, the consumer public, generally think little about the darker side of corporate entities like Nike. For the most part, we are unfailingly loyal to companies like Nike that deliver us exciting experiences and sparkly consumer goods—too preoccupied with the immediacy of televised sports and other entertainments to notice . . . or to care. Why would we?

Powerful forces labor tirelessly to ensure that we remain ignorant of the churning human machinery generating our shoes and tank tops. Many educational institutions, among them Christian high schools and colleges, maintain exclusive athletic contracts with Nike, proudly wearing their symbol (advertising for them) and cultivating the next generation of loyal customers, in exchange for benefits ranging from vast sums of money to discounted rates on shoes and other gear. Even churches are not immune to spreading the "good news" of Nike. I once visited a seeker-friendly style church that, on the sanctuary video screen offering inspirational preservice messages, displayed a large Nike swoosh with the message "Christianity—Just Do It" in the rotation. "Today's sermon brought to you by the Nike corporation—shoes for sale in the vestibule for 25 percent off" was probably not far behind! The disconnect between Christian mission statements and the harsh labor practices supporting the pop-culture symbols we associate with excellence and goodness rarely crosses our minds, let alone deters us. But in supporting these and other similar symbols, we, albeit unwittingly, reinforce modern-day racism and slavery. While Nike announces itself as the solution to racism and sexism (something made manifest in the Nike commercial referenced earlier), it makes its shoes and athletic gear almost exclusively through the exploited labor of people of color—mostly young women who fall well below the legal age to work full time in the United States and Canada.

It should not escape notice that the most powerful spokespeople for Nike products and the "Nike worldview" have been superstar athletes who are

interest. Hegemonic control thus renders invisible the underbelly of the cultural systems we enjoy and love, allowing structures constructed by and for elites to continue unchallenged.

10. Nike, "Nike Better World."

themselves people of color—Michael Jordan, LeBron James, Kevin Durant, Tiger Woods, Serena Williams, Cristiano Ronaldo, Michelle Wie, newcomer Zion Williamson, and many others. Athletes are truly successful when they get a piece of this action. Worldwide, Nike spent $3.75 billion on advertising and promotion costs in 2019 and $3.59 billion in 2020.[11] However, their "success" requires the continual exploitation of ever more distant nameless and faceless strangers.

In the rest of this chapter, I offer a brief overview of Nike's labor practices, and I raise questions about the relationship between the athletes of color who have lucrative Nike contracts and the oppression of (mostly) female Asian workers—also people of color—who their highly visible endorsements require, legitimate, and obfuscate. My interest is in how global capitalism and the metanational corporations that structure it draw influential people of color—like high-profile athletes—into solidarity with them, bringing their images, voices, and messages into hegemonic lockstep. Those who might speak for the powerless now identify with, represent, celebrate, stand alongside, promote, and defend the oppressor. Those who might help are instead looking the other way, snatching up profits as they do so. Those who might raise a powerful collective voice on behalf of the downtrodden do little more than cultivate strangers. And we, in turn, so often regard these people with an adoration approaching worship. No wonder some incorporate Nike symbols into their churches.

In developing the connection among Nike, the athletes of color who serve as their spokespersons, and the poor "strangers" of color who make our shoes, I draw on Immanuel Wallerstein's world-systems theory, as well as W. E. B. Du Bois's[12] vision for a pan-African movement. Both of these sociological thinkers offer us ways of better understanding the implications of our "trading in cedar." Both offer a prophetic voice amid the deafening roar of the sports stadium. First, let's examine the Nike way of doing business.

Supply Chains Supplying Their Chains: Understanding the Nike Model

The global sports-apparel industry totaled almost $174 billion in 2018. In 2014 the North American share of the global market was $60.5 billion, an amount predicted to rise to $73.5 billion by 2019.[13] Sport sociologist George Sage observes that the production of sporting goods is a key component in the sport

---

11. Sabanoglu, "Nike's Advertising and Promotion Costs."
12. Du Bois was the first Black man to earn a PhD from Harvard University.
13. "Sports Industry to Reach $73.5 Billion."

industry—we simply cannot understand sports without accounting for this factor. Though we take it for granted, apparel (which includes equipment) is an indispensable ingredient in sporting activities. However, apparel does not come from nature—people, human beings like you and me, stitch it together. Accordingly, the labor of those who make our shoes, uniforms, and other goods is the foundation on which our sporting experiences are fashioned.[14]

That sporting goods and athletic apparel make up such an enormous industry, one that locates almost all its production outside North America, should lead us to ask what life is like for those who make Nike apparel and other sporting goods. Lamentably, the answer to that question is a discouraging one.

Our lives are enmeshed with a global economy. Everything we have or use, with few exceptions, involves globalization and multinational or transnational corporations.[15] Most of the food we eat, clothes we wear, electronics we use, vehicles we drive, and so on are produced through the various structures of this highly complex and integrated economy. Among other things, globalization results in our (I write as a North American) having access to a tremendous variety of relatively inexpensive consumer goods and services. As noted earlier in the chapter, a few years ago, I bought a pair of hiking boots at Walmart. They were on sale for $12. How in the world can anyone afford to sell me a shoe for $6?

My Walmart experience is made possible only through low-wage labor. Globalization provides fertile conditions for an almost endless supply of exploitable workers. Sport sociologist D. Stanley Eitzen writes that "not everyone experiences globalization in the same way. For some, it expands opportunities and enhances prosperity, while others experience poverty and hopelessness. Jobs are created and jobs are destroyed by globalization."[16] There is little chance that Walmart could sell boots for so little money were they produced in North American factories for a fair wage. Globalization provides companies with the ability to control labor costs by moving production to countries that have lower (or almost no) standards for worker treatment or, usually, for human rights in general. For example, most people in my circles would be disturbed to learn that their shoes had been made by a fourteen-year-old girl who worked full time, plus forced overtime, for a couple of dollars a day— especially if it happened in one of "our" cities. However, when low-wage production happens outside of our borders, away from our communities, and

14. Sage, "Corporate Globalization."

15. Multinational corporations are based in one particular country but operate in many countries, while transnational corporations are "borderless" and do not generally recognize any one nation as their home.

16. Eitzen, *Fair and Foul*, 238.

in places where workers cannot tell us their stories or the conditions of their lives, we rarely think about it—or about them. "Low-wage" is generally the most significant factor (there are others) in "low-cost." We search for low-cost stuff and revel in finding a bargain. It feels almost virtuous to snag a "deal," and for the most part, the backstory of production is something we rarely encounter. In fact, we tend to locate ourselves on the right side of justice when we choose the fair-trade Starbucks coffee over their more questionable free-trade (not fairly traded?) offerings.

Nonetheless, for scant wages and benefits someone had to make the shoes and other products that we come to possess. And that someone will remain a stranger to us because the only way this production arrangement works is if the buying public is shielded from the reality of its labor force. The hegemonic control that multinational corporations like Nike exert derives from their ability to direct our focus to the exciting experiences they offer us while shrouding the infrastructures on which those experiences and products are fashioned. Furthermore, the meager remuneration that companies like Nike offer to workers has little to do with the company's ability to pay a livable wage that considers "their" workers' present and future needs.

When Nike sells shoes for amounts in excess of $125, the profit does not end up in the pockets of the workers who made them. The overseas labor utilized by the apparel industry—primarily concentrated in China, Indonesia, and Southeast Asia—is bid lower and lower by brokers who locate and contract the lowest-cost labor available for the Western companies that hire them. In effect, the poor of these "peripheral" countries are treated as commodities on the global markets. Brokers obtain labor much like they barter for the lowest-priced steel or cotton. In procuring this human commodity, Nike serves as the leader in what apparel workers' advocacy groups call "the race to the bottom."[17] Not "our workers," just "labor." Young woman . . . foreigner . . . laborer . . . stranger. But who cares? It's just business, and the basketball game is on. As one image sporting the Nike swoosh in the shape of a whip proclaims, "Slavery, Just Do It."

17. The documentary *No Logo* offers a clear, helpful, and sobering explanation of how supply chains insulate companies like Nike from responsibility for the workers who assemble their products. For example, Nike owns no factories overseas—it just contracts the production of goods via supply chains. Every link in the chain further distances them from responsibility for workers. Nike might connect with a particular broker who knows the labor landscape in Indonesia. That broker would contract with another, who would contract with another and another. At the end of this "race to the bottom" is the lowest-wage labor available. This approach enables Nike and others like them to deny their complicity in human labor abuses with the argument that it is really the factory owners and the standards in foreign countries that bear responsibility. Consequently, they can reap the financial benefits of exploitation while denying culpability.

Although we contemplate diversity, racial integration, fairness, and equality in Canada and the United States, our concerns seldom reach beyond our own borders to the strangers who make our shoes. Almost all of the exploitation found in the overseas production of athletic apparel is absorbed by people of color, most of whom are female and most of whom are young. Yet we proudly wear the corporate symbols of those who engineer, reinforce, and profit from this arrangement, stand in awe of the athletes who consume the biggest slices of this exploitation pie, and associate the whole business with excellence. How would we regard such people if it were our daughters who stitched their shoes for next to nothing?

Sage writes that in China average wages are just 2.1 percent of US average wages. These jobs have taken away American jobs—2.7 million of them between 2000 and 2003.[18] According to some estimates, the United States loses about half a million jobs a year to overseas labor. Additionally, wages paid by Nike (and Adidas) to their mostly Asian labor force have not increased to keep pace with the rising cost of living, among other factors, but have actually gone down.

How does a corporation based in the United States reduce their labor costs to almost nothing? They certainly can't do it in the US, where human-rights standards are monitored and are far too high to permit the levels of exploitation required to compel workers to work for unsustainably low wages in often-dangerous conditions (exposure to toxic chemicals, long hours, forced overtime, and even corporal punishment). Rather, the labor arrangements they desire require contexts where human rights are ignored or negated—something far more likely in less developed countries. Sage explains:

> The consequences of export-processing industrialization in developing countries has been dreadful. Although this system has provided employment for many workers, there have been adverse consequences as well: wages so low that workers cannot provide for their basic needs, unjust and inhuman working conditions, prohibition of union organization, and environmental devastation. Add widespread child labor to these conditions. According to International Labor Organization estimates released in 2002, some 352 million children (same as the entire US population) aged 5–17 are engaged in some form of economic activity in the world, with the Asian-Pacific region having the largest number of child workers.[19]

Moreover, despite claims by Nike and others, like Adidas, that their involvement helps improve conditions overseas, the meager wages they pay have not

18. Sage, "Corporate Globalization."
19. Sage, "Corporate Globalization," 394.

really helped these developing countries—the economic gap between rich and poor has widened dramatically. What they take is much greater than what they give. Although Nike trumpets its role in stimulating economies in the countries where they have located production, the evidence suggests that when wages begin to rise in those countries, even slightly, Nike relocates to countries where they can push their wage cost even lower.[20] Some Nike critics suggest that as countries like South Korea and Taiwan have democratized and begun granting workers more rights, Nike has relocated production to places like China and Indonesia where labor laws are negligible and often not enforced, and the governments are more repressive.[21] Writing for the *Washington Post*, Anne Swardson and Sandra Sugawara offer this summary: "No company symbolizes the mobilization of American companies overseas more than Nike. Its 30-year history in Asia is as close as any one company's story can be to the history of globalization, to the spread of dollars . . . into the poor corners of the earth. From Japan through Korea and Taiwan and then into China, Indonesia, and Vietnam, it is a story of restless and ruthless capital, continually moving from country to country in search of new markets and untapped low-wage labor."[22]

About Nike

Over 90 percent of the sneakers and sporting goods sold in the US are made in foreign countries, primarily in China. Nike, of course, isn't the only company making athletic shoes and apparel under dubious labor arrangements, but it is the industry leader and as such is in a position to act more responsibly and justly around the world. They set, and are responsible for, the trend. Some speculate that if Nike, who has the most clout in the sports-apparel industry, were to back off a bit, other athletic-apparel manufacturers would experience less pressure to follow suit as they compete for market share.

A long way from the company's 1964 waffle-iron shoe sole beginnings, Nike's current (2018) worth stands at $32.4 billion worldwide.[23] Philip Knight, the company's cofounder, is its largest stockholder, and his estimated net worth is $50.1 billion (as of June 2021).[24]

Although Nike is an American company, it has not manufactured an athletic shoe in the US since 1984.[25] Using an export-processing system, the

20. Macaray, "Nike's Crimes," 321.
21. Wokutch, "Nike and Its Critics," 216.
22. Swardson and Sugawara, "Asian Workers Become Customers."
23. O'Connell, "Brand Value of the Sports Company Nike."
24. "Phil Knight."
25. Macaray, "Nike's Crimes," 320.

intellectual work of design and marketing takes place primarily in the US, and the labor-intensive assembly work takes place in the company's seven-hundred-plus factories spread throughout Asia. Because Nike does not own the factories that produce their goods, they have been able to insulate themselves from responsibility for their workers. Accordingly, there are numerous accounts of the abysmal working conditions and human rights abuses taking place in Nike manufacturing facilities. In a short piece titled "Nike's Crimes," David Macaray writes:

> By now most people are familiar with Nike's glitzy corporate history. They burst upon the scene, then left the country. When Nike shuttered its last shoe factory in the U.S., more than a quarter-century ago, it was estimated that 65,060 American shoe workers had lost their jobs. Worse, of course, was the domino effect it had on the economy. When you relocate your entire manufacturing base to the Third World, you not only cause your own employees to lose their jobs, but you start the dime rolling; you induce your competitors (Reebok, Adidas, Puma, etc.) to move their facilities as well, as they seek to compete with the near slave-wages you're now paying your new employees. By the time the smoke settles, you have what we have today: $100 shoes being assembled by Vietnamese children making 20-cents an hour . . . *literally*.[26]

In a 1992 interview in the *Harvard Business Review*, Phil Knight, cofounder and then CEO of Nike, explained the shoe company's strategy of moving their manufacturing from one country to another: "We were also good at keeping our manufacturing costs down. The big, established players like Puma and Adidas were still manufacturing in high-wage European countries. But we knew that wages were lower in Asia, and we knew how to get around in that environment, so we funneled all our most promising managers there to supervise production."[27] Abysmal working conditions in these low-wage factories appear to be common. Summarizing a number of investigative reports by a wide variety of organizations, Sage notes the following as typifying working conditions in a Nike factory:

- In the late 1980s, minimum wage in Indonesian shoe factories was 83 cents per day . . . just 56 percent of the wage the government considered as meeting minimal physical needs.
- Horrendous working conditions, extremely long days, mandatory overtime, and abuse by supervisors.

26. Macaray, "Nike's Crimes," 321.
27. Willigan, "High Performance Marketing."

- 75–80 percent of Nike workers during the 1990s were women—something that appears to be the case up to the present day. Most were under 24, and it was normal to put in 10–13 hour days, six days a week. The typical worker was paid 13–20 cents per hour.[28]

While all this was going on, Nike was doing quite well, and paying out $1.13 billion on advertising alone in 1998. Since then the money Nike pays out for product and brand promotion has risen sharply and consistently. The 2019 figure for advertising and promotion, as noted earlier, stands at $3.75 billion.

Collective movements started arising with the intent to create public outrage against Nike to pressure them into changing their practices and improving conditions. Among them, the Nike social movement—a variety of organizations that connected online—set to work documenting below-subsistence wages, abysmal working conditions, employment of very young girls, abuse of workers, and antiunion practices, among other offenses, in Nike factories.[29] Some of this pressure seemed to produce results. For example, in 1992 Nike drafted a code of conduct stipulating new and improved standards for its labor suppliers, but subsequent research showed that many of the workers in its factories were largely unaware of the existence of the code. "Interviews with Nike's workers about the Code suggested that it was chiefly an instrument of damage control rather than a legitimate effort to protect workers who labored in Nike factories."[30]

So how are things looking today? Has Nike reformed and turned their considerable influence and vast fortunes to cultivating safe and humane workplaces and a living wage that provides for the present and futures of their workers in faraway places? Not really.

After noting the astronomical increase in sponsorships and endorsements by Nike and Adidas in recent years, the 2018 report written for CleanClothes-Campaign—an alliance of labor unions and nongovernmental organizations that focuses on improving conditions for workers in the global garment industry—reports that "leading sportswear brands, like Nike and Adidas, continue to withdraw from China because of the rising cost of labor, despite the fact that wages are only now barely enough to allow workers' families to live with dignity." Between 1995 and 2017, the worker's share of "the price of a pair of Nike or Adidas shoes sold to a consumer . . . has fallen by 30%." These brands shifted most of their labor to Indonesia, Cambodia, and Vietnam, where "incidents of human rights violations are more prevalent, and

28. Sage, "Corporate Globalization," 396.
29. Sage, "Corporate Globalization," 398–99.
30. Sage, "Corporate Globalization," 399.

workers' average salaries are 45 percent to 65 percent below the living wage," which is not sufficient for people to provide for even the basic needs of their family. The report continues:

> The apparent contradiction between the creation of downstream value and the precarious situation of garment factory workers can be explained by the business and financial model of sportswear makers Nike and Adidas. The central objective of this model is the maximization of profits in order to generate greater and greater returns for shareholders, as evidenced by the extraordinary dividends paid to shareholders each year (as high as 10 percent of gross revenue in the case of Nike). Nike has thus become a shining example of stock market success that its competitors strive to emulate. . . . Their ability to create profit rests as much on their ability to control and decrease production costs.[31]

These companies can save a lot of money, produce more, and increase economic pressure on suppliers by using "multi-level, transnational subcontracting supply chains based on the principles of lean management."[32] Working conditions in such factories are attracting greater scrutiny, but as that happens, brands move production to countries where labor is even cheaper and where they have less risk of scrutiny.

Journalists at *Tribune de Genève* report Nike's annual tax evasion figures to be an average of $60 billion per year, which "corresponds to what it would take to pay living wages to 287,000 workers in Vietnam and 241,000 in Indonesia." While this model increases profits for the company, these profits "do not 'trickle down' to the workers in the garment factories, despite the promises of sportswear brands, notably about the payment of living wages to their suppliers' workers."[33]

In recent years, if Nike and Adidas had set a goal of paying the workers in their supply chain a living wage, they could have done so by maintaining, not increasing, the amount of dividends they paid to shareholders and by leveling off the staggering amounts they spent on advertising. To pay workers a living wage, "the very logic of the system would have to be inverted; guaranteeing workers adequate wages and working conditions would need to be the objective—not brands' profit margins. As this study shows, this is not a matter of insufficient financial means—Nike and Adidas generate enough revenue to be able to pay living wages across their supply chains—but rather one of priority."[34]

31. CleanClothesCampaign, "Foul Play 2," 3–4.
32. CleanClothesCampaign, "Foul Play 2," 4.
33. CleanClothesCampaign, "Foul Play 2," 5.
34. CleanClothesCampaign, "Foul Play 2," 5.

Taking Their Labor, Keeping Them Poor

Marx's analysis of capitalism focused on the division of labor that characterized the exploitive relationship between the bourgeoisie and proletariat primarily within the nation-state itself. Wallerstein sees the current "world-system" as connected by this same capitalist division of labor. However, in the world-system, the global division of labor reaches far beyond national borders to connect very different cultures and societies, drawing them together in relations of dependency. Thus, where Marx focused on how the owner class exploited the worker class for profits, mostly within nation-states, Wallerstein sees the global economy—the entire world—as the new arena where this exploitation-drama plays out.[35]

Capitalism rests on a logic of energetic, progressive expansion. Accordingly, capitalist systems require an endless supply of low-wage labor. When the standard of living rises in a "core" country (like the United States) such that workers expect higher wages and benefits, human rights are prioritized, and profits decrease, nationally bounded capitalist systems reach their limits. To move forward, capitalists begin to push beyond national borders into new territories where they can obtain the cheap labor needed to continue expansion, enabling them to maintain or increase profits. The world-system that emerges from these activities constitutes a stratified system of class relations on a global scale. In effect, the world contains (and maintains) upper, middle, and lower classes (or castes) by country or political region.

For Wallerstein the exportation of exploitation is the key factor structuring the division of labor on which the world economy is based. Labor is more easily exploited in countries with less robust economies and with nondemocratic governments that tend not to police human rights. Ken Allan explains, "Exporting exploitation implies the movement of specific goods outside the national boundaries, and product movement from the most profitable to less profitable firms explicitly entails such a shift. Both of these processes move goods and labor from advanced capitalist to rising capitalist countries. In addition, both processes lead to the collapse of small businesses, and the centralization of accumulation—that is, capital is concentrated in fewer and fewer hands."[36] This results in "the stability of the modern world-system [being] based on a fundamental inequality in which some regions of the globe accumulate wealth at the expense of the continuing impoverishment of other regions."[37] In effect, the essential characteristic of the system is the inequal-

35. Allan, *Social Lens*, 455.
36. Allan, *Social Lens*, 458.
37. Appelrouth and Edles, *Sociological Theory in the Contemporary Era*, 575.

ity of relations it maintains. This inequality is vigorously reinforced by the prosperous core countries, who direct global production and who achieve the greatest gains from it. Global stability is achieved through pervasive instability. Rationality in the world-system is a product of the irrationality structuring global economic relationships. As we will see, racism and sexism provide legitimating mechanisms that minimize challenge that might disrupt or compromise the system.

In fleshing out the characteristics of world-systems, Wallerstein offers a typology that includes "core states," "periphery states," and "semi-periphery states." Core states have well-developed economies, a higher standard of living, higher wages, and so on. Because capitalists in core states have reached the limits of exploitable labor in their own countries, they turn to periphery states in the quest for profits. "These shifts result in a constant flow of surplus-value from the producers of peripheral products to the producers of core-like products."[38] Periphery states are those whose labor is forced (little occupational choice or worker protections) and underpaid. They are the weakest and most vulnerable players in the world-system. The semi-periphery emerges as periphery economies begin to stabilize and their standard of living rises even marginally. These states "both export exploitation and continue to exploit within their own country."[39] However, the transition from periphery to semi-periphery prompts core countries to abandon current production locations and search for new sites still entrenched in the periphery.

This tripartite categorization of nation-states and the systemic relationship between them helps explain what critics of the Nike model call the "race to the bottom." Core countries, then, are in the business of "extracting" surplus from the poor, periphery ones and then abandoning them once the standard of living rises there. In this process, the semi-periphery states play a critical role in maintaining the system. Because they function as both exploiter and exploited, they act as a sort of middle class, preventing unified opposition against the core countries. In the end, there will be no revolution, no real change, no future for poor shoe and garment workers, just a restless and relentless drive to secure perpetually impoverished, exploitable labor.

Kenneth Allan offers a compelling example to illustrate Wallerstein's theory:

In the 1800s, textiles were produced in very few countries, and it was one of the most important core industries. But, by the start of the twenty-first century,

38. Allan, *Social Lens*, 459.
39. Allan, *Social Lens*, 459.

textiles had all but moved out of the core nations. . . . In 1976, Nike began moving its manufacturing concerns from the United States to Korea and Taiwan,
which at the time were considered periphery states. Within 4 years, 90 percent of
Nike's production was located in Korea and Taiwan. . . . However, both Korea
and Taiwan were on the cusp, and within a relatively short period of time they
had moved into the semi-periphery. Other periphery states had opened up, most
notably Bangladesh, China, Indonesia, and Vietnam. So, beginning in the 1990s,
Nike began moving its operations once again. Currently, Indonesia contains
Nike's largest production centers, with 17 factories and 90,000 employees. But
that status could change. In 1997, the Indonesian government announced a
change in the minimum wage, from $2.26 per day to $2.47 per day. Nike refused
to pay the increase and in response, 10,000 workers went on strike. In answer
to the strike, a company spokesperson, Jim Small, said, "Indonesia could be
reaching a point where it is pricing itself out of the market."[40]

Yes, the proposed wage increase—so alarming to Nike—was twenty-one cents
per *day*, not per hour.

Wallerstein's emphasis is on praxis. He is convinced that the world as we
know it—the capitalist world-system—is coming to an end. Historically, all
worlds do. What "we" are doing—what we see so clearly in the Nike model—is
unsustainable on a number of fronts. "The structural supports upon which
capitalism has been built are limited and nearing exhaustion."[41] The chaos we
see all around us, economic and otherwise, provides evidence that the present world as we know it is coming apart. Wallerstein wants us to see, hear,
and understand the Marxist dynamics still at work within the system and to
translate this into action. Allan writes,

> Wallerstein is not saying that these changes are beyond our ability to influence
> or control. Rather, he means that "fundamental change is possible . . . and this
> fact makes claims on our moral responsibility to act rationally, in good faith, and
> with strength to seek a better historical system" [Wallerstein, *End of the World*,
> 3]. According to Wallerstein . . . , we must make diligent efforts to understand
> what is going on; we must make choices about the direction in which we want
> the world to move; and we must bring our convictions into action, because it
> is our behaviors that will affect the system.[42]

I remain pessimistic. The hegemonic control exerted by the Nike model
is so powerful, pervasive, and unassailable that its undoing requires all but a

40. Allan, *Social Lens*, 459, 60.
41. Allan, *Social Lens*, 465.
42. Allan, *Social Lens*, 467.

complete dismantling of the current system. Our allegiance to "big sports" and all that they include, and our sense that they represent excellence and the best things in life, offers Nike, Adidas, and others the cultural supports they need to continue with business as usual. Even religion is co-opted to bless the sport institution as holy among human endeavors. At the end of the day, we're just sports fans. Fanatics. And fans keep things going. No matter the cost.

Sourcing Labor from the Marginal and Despised

As we have seen, capitalism requires a supply of labor that can be readily exploited. In national capitalism, the level of exploitation is limited to the confines of the state itself.[43] As the economy expands in a nation like the United States, wages increase and profits go down. However, with global capitalism, exploitation can be exported. The cost of our shoes and athletic apparel stays about the same or goes up, but the wages that companies pay through their ceaseless colonial adventures go down. Although Nike appears to pay more wages in dollar figures, they actually pay less now (their exploitation of Asian workers is greater) than they did a decade ago.[44]

Wallerstein argued that core nations exploit periphery nations in this ongoing quest for profits. Where Wallerstein sees nations, W. E. B. Du Bois sees color—the reality of these exploited nations is one of color. "Thus the world market most wildly and desperately sought today is the market where labor is cheapest and most helpless and profit is most abundant. This labor is kept cheap and helpless because the White world despises 'darkies.'"[45] In how many factories is Nike paying primarily poor White women a few dollars a day to make shoes? Googling "Nike labor" and looking at the images is instructive. They are all of women of color.

As W. E. B. Du Bois writes, "There is a chance for exploitation on an immense scale for inordinate profit, not simply to the very rich, but to the middle class and to the laborers. This chance lies in the exploitation of darker peoples."[46] These are "dark lands," ripe for exploitation, "with only one test of success—dividends!"[47] Thus in a global economy, increasing profits rests on the symbolic meaning of color as constructed in race. "While Du Bois perceives distinct differences between Blacks and Whites that can be

43. Allan, *Social Lens*.
44. CleanClothesCampaign, "Foul Play 2."
45. Du Bois, *Darkwater*, 23.
46. Du Bois and Sundquist, *Oxford W. E. B. Du Bois Reader*, 504–5.
47. Du Bois and Sundquist, *Oxford W. E. B. Du Bois Reader*, 505.

characterized in spiritual terms (the souls of Black and White folk), he also argues that the color line is socially constructed and politically meaningful. . . . Race . . . is perceived as immutable and therefore a much more powerful way of oppressing people."[48] Accordingly, race functions as a means by which the oppression inherent in the capitalist world-system is legitimated and institutionalized.

In an essay titled "The Ideological Tensions of Capitalism: Universalism versus Racism and Sexism," Wallerstein affirms Du Bois's lament about "dark lands" and exploited labor hinging on color, and extends the analysis to include sex. According to Wallerstein, "The modern world, we have long been told, is the first to reach beyond the bounds of narrow, local loyalties and to proclaim the universal brotherhood of man. Or so we were told up to the 1970s. Since that time, we have been made conscious that the very terminology of the universalist doctrine, as for example the phrase *the brotherhood of man*, belies itself, since this phrase is masculine in gender, thereby implicitly excluding or relegating to a secondary sphere all who are female."[49] Wallerstein explains that the doctrine of universalism stands as the primary challenge to racism and sexism. The universalist ideology is seen in the concept of natural law, which proclaims that people are fundamentally equal and should not receive privilege or disproportionate rewards based on genetics or inherited position. Rather, universalism emphasizes merit. On the other hand, the racist/sexist ideology that legitimates precisely those things universalism opposes is alive, well, and currently structuring the world-system. These two ideologies—universalism and racism/sexism—exist in tension, forming a paradox.

Universalism, Wallerstein contends, is well suited for maintaining the capitalist world economy, for it assigns value and worth to all persons—offering a doctrine that, at least theoretically, includes (and uses) "all" in the ever-expanding capitalist vision. By contrast, particularisms (for example, excluding a people because of their religion or race) are incompatible with the logic of the capitalist system for which expansion and commodification are central (and possibly solitary) values. Exclusion through banishment, shunning, death, or some other means can work at odds with capitalism's thirst for expansion and the never-ending search for labor. Hitler's extermination of the Jews serves as an example. Killing millions of Jews eliminates the possibility that "they" could serve as workers. "It would follow then that, within a capitalist system, it is imperative to assert and carry out a universalist ideology as an

48. Allan, *Social Lens*, 208.
49. Wallerstein, *Essential Wallerstein*, 344.

essential element in the endless pursuit of the accumulation of capital. Thus it is that we talk of capitalist social relations as being a 'universal solvent,' working to reduce everything to a homogeneous commodity form denoted by a single measure of money."[50]

Within a meritocratic system, inequality is tolerated when it is presumed to be the result of merit and not inheritance or some other privilege. Racism, Wallerstein explains, is not simply "disdain" for the "other." Ultimately, racism involves the "ejection of the barbarian" from the community. Racism taken to such an extreme presents a problem for capitalism in that it leads to a loss of the labor that the expelled might have provided. Capitalism needs all the labor it can get. Thus, "ejection out of the system is pointless. But if one wants to maximize the accumulation of capital, it is necessary simultaneously to minimize the cost of production (hence the costs of labor power) and minimize the costs of political disruption (hence minimize—not eliminate, because one cannot eliminate—the protests of the labor force). Racism is the magic formula that reconciles these objectives."[51]

According to Wallerstein, racism "ethnicizes" the workforce. For example, when Europeans came to the New World, they slaughtered large numbers of native peoples. When they became convinced that the "Indians" had souls that needed to be saved, it altered their posture toward them. "Since Indians had souls, they were human beings, and the rules of natural law applied to them. Therefore, one was not morally permitted to slaughter them indiscriminately (eject them from the domain). One was obliged instead to seek to save their souls (convert them to the universalist value of Christianity). Since they would then be alive and presumably *en route* to conversion, they could be integrated into the work force—at the level of their skills, of course, which translated into meaning at the bottom level of the occupational and reward hierarchy."[52] In this way native peoples were not excluded or ejected but rather incorporated into the so-called meritocratic system—albeit at the bottom, where they would remain. And so, by virtue of racism, the workforce becomes ethnicized. This general approach, though it varies in form, "allows one to expand or contract the numbers available in any particular space-time zone for the lowest paid, least rewarding economic roles."[53] Furthermore, this racist system socializes children into internalizing and playing the "appropriate" roles that help sustain the system. And "it allows a far lower reward to a major segment of the work force than could ever be justified on the basis of

50. Wallerstein, *Essential Wallerstein*, 347.
51. Wallerstein, *Essential Wallerstein*, 348–49.
52. Wallerstein, *Essential Wallerstein*, 349.
53. Wallerstein, *Essential Wallerstein*, 350.

merit."[54] Finally, it allows the disparate doctrines of universalism and racism/sexism to be combined into a single system.

In the capitalist world-system, racism and sexism are intimately linked. Wallerstein indicates that "the ethnicization of the workforce exists in order to permit very low wages for whole segments of the labor force."[55] This entire arrangement is only possible because of the unpaid labor that women perform within a system that sees this as normative. Thus, when males, functioning in households as primary wage earners, provide low-wage labor in ethnicized systems, their wages can provide only a portion of the resources required by the household. Their low-wage situation is only sustainable because women (and children and the elderly) input labor into "so-called subsistence and petty market activities."[56] In short, capitalists rely on the normative system within which the unpaid labor of women is legitimated. "In such a system, this labor input in nonwage work 'compensates' the lowness of the wage-income and therefore in fact represents an indirect subsidy to the employers of the wage laborers in those households. Sexism permits us not to think about it. . . . As racism is meant to keep people inside the work system, not eject them from it, so sexism intends the same."[57] Furthermore, women's work in these situations is frequently viewed not as critical to the household but as something supplementary—something that need not be taken too seriously.

When we see young women of color working in Nike factories for extremely low wages, we are witnessing a system that exploits and ensnares them from multiple angles even as it provides and reinforces legitimating mechanisms that ensure few notice and even fewer care. These women exist within a system that preaches an ideology of universalism, even as it employs racism and sexism to fuel and sustain that system. Recalling the words of George Sage, our sporting experiences depend on the labor of those who make our shoes and tank tops—women of color, who work in periphery countries that are endlessly mined by the core and semi-periphery. These are the women who Nike thinks price themselves out of the market when they want a twenty-one-cent-per-day raise. We don't tolerate it here, but we seem to support it there.

As Du Bois said, "The White world despises 'darkies'"[58] . . . especially when they are women.

54. Wallerstein, *Essential Wallerstein*, 350.
55. Wallerstein, *Essential Wallerstein*, 350.
56. Wallerstein, *Essential Wallerstein*, 350.
57. Wallerstein, *Essential Wallerstein*, 350.
58. Du Bois, *Darkwater*, 23.

Not So Innocent Ourselves

Big sport offers a powerful and seductive way of veiling the ugly underbelly of global consumer capitalism. It is easy to see Nike's Phil Knight as an objectionable and greedy capitalist. That is what he is. Knight and his people have fought for many years to keep Nike wages low, labor young, unions out, and workers unprotected and vulnerable. It is less easy to see Michael Jordan, LeBron James, Kevin Durant, or Colin Kaepernick as the faces of greed who oppress people of color. In the United States, these athletes are vocal proponents for racial and gender equality, sometimes at cost, and they give to philanthropic causes that address various types of inequity. They entertain us, they inspire us, and through their example, we sometimes rise to greater heights ourselves. But they take Nike money. And they spend it on themselves. A lot of it.

The current top five Nike athletic endorsements as of 2021 stand as follows:

- Michael Jordan: $100 million/year (for life)
- LeBron James: $30 million/year
- Cristiano Ronaldo: $30 million/year
- Kevin Durant: $30 million/year
- Tiger Woods: $19 million/year[59]

Note that all of these athletes are people of color. All are African American, except for footballer Cristiano Ronaldo, who is Portuguese.

Michael Jordan reportedly "earned" $110 million from Nike in 2017 alone.[60] They pay him more when they do "well." The young women of color who provide the labor by which they prosper do not receive bonuses when Nike has a banner year. No "signing bonuses" for them. Jordan maintains a luxury yacht and flies in a private jet that looks like a sneaker, with his accolades, N236MJ (number 23, 6 NBA championships), painted on the tail. LeBron James lives a life of opulence and stands to make more than a billion dollars from Nike during his lifetime. A story in *USA Today* offers details about Kevin Durant's $12.15 million beach house.[61] This is but a small glimpse of the conspicuous consumption enjoyed by these "gods among men." However, the money they acquire from Nike comes to them as a direct consequence of the unpaid labor of mostly young, mostly Asian women. People of color.

59. Pereira, "Top 5 Nike Endorsements."
60. Badenhausen, "Michael Jordan Leads the NBA's Biggest Shoe Deals."
61. Im, "Kevin Durant Sells Gorgeous $12 Million Malibu Beach House."

Of course, Nike contracts with White athletes as well—and they are no less culpable for the role they play in maintaining this system of oppression.

My point is that elites such as Phil Knight—who influence and, with like others, set the agenda for the capitalist world-system—co-opt the very forces that might offer a compelling counternarrative to this hegemonic system that colonizes the entire world. Athletes of color—who might stand as powerful voices of opposition to the deplorable labor practices foisted upon poor people of color—are recruited to fortify and secure the fortunes of those who would pluck the last dime from girls who make their shoes and who, by extension, build their yachts, beach houses, and Lamborghinis. As spokespersons, these athletes, who we so admire, assist us in buying into and even celebrating the economic systems tuned to benefit the Phil Knights of the world, and they help divert our gaze away from the wretched things these global monopolies leave behind. When Nike recently acquired Colin Kaepernick's endorsement, their stock rose to a record high.[62] Kaepernick will take a knee in protest of American racism—and good for him. But I wonder if he ever thinks about the young women of color who make the shoes on which he stands. His Nike ad reads, "Believe in something, even if it means sacrificing everything." Indeed. Someone did sacrifice—we just don't notice, and we mostly don't care. For his endorsement, Kaepernick receives a lot of Nike money—and this makes it awfully difficult to raise a prophetic voice against this oppressive company.

Jordan, James, Durant, Ronaldo, Woods, and Kaepernick do not need the Nike money. I do not think they should take it. We should not be impressed or enchanted when they do. Instead, we might mourn the great loss that Nike and similar strong-arm metanationals represent to young women of color who are offered no voice, no recourse, no options, and no futures. What do these nameless women think about the slogan "Just Do It"? Do they cheer when LeBron dunks a ball or Ronaldo scores a goal? Do they surf the web to marvel at the interior of Kevin Durant's beach house? Likely not.

What would happen if any one of these powerful athletes turned down the money and brought to public attention the reality of the system? What if both Michael Jordan and LeBron James would visit a Nike shoe factory and live and work beside the laborers for a week? What if Jordan, James, and Ronaldo offered their voices to the oppressed, rather than the oppressor? What if they quit competing in cedar?

Du Bois was deeply involved in pan-African movements, and between 1919 and 1927 he engineered four pan-African congresses. Pan-Africanism func-tioned as both a cultural and a political ideology that called for solidarity

---

62. Kelleher, "Nike Shoes Close at All Time Record High."

between people of African descent on the basis of their common interests. Du Bois's famous line "The problem of the twentieth century is the problem of the color line" was written with this in mind.[63] While Du Bois's writing centered on the interests of people of African descent, his concerns can be easily extended to envision all people of color being bound together by the interests and issues they share in common.

In spring 1949, he spoke at the World Congress of the Partisans of Peace in Paris, saying to the large crowd, "Leading this new colonial imperialism comes my own native land built by my father's toil and blood, the United States. The United States is a great nation; rich by grace of God and prosperous by the hard work of its humblest citizens. . . . Drunk with power we are leading the world to hell in a new colonialism with the same old human slavery which once ruined us; and to a third World War which will ruin the world."[64]

We still colonize the world in search of profits. As Du Bois notes, we do it by color. As Wallerstein observes, we do it by gender too. We, especially we who see ourselves as the people of God, must recognize and take responsibility for our complicity in sustaining the systems that oppress distant strangers. Nike's business practices exploit people of color, leaving them with want, poverty, and hopelessness. And through all this, we sit enthralled, entertained by those who provide the cultural legitimation for taking so very much from these faraway neighbors. We cheer as iconic athletes and the hegemonic package of big sport help us look the other way, so that people like Phil Knight can keep getting richer—no interference from us.

> Even if you take the position that Nike is, ostensibly, no worse than any other shoe manufacturer when it comes to trolling for poverty wages, you have to admit that its Chairman of the board, Phil Knight is a supreme hypocrite. Vehemently anti-labor union, Knight nonetheless tries to come off as this above-the-fray enlightened philanthropist/humanitarian. He does charity work; he gives money to colleges. But in truth, Knight is as hard-bitten a businessman as any sweatshop foreman. The only difference is image. And image is everything to Nike. The company spends an estimated $280 million a year on celebrity endorsements [way more now], including those of superstars Michael Jordan and Tiger Woods. It's no exaggeration to say that Knight, the "humanitarian," could feed and clothe all the children of an African city for less than he's paying Jordan for one year.[65]

I fear we're not so innocent ourselves. At least not if we compete in cedar.

63. Du Bois, *Souls of Black Folk*, 9.
64. Lewis, *W. E. B. Du Bois*, 687.
65. Macaray, "Nike's Crimes," 321.

Postscript: A Profound Undoing

What do we do with such unsettling information, when disentangling ourselves from one corrosive capitalist enterprise usually necessitates turning to
another that is likely as bad? What difference does it make to ban Nike but
then embrace Adidas or Puma? Should we go barefoot? Are there alternatives?
When I click through Facebook, I find some of my "friends" posting witty
aphorisms that disparage any who would criticize even egregious examples
of corporate greed and human neglect found in the *capitalist* world-system.
Positioned against the dreaded socialism, many accept the capitalist system as
something that is fundamentally just and unquestionably best. With the "at
least it's not socialism" standard, the practices of Nike (and others who profit
from racism, sexism, and engineered poverty) become accepted as virtue—
evil becomes thought of as good. We are caught between bad choices. How
do we live as God's people in a world where simply enjoying a professional
basketball game, wearing shoes, or drinking coffee implicates us in slave-level
wages, coercive labor practices, and celebrating that of which we should repent? There is no clear answer to such a question. These matters are complex
and multilayered. There is simply not a correct form of social organization
that will eradicate evil in the world.

The Old Testament prophets were up against the same things we are.
They, like us, faced deeply entrenched social systems, exploitive practices,
and interests of powerful people that ran counter to the demands of God's
justice. Still they said, "Repent." Still they told God's people to fight injustice,
to put away worldly things, and to seek and desire the righteousness of God.

Society is an act of imagination. What you see around you represents the
limits of what "society" has envisioned. The people of God, however, are to
imagine things differently from the culture around them. Our imagination
should not function in service of selfish ambition, violence, or neglect of the
other. When the prophets called God's people to repentance, they were, in
part, issuing a call to fresh imagination. We might hear them saying, "Look
at yourselves. You are oppressing the poor, forgetting the stranger, hoarding,
hating your brothers and sisters, exercising greed, using violence. Shall I go
on? God hates these things. Repent, and have a little more imagination. You're
the people of God after all. What sort of world do you want?"

God's people are to offer an alternative to the dominant reality of the society around them. A world where Jesus is Lord requires a profound undoing of
society as we know it. We are not to be the people of "business as usual." Our
imagination, animated by nothing less than the Spirit of God, should call into
question the structures and priorities of this world. If we fail to question the

dominant secular reality, instead competing for the prizes this world offers, we *are* the world. And then, what is the point of being the people of God?

Framing these ideas in the language of sports, we should resist being fans of the practices and structures of this world. *Fan* is short for "fanatic," and fanatics develop ideological commitments that can compromise their allegiance to the ways of God—to doing justice, loving kindness, and walking humbly. In this world, it is very easy to be a sports fan or a fan of some other socially valued endeavor. It's easy to be "all in." Fanaticism can produce a loss of perspective, and this can deter us in our efforts to resist the patterns of this world. When we love the things of this world, when we become over-committed to the social systems that support our lives and our lifestyles, our critique of those things can fall away, and we can become blind to injustices built into them.

So a Christian approach to addressing such complex matters as labor abuses in supply-chain global capitalism is found not in a moral list of dos and don'ts but rather in the distinctive life ethic of a people of imaginative faith, who by doing justice, loving kindness, and walking humbly with God question the things of this world and, by example, offer society an alternative to the dominant reality. In the spirit of such an ethic, I offer one practical suggestion: pick something from which you can abstain. For me, it is Nike products. I know how they're made, and our family no longer buys them. I have no illusions that this makes even a small dent in the Nike machinery I've questioned in this chapter, but I offer it to God as a small act of fasting from one of the things of this world. As I do so, I try, every so often, to pause, remember, and mourn for the young people of color who in faraway, hidden places make my shoes for less money a day than I spend on coffee. And just maybe, as I—as the people of God—do this sort of thing, a distinctive life ethic will settle over us.

Who knows, maybe together we will accomplish a profound undoing.

PART 3
INVITING STRANGERS

CHAPTER NINE

CHALLENGING THE NORMAL

The Strange(r) Reality of the Gospel

Walls, Border Crossings, and Threats to the Normal

I grew up in Southern Ontario but went to college in North Georgia. Unable to afford a car, I drove the considerable distance from Ontario to Georgia on a motorcycle—something far less romantic than it sounds. I remember traversing the US-Canada border multiple times without giving the crossing much thought. It was the late 1980s, I was an eighteen-year-old with a mullet and an old suitcase tied to the backrest of my motorcycle (there are pictures!), and the possibility of being detained by border authorities never occurred to me. And I never was, despite the fact that besides my Ontario driver's license, I carried no passport or other official document to validate my identity.

Things are different in the post-9/11 world of walls, barbed wire, and drawn weapons. In 2015, US border authorities held a Somali-American family of six for eleven hours at the Canadian border as they were attempting to return home to Minnesota after visiting relatives in Saskatchewan. Why? Apparently, the father's name, Abdisalam Wilwal, had appeared on a terror watch list for reasons the US government has, to date, refused to divulge. At the border, the family produced their US passports as well as the children's birth certificates. Moments later, three border officials emerged with guns drawn and pointed at the family.[1] Various legal documents and news reports detail

---

1. Hauslohner, "U.S. Family Suing Federal Government."

the harrowing experience that followed. "The lawsuit filed by Abdisalam Wilwal, his wife Sagal Abdigani, and four children—then ages 5 to 14—says the family was denied food for hours, Wilwal passed out after hours of having his hands cuffed behind his back, and the ordeal caused so much fear that at one point the eight-year-old girl told her mom, 'maybe they'll kill us after sunset.'"[2] "Maybe they'll kill us?!" How terrifying this must have been—especially coming from the very authorities responsible for protecting and caring for US citizens. The lawsuit also divulges that Wilwal was questioned about his religious practices and travels and was denied access to a lawyer or interpreter. During their ordeal, the Wilwal-Abdigani family's oldest son was separated from the family, patted down, and told to remove his clothes for a strip search—something he successfully resisted.

In 2018, a federal judge presiding over Wilwal's lawsuit rejected the government's argument to have the case dismissed. Hugh Handeyside, a senior staff attorney for the ACLU National Security Project, explains, "In this case, the court recognized that we don't forfeit our due process rights at the border. Abdisalam can now pursue his legal claims to force the government to tell him why it put him and his family through this ordeal—and prevent the government from ignoring the Constitution again in the future."[3]

How frightening for this family. "Are you one of us . . . or one of them?" How vulnerable and helpless they must have felt.

What self-respecting terrorists would vacation in Saskatchewan anyway?!

More recently, in the summer of 2019, my (American) uncle and aunt who were in their late sixties faced a tense situation while trying to cross back into the US after visiting my parents in Ontario. After they pulled up to the border gate and had their passports scanned, border personnel suddenly surrounded their car. They pulled my uncle out of the vehicle, frisked him, and then escorted him into a building while instructing my aunt to move to the driver's seat and park the car before joining him. After a short period of questioning, they released them, satisfied that my aunt and uncle posed no imminent threat, but without apology. Apparently, my uncle shared some characteristic in common with a nefarious person the border guards were trying to catch. In "casting a wide net," they were treating all they ensnared as hostiles. As they processed my relatives out of the building, permitting passage back into the States, the officials explained that my uncle's passport would likely trigger this sort of event whenever they crossed the US-Canada border. Oh, bureaucracy. How unsettling to have constitutional rights suspended while

---

2. "Somali-American Family Sues after Detained for 11 Hours."
3. Handeyside, "Judge Just Reminded CPB That the Border Isn't a Rights-Free Zone."

powerful people determine "we" or "they" status. How vulnerable you feel, even as a citizen with legitimate documentation. How much more frightening such experiences must be for those who struggle to speak English or who have brown skin. These are sobering stories, and my wife and I take them quite seriously. Now when our family moves between countries visiting relatives, we feel anxious about crossing the border, and we double-check that our passports are up-to-date and opened to the right page. We even bring our children's birth certificates and various adoption documents along in case authorities question our parental ties to them. They're from Bulgaria and China and look nothing like us.

How important it is to belong.

The apostle Paul hazarded various we-or-they "border" crossings that sometimes required him to pull the "Roman citizen" card to mitigate threats from the Jews and Roman authorities. In Acts 21 and 22 some of Paul's fellow Jews seize him and accuse him of opposing their teachings and defiling the temple (they correctly perceive Paul to be challenging important boundaries that defined their identities). In response to the civic unrest this provokes, the Romans authorities get involved, arrest him, bind him with chains, and only then ask who he is and what he has done—perhaps people detained at the US border can relate! At this point, the writer of Acts notes, the Roman soldiers had to carry him away because the violence of the mob was so intense (Acts 21:35). Just before they cart him off, Paul asks the Roman commander for permission to speak to the people. Permission granted, he addresses the crowd-turned-mob in Aramaic (a language Palestinian Jews were most likely to speak and understand). He offers them his rather unusual testimony, and they appear to listen. However, in Acts 22:21, when Paul says, "Then he [the Lord] said to me, 'Go, for I will send you far away to the Gentiles,'" their rage sharply escalates, quickly obliterating any remaining inclination to listen. Whereupon all you-know-what breaks loose. Acts 22:22–24 details their over-the-top response to Paul's announcement: "Up to this point they listened to him, but then they shouted, 'Away with such a fellow from the earth! For he should not be allowed to live.' And while they were shouting, throwing off their cloaks, and tossing dust into the air, the tribune directed that he was to be brought into the barracks, and ordered him to be examined by flogging, to find out the reason for this outcry against him."

Wipe him from the earth? For what offense? For the same one we've examined in the previous chapters of this book. Paul had transgressed a critical we/they, in-group/out-group boundary. Though a well-credentialed insider, Paul dared to invite outsiders, whose mere presence violated temple protocol, into the religious community, claiming that God had told him to begin tearing down the walls separating Jew from gentile, good people from "dogs." This was no small matter. These walls defined Israelite identity as *the* people of God. Foundational theologies and cultural tradition rested on them. The gospel that Paul proclaimed was an invitation to set aside these barriers and unfurl a banner reading "Welcome to the neighborhood!" Paul was trying to inspire his compatriots to anchor their identities in something besides the same social hierarchies that have structured human existence across all of history. He was asking them to reimagine and redraw the contours of the "people of God"—to rethink "we" and "they." Paul's wall-demolition initiative posed a threat to in-group identity. "Who are we if we're mixed up with . . . them?" We all face this disorienting question in one way or another.

Recall from chapter 4 the image of the angry White mob flanking young Ruby Bridges as she walked, under guard, into William Frantz Elementary School. Ruby was a stick of dynamite in the foundation of White identity. How similar that ugly scene was to the one facing Paul—both represented change and threat to the existing order. The Israelites in the Acts 21–22 narrative were willing to use violence to keep important socioreligious identity-walls intact. So are "we," if we're honest. Opening ourselves to strangers is not benign. Paul's mission and ours, if we're successful, will change the "family" and neighborhood in all kinds of important ways.

- "They" will bring new norms.
- "They" will question "our" ways.
- "They" may resist learning "our" language.
- "They" may require resources "we" had grown accustomed to dividing among ourselves.
- "They" may need health care.
- "They" will challenge some of "our" traditions.
- "They" may want to be among the decision-makers in the group.
- "They" represent the end of one thing and the beginning of something new.
- In the end, "we" will not be the same as we are now.

Including strangers destabilizes a settled group, and we humans crave stability and predictability. You can see why what Paul called the gospel—the good news—might not be received as something good to those whose identities it threatened. You don't have to look far to see that you and I, like the Israelites in Acts 21 or the White mob pushing in on Ruby Bridges, don't frequently receive the "include strangers" part of the good news with gladness, anticipation, and a word of welcome on our lips.

When you hear these stories, where do your sympathies lie? Who do you side with? There's a good chance that Christians will identify with Paul, hoping the Jews will see the light, accept the gospel, and change their insular ways. But what if you're Jewish? How then do you hear that story? In hearing the story about Ruby Bridges, many African Americans undoubtedly root for young Ruby as they remember her courageous walk to school. But what if you're from New Orleans and your relatives were among those protesting school integration efforts in your community? How did you feel about reading chapter 5, which offered perhaps unsettling information about some of the ways gender is socially constructed? Maybe you came away sympathetic to intersex people (who are few in number) but also a bit uneasy that this might be part of some "agenda" to chip away at what you see as clear, biblical teaching that God created "male and female"? Is there no firm ground on which to stand? Finally, if you have been struggling to find employment, how did it feel to reach chapter 6 and think about inviting migrants—legal or otherwise—over to enjoy resources you felt denied? Does being a citizen mean nothing?

We all exist in particular social locations replete with values, norms, and cultural perspectives. It's easy for people in my social location (remember, I'm White, heterosexual, married, American, educated, middle class, and currently employed) to envision ourselves in dominant positions relative to others, especially strangers. I'm accustomed to being part of the group that makes the decisions in various institutions. When I'm not, I can usually gain access to people in authority. This tendency to identify with the powerful ones in a social structure influences how I read the Bible and think about God. I readily see myself enjoying fellowship with Jesus and the disciples, refusing to be lured into arguments over which of them is the greatest, showing mercy to the woman with the issue of blood, and shielding the woman caught in adultery from her accusers. In locating myself in the biblical story, I'm one of the "good guys," I'm on the right team, and we all know how my story concludes. Accordingly, reaching out to strangers through practices of evangelism or what some call mercy ministry tends to mean inviting others (strangers) to join me in *my* ways, my perspective, my church, and so on. Come on over to my place, but I'm still in charge . . . at least until you're a lot like me. For example, when predominantly White institutions, like colleges, work to increase their racial diversity by recruiting minority students yet maintain the same racial disparities in the powerful parts of the organizational hierarchy, the minority "outreach" can reinforce the very disparity that stimulated it.

In the end, the "strangers" may feel just as marginal inside the group as they did outside of it.

At present, many organizations—churches, colleges, hospitals, manufacturers—voice a commitment to cultivating diversity within their ranks. I wonder whether the commitment reflected in an organization's promotional literature anticipates the profound change that may occur as it becomes more "diverse." Real diversity begins with including strangers, and including strangers is risky. Cultivating diversity means inviting strangers in with the understanding (and ideally the hope) that they will change us—sometimes in fundamental ways. Maybe "inviting in" is the wrong terminology—it implies a one-way relationship that moves "toward us." You, the stranger, may join "us" on our side—the right side—of the wall, but the walls remain intact. I once heard a minister at a mostly White church talk excitedly about the priority his denomination was putting on drawing Black ministers into their ranks, saying, "We're working really hard to recruit Black people into our seminaries to bring them up to speed on our theology." Hmm. On the one hand, I appreciate the recognition that the denomination had something to gain from greater African American presence and leadership. On the other, the "join us and be like us" message suggests allegiance to the existing social/theological/ecclesial order. This minister's announcement, though sincere, seemed to underestimate how minority clergy might help the denomination identify and understand some of their own problems—theological and otherwise—that social location had rendered invisible. I imagine a Black seminarian or minister would hear such an appeal as "Come sit with us and let us change you." That's not diversity; it's just a settled monologue directed at a multiracial group. Real diversity— the risky kind that invites strangers—offers the possibility of something new, disruptive, and potentially wonderful.

An Alternative to the Dominant Reality

Theologian Walter Brueggemann writes that the gospel offers a "genuine alternative" to the dominant (social) reality, or what we call "the status quo."[4] It makes sense that the gospel's "good news" and the social arrangements it promotes would be attractive to those pushed aside or exploited by the system—those who desperately need an alternative. But why would people thriving within the dominant system embrace change? For the rich young rulers occupying the better seats in society's banquet hall (people like me?), "accepting" the gospel may require setting aside material advantage and possibly

4. Brueggemann, *Word Militant*, 27.

taking a seat of lesser honor. Pretty disruptive. Groups advantaged by a given social system tend to embrace the status quo that forms the basis for their identities. With identity at stake, how would those near the top of the stratified order perceive "good news" that offers to "undo" present arrangements?

For people deeply vested in the dominant culture, countercultural movements pose a threat. Furthermore, if the present system is perceived as a kind of kingdom of God on earth, then Christians positioned to control and enjoy its bounty may simply refashion the gospel to support the existing reality. In this way, the dominant social system and the gospel simply join forces against whatever else is out there, whether it's the "axis of evil," those with a "Marxist agenda," or "illegal immigrants." In effect, the dominant social reality *is* the alternative, and the gospel becomes synonymous with God's in-group blessing on God's chosen people—"good news" that supports existing cultural us-against-them divisions.

We observe this phenomenon when nationalists appeal to, say, "Christian America," or when some Christian groups defend a cherished cultural practice as stemming from "Christian principles" or "absolute truth." The idea is that the current system just needs the influence and support of good Christian people rather than an alternative that represents a fundamental break with the dominant reality. Perhaps this is why some Christians use the language of "accepting" the gospel. *Accepting* is a passive term that is far more conservative than the radical, world-altering, sell-all-you-own gospel that Brueggemann calls a "genuine alternative."

Genuine alternatives are good news to disenfranchised strangers, even as they are generally met with resistance by those advantaged by the status quo. Remember that the rich young ruler of Matthew 19 "went away grieving, for he had many possessions" (v. 22) when Jesus offered him a genuine, though radical, alternative to the dominant reality on which his identity depended. In a more contemporary example, a recent *Newsweek* article examined Pew data showing that 65 percent of Americans who claim no religious affiliation felt that the US had a special responsibility to provide care for people displaced by violence or war, while "only 25% of White evangelicals felt a responsibility to help people who have been forced to leave their country due to horrifying circumstances." The author, Heather Thompson Day, points out that "White evangelicals were the least likely of all groups to feel any responsibility for the very same people scripture says in Deuteronomy 10:18–19 that God loves." She concludes, "If you want to hide from God and His word, religion increasingly looks like a good place to start."[5] Sadly, one of the more privileged groups

5. Thompson Day, "Evangelicals Are Less Likely to Welcome Refugees Than Non-believers."

in American society (White evangelicals) sometimes show the lowest level of concern for the most victimized and destitute.

Just a few months before this *Newsweek* article was published, the *Washington Post* published a piece by Greg Sargent noting that from 2016 to 2018 support for building a southern (US-Mexico) border wall grew from 58 percent to 67 percent among White evangelical Protestants in America. Sargent suggests that this wall stands as a "significantly potent totem" that has little to do with national security or economic threat and plenty to do with a fear that the sun may be setting on White, Christian dominance in the country.[6] He further draws attention to a growing schism between White evangelicals who support the wall and non-evangelical Whites who oppose it. Taken together, these two articles seem to suggest an inverse relationship between holding an advantaged position in the social structure and identifying with the suffering of those in lower social positions. Just as the rich young ruler struggled to embrace the genuine alternative Jesus offered, privileged groups in a society may struggle to embrace the "sell all you own and give the money to the poor" alternative reality to which God's people are called. Furthermore, this raises troubling questions about whether affluent people of faith are more likely to identify with those who share their social class, but not their faith, than with those who share their faith but not their social class.

Sociologists Keith Roberts and David Yamane explain how hymns popular among the affluent reflect different priorities than hymns popular among the poor. "In upper- and middle-class churches, the hymns frequently express a positive value of this-worldly activity, an affirmation of individual self-worth, a high valuation of individual initiative and accomplishment, and a sense that persons are in charge of their own destinies."[7] The fourth verse of "Rise Up, O Men of God" provides a good example:

> Rise up O men of God
> The Church for you doth wait,
> Her strength unequal to her task;
> Rise up, and make her great![8]

By contrast, the hymns of the poor tend toward an otherworldly orientation, emphasizing a desire to leave the sufferings of this world for heaven, a better place, an alternative to their present reality. Consider lines from several verses of "Alas! And Did My Savior Bleed?":

6. Sargent, "Walls around Trump Are Crumbling."
7. Roberts and Yamane, *Religion in Sociological Perspective*, 314.
8. Merrill, "Rise Up, O Men of God."

> Alas! and did my Savior bleed? And did my Sov'reign die?
> Help me, dear Savior, Thee to own, And ever faithful be;
> Would He devote that sacred head, For such a worm as I?
> And when Thou sittest on Thy throne, Dear Lord, remember me.[9]

Roberts and Yamane further observe that popular hymns in churches of the affluent tend to embrace conventional, secular norms. This may be because those in the middle and upper classes are frequently in a position to establish and reinforce cultural norms in a society. For the more affluent, "what is" is good, and change is normally resisted and suppressed. For the privileged, an alternative to the existing order that requires including strangers and deprioritizing the things of this world is intrusive and threatening. With so much at stake (at least for those who see themselves as the people of God), the status quo is simply equated with the will of God, and those who threaten it—even the poor—are ignored or labeled as the enemies of God.

Sociologist Russ Heddendorf offers a helpful insight into the boundary-making dynamics of the people of God. He argues that although Romans 12:18 offers the counsel, "If it is possible, so far as it depends on you, live peaceably with all," maintaining conflict with society (the world) is essential because it provides an important boundary for the group: "In John 15:18–20, for example, Jesus implies that conflict with the world helps to define the group. The disciples gain an identity as Jesus's followers when the world hates them as it hated him. Conflict provides a boundary for the group, that they might not be 'of the world' while being 'in the world.'"[10] He explains, "The problem comes in trying to understand when group goals or actions represent the transcendent will of God and when they merely represent some group or individual needs."[11] We must take care not to fashion a cheerleader god who supports our group but rather be willing to change our ways, perhaps abandoning social advantage, as we submit ourselves to the God of the "genuine alternative." The people of God should oppose evil, but sometimes our opposition to others may be little more than guarding our resources and fortifying our identity by scapegoating. Instead of "we're with God," we come to think, "God's with us." There's a difference. In a clever bit of wordplay, Heddendorf writes that believers are to be separate but are not to separate themselves. Allegiance to the kingdom of God requires that God's people be accessible to those who are not like-minded—accessible to strangers.

9. Watts, "Alas! And Did My Savior Bleed?"
10. Heddendorf and Vos, *Hidden Threads*, 80.
11. Heddendorf and Vos, *Hidden Threads*, 80–81.

In exploring self-interest as a powerful determinant of a group's actions, Brueggemann points to our tendency to read the Bible (and thus hear "the gospel") in ways that reflect and support the "old hegemony."[12] If you're unfamiliar with this term, you can think of it as the dominant reality that is internalized, accepted, taken for granted, and reinforced through various cultural supports. The concept of cultural hegemony is associated with Karl Marx, who famously said, "The ideas of the ruling class are in every epoch the ruling ideas, i.e., the class which is the ruling *material* force of society, is at the same time its ruling *intellectual* force."[13] Through powerful cultural mechanisms, even people disadvantaged by a social system come to agree with the dominant reality that surrounds them. When we passively accept "our" world as the best possible, offering a serious critique of it becomes difficult. In fact, most people work rather tirelessly to prop up and defend the cultural supports that hold society in place. Oddly, we Christians can complain about the encroachment of the so-called secular world even while we work tirelessly to maintain, enjoy, and support that world.

One example I can offer concerns violence in American contact sports. In my Sociology of Sport class, after looking at the concussion crisis in the National Football League, acquainting students with disturbingly high injury statistics, and reading quotations from NFL players that testify to how much they love breaking the ribs of their opponents (really!), I read a variety of Bible passages from both Testaments that address violence. I teach at a Christian college, and I have a difficult time finding support for my idea that there is disconnect between what the Bible says about violence and the way Christians support it in football. Almost every year a student in my class will respond to my promptings about NFL players and violence with the words, "But it's within the rules of the game." Recently, a student said, "But he's paid huge amounts of money to crush his opponents—that's his job!" My point is that in American culture we accept violence as legitimate, exciting, and necessary. When I suggest an acute disjunction between the theology we voice about people being made in the image of God and our enthusiastic support for "brutal body violence" in football, many students are at a loss about how to interpret my statements. Taking me seriously requires a deconstruction of much of the reality of big sports that they have come to accept, internalize, take for granted, and enjoy.

In 2019 I attended a conference about Christianity and sports that hosted a very likable, well-known evangelical football player who, in talking about his experiences competing against another player, remarked with a good-natured

---

12. Brueggemann, *Word Militant*, 24–25.
13. Quoted in Farganis, "Karl Marx," 45.

grin, "I really wanted to hurt him!" . . . and the Christian crowd filled with Christian faculty and Christian coaches roared with approval. His comment upheld both entertainment violence and patriarchal masculinity norms, with the effect of powerfully reinforcing their compatibility with the gospel and the will of God. In this and other ways, religion—perhaps faith itself—can be co-opted to support the dominant model of reality that many have come to love and accept. My students frequently express that sports are an excellent platform for "witnessing" and for "winning people to Christ" (note the competitive sport language employed to describe spiritual realities). However, this style of bearing witness rarely requires modifying many aspects of the dominant sport machine or the worldview that sustains it. There is little critique. It all fits together nicely, and conformity to a "biblical worldview" requires only minor modifications to the dominant model. No alternative needed.

Brueggemann further explains that, in reading the Bible through the "dominant text" of the Enlightenment tradition, we easily cultivate support for our consumptive lifestyles, love of self over neighbor, ruthless competition, relentless production, violence, dominance, environmental degradation, and a multitude of other factors that compose our hegemonic normal. In conforming the ways of God to the ways of society, dominant text readings permit us to disparage or even persecute desperately poor migrant-strangers who require our help unless they have followed "our" complex laws to the letter. "No illegal immigrants for us; we're law-abiding citizens!" What Brueggemann calls the "dominant text" reading of the Bible supports inequalities that are clearly incompatible with the gospel, and it deters us from caring for strangers as brothers and sisters. As a result, we learn to see the good news as an extension of present social arrangements, and we co-opt and distort "gospel" in support of "we" over "they." Brueggemann offers the following summary:

> The biblical text is indeed a profound alternative to the text of the Enlightenment and therefore alternative to the dominant text with which most of us came to church. For a very long time we have assumed that the "American Dream," which is our version of Enlightenment freedom and well-being, coheres with the claims of the gospel. It is the United States that is God's agent in the world, God's example, and God's most blessed people. . . . Now we are coming to see belatedly—indeed, we are required to see—that the American Dream as it is now understood has long since parted company with the claims of the gospel. Whereas the dominant text finds human initiative at the core of reality, the gospel witnesses to holiness as the core, and whereas it is the self that arises out of the hegemonic text, in the gospel it is the neighbor.[14]

14. Brueggemann, *Word Militant*, 27.

The gospel as a counter-text pushes against rather than supports the dominant society, offering a "genuine alternative" to the hegemonic normal. Brueggemann's point is that you have to look for the gospel, and you find it, in part, through a particular mode of reading. *How* we read the Bible from our respective social locations has profound implications for what we find there and what the text helps us to see. Our approach to reading the Bible can stimulate or stifle our imaginations. As we read (if we read), do we look to support the dominant perspective, or do we search for an alternative that invites us to be involved in freeing captives, lifting up the downtrodden, canceling debt, sacrificially caring for neighbor, and generally deprioritizing the things of this world? Accepting the challenge of this alternative way of reading the Bible requires thinking deeply about identity and, consequently, about strangers. Do we read to keep strangers in their place, or do we read to participate in the genuine alternative of the gospel? Bruce Cockburn sings,

> Depends on what you look at, obviously,
> but even more it depends on the way that you see.[15]

Echoing this sentiment, Brueggemann alerts us to two possible "texts" we can find in the Bible and thus at least two discernible patterns we can choose to follow: hegemony and counterhegemony (see fig. 9.1).

The critic may raise a hand and object that the two patterns depicted in figure 9.1 offer little ground on which the real person in the real world can stand. These alternatives suggest an "all in" or "all out" approach that some may see as little more than academic posturing. Were the critic to step into my life, he or she might catch me enjoying Netflix programs that reinforce gender stereotypes and glamorize the same sort of violence I just criticized in the sport-conference example. She might point out the duplicity evidenced by my choice of shoes, which, while not made by Nike, were probably manu-factured using equally exploited labor. He might note that I participate in a 401(k) retirement plan, hope it grows, but have little idea which companies are represented in its holdings. She might observe that although I wrote a chapter addressing the needs of poor migrants, I just spent more money fix-ing my driveway than I've ever given to organizations that offer legal help to those languishing at the border.

At the extreme of the "all out" (counterhegemonic) side, we have Walter Brueggemann joining forces with the sociologists who, let's face it, mostly complain for a living(!), telling us to read the Bible better, reject the modern

---

15. Cockburn, "Child of the Wind."

Pattern 1 (supports the dominant system and resists change)

dominant reality ➡ dominant text ➡ dominant reading ➡ hegemonic normal

Pattern 2 (challenges the dominant system and promotes change)

gospel/alternative reality ➡ counter-text ➡ alternative reading ➡ counterhegemony

Figure 9.1. Hegemony and counterhegemony

world with its neighbor-alienating excesses, and imagine and embody some completely different way of living that most likely rejects professional sports and Netflix. Well . . . good luck with that! At the extreme of the "all in" (hegemonic normal) side, we have a bunch of reasonably well-to-do Christians selectively reading the Bible in ways that affirm their consumptive, self-oriented, God-is-my-copilot approach to life while slapping WWJD bumper stickers on their cars, building a wall to keep out the poor, and muttering about secularization as God whisks them away to heaven.

I suggest a third approach we might consider. This approach acknowledges the tension inherent in living "in the world," while being "not of the world." It seems to me that an "in, not of" approach to living in God's world helps avoid the traps of unrealistic social utopias while still taking seriously the importance of maintaining perspective on one's situation in the world. I want to argue that strangers play an essential role in helping a group—like the community of the people of God—live in their world(s) while cultivating a critical perspective and loosening their grip on the things "of" this world just a bit. How could a group see what they're *not* seeing about themselves without allowing an outsider to penetrate their boundaries? The material on Simmel's stranger from chapter 1 explained how strangers represent a social position that can help a group gain perspective precisely because they stand peripheral to the group.

If we wish to take Brueggemann's counsel, the stranger can help us see the biblical text anew, perhaps from the position of a subordinated person or group. How could "we" start reading the Bible differently unless a stranger would show us new ways to think about it? The stranger, however, is also a person in his or her own world, with commitments to culture, social networks, and various structures that are both good and bad. Understanding this can help us better apprehend the reality of living in a world where we are not free to exist outside of culture, as though living a life free of compromise with the modern world were possible. A stranger can help us to identify and acknowledge various points of tension in our cultural lives that represent living for self in disregard of neighbor. In the end, without rejecting our own "world" as all bad, or placing it beyond critique, the stranger can help us edge toward loving our neighbor, giving not taking, repenting not justifying, and as we do so, we may become just a bit more like the Jesus we call Lord.

The earlier quotation that questions commitments to the Enlightenment text is from a chapter in Brueggemann's book titled "Preaching as Reimagination." By emphasizing the prophetic mode of preaching and envisioning the preacher as one who ignites imagination for change, this chapter pushes into sociological territory. I tell my undergraduate students that sociology is mostly about looking at old things in new ways. My colleague (in our two-professor department) explains it a bit differently, saying that we all look down

Figure 9.2. Old/young woman optical illusion (dated to the nineteenth century)
(Source: Universal History Archive/Universal Images Group via Getty Images)

the dominant path, but sociology tries to get us to tilt our heads just a bit to see things from a new angle. The effort to refocus your gaze is a bit like the effort required to decipher an optical illusion or find the hidden picture in a stereogram.[16] If you search the internet for optical illusions, you'll come upon the classic old/young woman drawing that dates back to the late 1800s. Viewed one way, the cartoonish figure resolves into an old woman reminiscent of Hansel and Gretel's witch, with a large nose, a pronounced chin, and a headscarf concealing her voluminous hair. Viewed another way, the image depicts a delicate, beautiful, and demure young woman with a graceful jawline and an aristocratic bearing, turning ever so slightly away from the observer. When I display the image on a classroom screen, after a bit of gazing, squinting, and rearranging of their own facial features, most students can see both women. However, there are always a few who, try as they might, can see one but not the other.

During the same class, I place stereograms (google them!) on the screen and let students pull out their phones to look at them up close. To the untrained eye, stereograms appear to be just a sequenced, abstract pattern. However, move within a couple inches of the colorful swaths, then back away, relax your focus, "widen" your eyes, and "enter in," and you may find yourself inside the picture, where you will discover well-defined, three-dimensional objects

16. The optical illusion/stereogram example is excerpted and adapted from Vos, "Way That You See." Used with permission.

Figure 9.3. Zebra stereogram (Source: © Gene Levine, Eyetricks 3D Stereograms, www.eyetricks3dstereograms.com)

previously hidden from view. The stereogram in figure 9.3 contains a zebra with wavy stripes. Seeing the object hidden within the pattern is astonishing and delightful, and the difficulty in finding it makes it all the more pleasurable.

These examples, both of which require a bit of imagination and adjusting one's gaze to see the unseen, visually illustrate Brueggemann's ideas about reading the Bible to find the alternative text of the gospel. Once I learned to see both the old and young woman in the optical illusion—the alternate realities it contains—I could no longer see only the "dominant" image I once saw. Now, both images are always present—I simply need to focus on one or the other. I have a similar experience with the stereograms. Likewise, once you begin to see the priority that the alternative text of the Bible places on both inviting strangers into "our" worlds and being found in "theirs," it's hard to unsee it. The previously hidden reality of the gospel counter-text becomes the important reality—one that calls you to a new identity that finds fulfillment in serving over being served, pouring out over filling up, giving over hoarding, and including over excluding. This inversion of the dominant reality is precisely what Jesus modeled, even to his death. To die to self is, in large measure, to live for strangers. And the message encoded in the biblical stereogram, if you widen your gaze and really learn to see it, offers a radical and potentially freeing escape from the hegemonic normal.

Brueggemann's ideas about looking for the alternative text, resisting the old hegemony, and exercising prophetic imagination are similar to ideas developed by sociologists since the discipline's inception. Though sociologists seldom frame issues in theological terms, their focus on social justice, change, imagination, exercising prophetic voice, and identifying with the oppressed can provide additional analysis that complements theological research. For example, where theologians might illuminate prophetic themes in the Bible that call God's people to care for the poor, sociologists can specify the location of hidden poverty, measure it, and even identify ways that religion sometimes functions to exacerbate it. Where theologians might help people identify and interpret parts of the Bible that address racial divisions, sociologists can offer insight into how race and social class are coterminous, and they can reveal the unrecognized racism hiding in our hegemonic normal. For example, chapter 8 of this book examined how Nike generates profits through a globally racialized system that exploits women of color who labor in hidden factories in Southeast Asia, and it also points out how the hegemonic forces of big sport legitimate the athletic apparel industry and blind us to this injustice. Sociologists, in this case, point out that eradicating race-based human-rights abuses in *America* does not eliminate racism and economic injustice but merely moves it to peripheral countries, where most of us cannot see it. In this and other ways, sociology can help elaborate that which theology brings to attention. Sociologists can help (God's) people better understand the group-level processes by which injustice is structured and sustained, the location of injustice, and the frequently unseen social forces that push us to sustain the injustice God calls us to oppose. God calls us to strangers, especially "the least of these," who are oppressed and victimized by social systems. Sociology offers a number of tools to help us locate and understand them, and to bring their needs to pubic expression.

Given this potential, and frequently untapped, resonance between theology and sociology, I want to identify and briefly develop three sociological ideas or analytic tools that can aid the people of God in the ongoing call to discover and live out the genuine alternative gospel, especially as that call relates to the embrace of strangers. These include role taking, the symbolic paradox, and violence and the character of the social bond. The first of these (role taking) comes from George Herbert Mead.

Role Taking: Adopting a Stranger's Perspective

George Mead was a University of Chicago professor who was formative in establishing the symbolic interactionism (SI) perspective in American sociology in the early part of the twentieth century. The SI tradition has a more fluid and dynamic conception of society than do the traditions that preceded it. Symbolic interactionists tend to think of society more as a process than as a thing. We can't, for example, empirically demonstrate the reality of what we call "social structures" or even of various concepts employed in the human sciences. Try to show me "capitalism" or empirically demonstrate an "attitude," for example. These aren't "things" in the sense that they exist in meaningful ways apart from human beings. The SI tradition, with roots in the pragmatist school of philosophy, contends that all we really have access to is people interacting on the basis of symbols. Accordingly, social structures are neither fixed nor inevitable—they're just people acting in patterned ways. If human interaction via symbols is the essence of what we call "society," you can see that what we call "the self" is right at the center of it all. For Mead, the self is the central organizing mechanism for society—all things social are based on it. But where does the self come from? What is a self, and how do you get one? Are you born with a self? These seem like ridiculous questions that may just confirm what many already believe about sociologists! But think about it. Why are you like you are, and how did you come to be that way?

Mead explains that we acquire a self through role taking.[17] He reasons that we are all born blank slates who receive selves through socialization. Mead defines the self as the peculiar ability to be both subject and object. Thus, having a self means that a person possesses (subjective) consciousness but also understands that he or she is an object of consciousness to others. Oddly, to "get" a self requires one to go outside of him- or herself. Mead explains three stages humans pass through in developing a self.

The first is the play stage. Here you can think of a very young child pretending to be someone else. When you were a child did you play "mommy" or perhaps pretend you were a character from Star Wars? I remember playing the Incredible Hulk, which included flexing enough to pop my shirt snaps open as I imagined a Lou Ferrigno–like physique bursting out of my size-small shirt! In this stage a child is learning to step out of him- or herself and into the place of someone else. For the duration of my play on some Saturday afternoon, I'm not Matthew, I'm the Hulk! The play stage thus functions as an elementary attempt to get outside oneself and see things from another's perspective.

The next stage, the game stage, is when an individual learns to organize a limited group of roles simultaneously. Mead uses the example of baseball. In baseball, if I'm the batter, I must simultaneously imagine how I look to

17. Strauss, *George Herbert Mead*, 216–28.

all of the opposing team's players. In a way, I must put myself into their consciousness and think as they might think. Success in baseball, or any team sport, depends on this ability to see yourself from the perspective of multiple others at the same time.

The final stage—something Mead calls the "generalized other"—involves internalizing the perspective of a community. For example, I am a professor at a Christian college. As I live my life and do my work, I have a general sense of the expectations and moral weight of the Christian college community in which I live. If I were to, God forbid, utter some vulgarity while teaching a class, I would instantly think, "Oh no, that's not the sort of thing a professor at this college should say," as I headed back to my office to clean out my desk!

Each of these stages in acquiring a self represents increasingly sophisticated levels of socialization. Role taking as the means of acquiring a self is pertinent to our discussion of strangers for a number of reasons. First, it suggests that apart from others there really is no self. The self is constructed as you progressively learn to see yourself from the perspective of others. For symbolic interactionists like Mead, the social produces the self, rather than the self producing the social. What we call "society" is located in the intersection between us, where our interactions take place. A person who cannot consider the impact of his or her actions on others represents a failure of socialization, is incomplete, and may have pathological consequences for society as well as themselves.

Second, role taking is an act of recognizing others, placing ourselves in their consciousness (in their shoes), and viewing the world and our own actions through their eyes. This offers the possibility of empathy and suggests that our own personhood depends on our recognizing the personhood and needs of others. We humans cannot survive apart from the social, something we participate in through role taking. The selfish person is one who for some reason cannot engage in role taking. Selfishness is thus destructive to society at a fundamental level. In an important way, society itself rests on people's ability and willingness to consider their impact on those in their orbits. Sounds a lot like the Golden Rule, doesn't it?

Let me provide an example. When one of my daughters was about four years old, she had her tonsils and adenoids taken out in the same operation. At first she seemed okay. But, in the days following the operation her throat became increasingly sore, and she refused to eat or drink anything. In a week she had lost 10 percent of her body weight, and we had to take her to the hospital so she could receive IV fluids. I remember my wife trying to encourage her to eat and drink using terms she might understand. She said, "Your tummy is so little. You need to eat so your tummy gets bigger." Seems innocent enough. But, what my young daughter had internalized was "little tummy bad; big tummy good." One Sunday a few weeks later at church, I was pulling her out of the silent prayer portion of the service for failure to comply with the silent part of the minister's instructions. As I held her little hand and walked to the back of the sanctuary, just before exiting the room, my daughter snaked out a hand and patted the "tummy" of a large woman who usually sat at the back because of difficulty fitting into a regular seating row. Before I knew what had happened, my child thoughtfully (and loudly) remarked (in front of God and everyone), "You have a big tummy!" She meant no disrespect or malice. She said this conspiratorially, with a kind of thumbs-up glance at the woman as if to say, "Your mom must be really proud." Well, needless to say, we had to find another church!

Imagine that rather than hurrying out of the sanctuary, kneeling down to my daughter's level, and talking to her about why she shouldn't say such things to others, I had high-fived her and shouted out, "Good one!" That would have been horrible and terribly negligent on my part. As her parent, it was my responsibility to say, "Hey little one, think about what life is like for that woman back there. She probably feels a bit sad that she can't sit with the others at church. That's difficult for her. You need to remember to think about how she might feel before saying something about her tummy." We, her parents, would undoubtedly face this again in the near future, but over time, our daughter would learn to pause, get outside herself, take the role of the other, and adjust her actions accordingly. It is a parent's job to help a child get outside herself. Model a disregard for the other, teach her to view the world as her own, encourage her to think only of her own needs, and she will fail to attain what we might call "full personhood." Moreover, if everyone stays inside him- or herself, failing to role take, there really is no possibility of society. Society emerges as we consider the needs of the other, the stranger.

Over and over again, the Bible, sometimes in obvious ways and sometimes covertly, calls us to role take. Consider how the following all evidence role taking:

- The parable of the good Samaritan (Luke 10)
- The parable of the lost sheep (Luke 15)
- Jesus's interaction with the woman who anointed him with perfume (Mark 14)
- Jesus casting a man's demons into a herd of pigs (Luke 8)
- Jesus talking with the Samaritan woman at the well (John 4)
- Jesus focusing on the woman with the issue of blood (Mark 5)

- Jesus healing the Roman soldier's ear (Luke 22)
- Jesus going to Zacchaeus's home for a meal (Luke 19)
- Jesus hanging on the cross as the scapegoat for humanity (Matt. 27)

Perhaps Philippians 2:3–4, which exhorts, "in humility regard others as better than yourselves. Let each of you look not to your own interests, but to the interests of others," should be on our lips more, as it might move us to see things through the eyes of a poor migrant, a girl at church, an intersex person, a young woman from Thailand who makes our shoes, a prisoner, a looter, a person from across the political aisle, or even someone we perceive as an enemy of God. In role taking, we can begin to imagine something different, and better, for the society we might become.

Strangers and the Symbolic Paradox

Symbols function in at least two important ways: (1) they provide essential anchors for our identities, and (2) they tell us what to avoid. As noted in chapter 4, symbols are simultaneously inclusive and exclusive.

The tragic symbolic paradox we face is this: While human life depends on symbolic identification with a group, those same symbols that give our lives distinctive character create boundaries with out-groups. As we seek to preserve identity, our allegiance to our own groups and the symbols they produce frequently results in suspicion, animosity, derogation of the other, denial of privilege, exclusion, hatred, and in extreme cases extermination of those we perceive as different from us. In effect, the very thing (group symbols) that makes human identity possible is the thing that destroys it. Examples abound.

Do you see the dilemma? A macro-level group like America is pluralistic in character, composed of a multitude of subgroups, each with their own identity-needs and symbols. There are some macro-level symbols like the flag or perhaps the Statue of Liberty that provide a basic cohesiveness for "Americans," but there is always the danger that subordinate groups will have to accept being trivialized and maligned or risk symbolic or even physical violence. There is always the danger that a minority group will be relegated to a "stranger" role if they choose to challenge the boundaries around which dominant American identity is organized. Brueggemann's comments about different modes of reading the biblical text are instructive in the symbolic realm of everyday life as well. How do we read these symbols? Do we look to support the hegemonic normal, or can we read the symbolic landscape with an eye on the marginal ones . . . with concern for the stranger?

Killing Strangers with Help from on High

The road that separates "us" from strangers is paved with violence. In chapter 3, we briefly examined Émile Durkheim's ideas about the nature of the social bond and the collective conscience (a group's sense of "we"). Durkheim was interested in the shift from the kind of social bond prevalent in premodern, preindustrial societies (a bond based on the similarity of group members, which he called "mechanical solidarity") to the kind of bond characterizing groups in the industrialized, modern world (a bond based on differences and the interdependence of group members, which he called "organic solidarity").[18] Groups with a mechanical bond held together because members saw themselves as similar—same religion, race, worldview, general approach to making a living, and so on. Groups with an organic bond, more like what we see in Western society now, hold together because of the way members' differences dovetail to maintain stability—like a factory where people do all sorts of different things in the collective effort to turn out some product. Ideally, then, in modern societies we should see higher levels of cooperation between groups and between individuals who are very different from one another. For example, it matters not a bit to me whether the individual who manages my retirement account is Black or White; Protestant, Catholic, or Jewish; or believes in evolution. If she manages my money well, I'm satisfied and quite unlikely to oppose her—she's played her role well, thus enabling me to play my role well. In the older sort of society bonded by a mechanical "sameness," the group (or society) holds together as a family does—seeing themselves as similar along important dimensions. I may not like my sister (in fact, I do!), but if you oppose my sister, speak badly about her, or threaten her in some way, you'll feel the force of my wrath because you've threatened "us." This is the basic plot of most revenge movies!

Durkheim noticed that these two different social types (mechanical and organic) were characterized by very different legal codes. Societies with a mechanical bond emphasized repressive or punitive law, while societies with organic-type bonds tended toward restitutive law. The function of punitive law is to excise the person who offends the community, while the function of restitutive law is to restore the offender to proper functioning. These, of course, are ideal types, and both approaches would be present in both kinds of societies to a greater or lesser extent. Mechanical societies hold together because of a strong collective conscience. Accordingly, competing worldviews, pluralism, and so on constitute a grave threat to the very existence of the group. Allan

18. Durkheim, *Division of Labor in Society*.

writes, "The function of punitive law is not to correct, as we usually think of law today; rather, the purpose is expiation (making atonement). . . . Punitive law is exercised when the act 'offends the strong, well-defined states of the collective consciousness.'"[19]

So, in the Old Testament, the Israelites' sense of themselves and their way of life (their collective conscience) was so threatened by any competing sexual ethic that their legal corpus included stoning the person caught in adultery. No counseling or rehabilitation programs, no chatting about what happened in an offender's childhood, mitigating circumstances, and so on. Likewise, Amish communities (which primarily emphasize a mechanical bond) shun (cut off from the community) the person who marries an outsider (the English). Clearly, this legal approach focuses on in-group/out-group, we/they, family/ stranger relations. No intermarriage, no foreign gods, no questioning gender roles or challenging accepted authority arrangements. The entire legal code centers on maintaining clear boundaries between insiders and outsiders. The goal of law in such a system is to maintain the social bond through a strong collective conscience—something extremely vulnerable to stranger-threat.

We can discern these two legal types—punitive and restitutive—in the progressive unfolding of God's revelation across the breadth of Scripture. Much of the Old Testament legal canon represents the repressive type. Think here of Levitical law, the practice of stoning, and commands that appear to aid the Israelites in carrying out genocide. Punishments for transgression are clear, swift, decisive, absolute, and directed toward maintaining the purity of the collective conscience. Of course, you also see hints at inclusiveness in passages such as Deuteronomy 10:19, where Moses commands the Israelites to "love the stranger." In the New Testament (which is full of punitive law), we see Jesus engaged in challenging legal precedent that functioned to shame, exclude, or shun the individual. Think here of the stories of the woman caught in adultery, the woman at the well, the man with the withered hand, or the woman with the issue of blood, as well as parables like the good Samaritan that represent sacrificial care for (or *by*, in the case of the good Samaritan) those who represent threat to the religious community. In 1 Corinthians 12, Paul synthesizes both types of bonds in a beautiful vision of the church, where the mechanical "we are all one in Christ Jesus" bond produces special love and care for the more vulnerable members as all contribute their unique gifts and callings to the proper functioning of the whole. In this way, the organic bond of difference is celebrated, none are strangers, and the mechanical bond "in Christ" functions to draw in those who might remain peripheral to the

19. Allan, *Social Lens*, 141.

community. In Paul's vision, the focus of the community of the people of God is restorative, not punitive.

Lewis Coser (1913–2003), who contributed to the conflict perspective in sociological theory, focuses on discerning the place and function of conflict in human life. Counterintuitively, Coser was interested in the functional *benefits* that conflict has for society.[20] Although most of us like to avoid it, conflict is not all bad. For example, if my wife and I enter into conflict over my desire to spend our family's money on a new motorcycle (not much possibility of a mullet at this point, but the rest of the dream is still alive!), that conflict can help clarify what it is we value (lamentably, it's probably not the motorcycle). In this example, conflict performs a communication function through which, ideally, the marriage is strengthened and the family benefits. A marriage free of all conflict is not necessarily better than a marriage where the partners' differences are brought to expression and addressed. In effect, conflict can be constructive, even desirable, when contending parties remain focused on solving problems and not on injuring, depriving, or annihilating the other. However, as we all know, when the goal of conflict is to damage others and push them away—rendering them strangers—it can overwhelm an individual, group, or society, devolve into violence, and wreak devastation on all involved.

Coser observes that conflict is instinctual for us, which is why you can find it just about everywhere in human society—conflict is ubiquitous. However, he sees us as different from animals in that most of our conflicts are motivated by *cultural* values.[21] "Shared meaning" is a good, succinct definition of culture. As such, cultural values are not something simply lurking about in individuals. Rather, they originate and are maintained in groups, and as we learned in earlier chapters, groups negotiate their identities by comparing favorably with relevant out-groups. Groups can be college roommates, families, workplaces, denominations, nations, genders, sports teams, and so on. In each of these groups, the collective "we" develops ways of understanding, common goals, and so on. Accordingly, many of our conflicts arise when we feel deprived relative to other groups, or when we feel threatened or subordinated by them, especially when their ways and understandings (culture) challenge our ways and understandings. Furthermore, things in our shared world are scarce—whether those things are desirable positions in a workplace hierarchy, oil, jobs, respect, or the shared sentiment that God is on *our* side. As we are all members of a variety of groups (gender, family, church, political party, nation) and all of these groups compete with other groups for valued

20. Coser, *Functions of Social Conflict*.
21. Allan, *Social Lens*, 260.

resources, potential for conflict is always simmering just below the surface. And, as pointed out earlier, it can be used in ways that strengthen the parties involved or that dehumanize and destroy them.

Conflict is unlikely to become violent as long as the parties involved are pursuing rational goals. For example, when workers go on strike in protest of low wages or difficult working conditions, they aren't hoping for a riot or fistfight. What they want is better pay and maybe safer conditions. These things are rational. If their requests are met, they will likely be satisfied with the progress they've made, head back to work, and be relieved that no one got hurt or arrested. However, sometimes in conflict, a group loses sight of rational goals and the conflict takes on a very different and more destructive character. Coser identifies two factors that help predict the level of violence that will emerge in a conflict: *emotional involvement* and *transcendent goals*. When we become emotionally aroused, winning a conflict can take on heightened importance as it fills an identity-need. Some communication scholars call this "ego-based" conflict. Let's say that as I'm driving along, I go out of my way to show kindness to another motorist by opening up space so that he or she can merge into slow-moving traffic. Later, however, when I need the favor returned, the other driver offers me the middle finger of fellowship and cuts me off. Now I'm angry, and I begin driving more aggressively (road rage!), looking for ways to assert myself over the idiot who dared be so rude. At this point, I'm all worked up, but what is my goal? Is it to get home safely? Is it to model decorum and restraint to my children in the back seat? Not at all. This is now full-blown ego-based conflict that is no longer focused on rationally solving the problem (which actually no longer exists). Rather, my goal becomes asserting myself. My goal is one of identity.

About transcendent goals, Allan explains that when people keep their concerns at an everyday level—just problems that need solving—they invest less emotional energy and conflicts stay at the rational level. However, when a group sees its goals as greater than the group itself, and their concerns extend beyond everyday life, the conflict is more likely to become violent. Thus, when a nation goes to war, the reasons for engaging in the conflict are rarely couched in rational terms. "We" don't announce we're going to war to take strategic oil reserves but rather to "serve justice," "defeat oppression," or "fight for democracy." Likewise, when a country's president invokes the name of God as part of the rationale for going to war, it is a sign that the violence is about to escalate. "Anytime violence is deemed necessary by a government, the reasons are couched in moral terms (capitalists might say they fight for individual freedoms; communists would say they fight for social responsibility and the dignity of the collective). The existence of the Right to

Life side of the abortion conflict tends to exhibit more violence than advocates of choice—their goals are more easily linked to transcendent issues and can thus be seen as God-ordained."[22]

Think back to the Acts 21 story that climaxed in Paul's fellow Israelites shouting that he should not be allowed to live. All the elements that escalate violence are present.

- The Israelites are together in a determined group (strong collective conscience);
- Paul threatens the group's identity by suggesting they change their membership requirements (emotion is heightened and rational goals set aside); and
- Paul, to their hearing, says, "*God* is on my side" (placing transcendent goals at the center of the conflict).

Backing away from his anger, one of the Israelite leaders might have said, "Okay, Paul, but we'll leave things as they are for now and take up your idea at our next quarterly board meeting. Who wants dinner?" While facetious, such a statement represents a rational approach to addressing conflict. Instead, in the face of such profound threat to the collective conscience, the only solution considered was one of violence—a solution that reinforced stranger boundaries between Jews and gentiles, and for which Paul was the scapegoat.

The situation facing the Wilwal-Abdigani family at the US-Canada border had the same elements. The border guard, acting with heightened emotion, probably fueled by nationalism (transcendent goals), and certainly reinforcing a we/they mentality, acted violently toward a family of US citizens who simply wanted to return home. Religion was part of this equation as well. You will recall that they asked Abdisalam Wilwal about his religious affiliation. We and they. Walls and borders. Kill the scapegoat. Such a simple formula that you think we would abandon it. But it's the formula that puts migrant kids in cages at the border, that allows us to incarcerate people at the highest rate in the developed world, and that led to the killing of George Floyd in late May 2020. We sure seem keen on scapegoating strangers. But it's a formula that will continue to fail us.

Strangers No Longer: On Earth as It Is in Heaven

The gold standard for opposing strangers is eternal damnation—the ultimate "we versus they." Banishment to hell has all of the elements we've examined

22. Allan, *Social Lens*, 262.

in this chapter, including repressive law, a focus on transcendence, and a strong symbolic component. Accordingly, the sociologist in me struggles with some of the traditional doctrines of heaven and hell that I hear promoted by various Christian people, in part because they tend to cultivate we-and-they divisions. For many reasons, I feel ill at ease with the simplistic "Heaven or Hell? You Decide" billboards—complete with illustrations of molten lava on one side and inviting sun-dappled clouds on the other—that grace the Georgia interstate near where I live.

"Heaven or Hell" billboards and other similar messages leave me wondering if we've imagined a God who's a lot like us. Does the Jesus who showed such beautiful compassion to the woman caught in adultery (John 8), who extended a hand of fellowship to the man with the withered hand (Mark 3), who gave us the parables of the prodigal son and the good Samaritan, and who instructs us not merely to tolerate but to *love* our enemies in the end permanently cut off those very strangers he calls us to embrace? The existential threat of everlasting torture reverberates with echoes of social control. Even some of our children's songs warn our young ones to take care lest the God who sees all make eternal strangers of them. "Oh be careful little eyes what you see / Oh be careful little hands what you do . . . / For the Father up above is looking down in love, so be careful . . ." seems illustrative of the tactics we employ in exacting social compliance from others. While we may not outright tell another to "go to hell" (though increasingly we do), much of the polarized speech I see on social media and from politicians, some of whom identify as Christians, may as well spell out those words.

Securing a spot in heaven as *the* goal of Christian discipleship seems flat and unidimensional to me. With some frequency I hear "the Christian life" (a construct I find problematic) reduced to "knowing where you're going." Less often do I hear God's children associate the primary aim of following Christ with loving strangers, caring at cost for the poor migrant, taking up the case of the oppressed against the powerful, or accepting economic disadvantage in the interest of social justice for those outside their/our immediate circles. Since the biblical record reveals Jesus continually moving *toward* strangers, it stands to reason that following him will land you in their company. Following Jesus should not primarily lead us to ourselves. If heaven is a place for "us" that offers escape from the strangers God loves, why bother with "them" here and now? If the successful Christian life is one that results in complete disengagement from the creation and escape to heaven, what does that say about the witness of the church, "our" understanding of mission in the world, or God's love for the creation and those who live in it? Is our purpose merely ourselves?

Explained earlier in the chapter, this-worldly religion correlates with social advantage, while otherworldly religion has greater representation among the disenfranchised who need a "genuine alternative." I see a notable deviation to this sociological pattern. Allegiance to another world, captured in the familiar sentiment "This world is not my home," can also hold currency among the socially *advantaged* in ways that support a commitment to the present worldly/social order. A commitment to ending up in heaven (arguably a commitment to self) can promote apathy toward this-worldly matters such as environmental justice, care for the poor, taking up the cause of the migrant, or working to heal the devastating aftermath of racial inequality. In the case of poor and disenfranchised Christians, feelings of deprivation and a lack of agency combine so that the hope of "heaven," however abstract, offers a glimpse of a desperately needed alternative reality. But for those who enjoy social advantage, leaving this world for "heaven" offers a kind of "have your cake and eat it too" existence. Those who are well off may feel the need for an alternative less acutely than the disenfranchised. If the ultimate goal of following Christ is to leave this earth for heaven, there is little motivation to stand against injustice, especially when doing so might compromise the social rewards one enjoys (remember the rich young man?). The belief that relationship with God is primarily about "getting saved" and "going to heaven" can undermine the believer's motivation to care for the earth and all its inhabitants. In fact, this world *is* our home. God has not abandoned creation but rather invites us to participate in its renewal with hope, anticipation, and the thrill of divine purpose.

Though her intentions were likely not theological in character, Belinda Carlisle, lead singer of the 1980s all-female band the Go-Go's, may have been on to something with her hit song "Heaven Is a Place on Earth." N. T. Wright says as much in his book *Surprised by Hope*, which addresses the related questions, "What is the ultimate Christian hope?" and "What hope is there for change, rescue, transformation, [and] new possibilities within the world in the present?"[23] Are "we" the people of God *for the world* or the people of God for another world? Our answer has profound implications for our engagement with the world and for the importance of mission in our lives. Thinking of this world as our home rather than just our launching pad has radical implications for how we live and what we think God is doing through us. Wright says,

> As long as we see Christian hope in terms of "going to heaven," of a salvation that is essentially away from this world, the two questions are bound to appear

23. Wright, *Surprised by Hope*, 5.

as unrelated. Indeed, some insist angrily that to ask the second one at all is to ignore the first one, which is the really important one. This in turn makes some others get angry when people talk of resurrection, as if this might draw attention away from the really important and pressing matters of contemporary social concern. But if the Christian hope is for *God's new creation*, for "new heavens and new earth," and if that hope has already come to life in Jesus of Nazareth, then there is every reason to join the two questions together. . . . We find that answering the one is also answering the other. . . . To many—not least, many Christians—all this comes as a surprise: both that the Christian hope is surprisingly different from what they had assumed and that this same hope offers a coherent and energizing basis for work in today's world.[24]

Wright argues that much of the "muddled" thinking that characterizes what Christians think about life beyond the grave is rooted in the "Platonic downgrading of bodies and of the created order in general, regarding them as the 'vain shadows' of earth, which we happily leave behind at death."[25] He writes, "Why try to improve the present prison if release is at hand? Why oil the wheels of a machine that will soon plunge over a cliff? That is precisely the effect created to this day by some devout Christians who genuinely believe that 'salvation' has nothing to do with the way the present world is ordered."[26] Furthermore, a faith focused on escape to heaven downgrades the centrality and importance of bodily resurrection in orthodox Christian belief and theology. If we view death as "going home at last" or being "called to God's eternal peace," then we will mount no opposition to "power-mongers who want to carve up the world to suit their own ends." But resurrection depends on "a strong view of God's justice and of God as the good creator. Those twin beliefs give rise not to a meek acquiescence to injustice in the world but to a robust determination to oppose it."[27]

To our purpose here, strangers are the heart of what we call "the world." If Jesus calls God's people to minister to strangers, capitulating to a belief that centers on leaving behind the least of these to rest with Jesus seems to miss the point of what Jesus came to do. Furthermore, a "leave earth for heaven" approach to Christian living trivializes the doctrine of election, which teaches that the people of God are elect both to be something and to do something.

Israel believed . . . that the purposes of the creator God all came down to this question: how is God going to rescue Israel? What the gospel of Jesus revealed,

24. Wright, *Surprised by Hope*, 5.
25. Wright, *Surprised by Hope*, 26.
26. Wright, *Surprised by Hope*, 26.
27. Wright, *Surprised by Hope*, 26–27.

however, was that the purposes of God were reaching out to a different question: how is God going to rescue the world *through Israel* and thereby rescue Israel itself as part of the process but not as the point of it all? Maybe what we are faced with in our own day is a similar challenge: to focus not on the question of which human beings God is going to take to heaven and how he is going to do it but on the question of how God is going to redeem and renew his creation *through human beings* and how he is going to rescue those humans themselves as part of the process but not as the point of it all.[28]

It was Jesus who taught us to pray that God's will be done on earth as it is in heaven—for Wright, "one of the most revolutionary sentences we can ever say."[29] He concludes that in the end, heaven comes to earth. This reframing of what ultimately happens to us and the world takes resurrection and renewal seriously, helps us think of strangers as neighbors, and proclaims that what we do matters now and in the anticipated age to come. Wright concludes, "Our task in the present . . . is to live as resurrection people in between Easter and the final day with our Christian life, corporate and individual, . . . as a sign of the first and a foretaste of the second."[30]

If he's right, there's no getting away from strangers. They are our mission. . . . At least until heaven comes to earth and there are strangers no longer.

28. Wright, *Surprised by Hope*, 185.
29. Wright, *Surprised by Hope*, 29.
30. Wright, *Surprised by Hope*, 29, 30.

CHAPTER TEN

PURSUING THE COMMON GOOD

Three Stories of the Neighbor

Apology Accepted

In 1993, sixteen-year-old Oshea Israel was at a party during which he got into a fight with twenty-year-old Laramiun Byrd, who he ended up shooting and killing. Israel was subsequently arrested, tried, and convicted of murder. He was sentenced to twenty-five years, and he ended up serving seventeen before his release in 2010. For more than a decade following Israel's conviction, Mary Johnson, Laramiun's single mother, was having a difficult time coping, especially with the conflicting feelings that accompany such a devastating experience. She remembers being full of hatred for the boy who had killed her son. She also struggled with the conflict that harboring hatred created for her as a person of Christian faith—one called to extend forgiveness to others. Years after Israel's sentencing, Johnson decided that she wanted to visit him in the Minnesota Correctional Facility in Stillwater. In a moving NPR interview where she dialogues with Israel, she explains, "I wanted to know if you [Israel] were in the same mindset of what I remember from court, where I wanted to go over and hurt you. But you were not that 16-year-old. You were a grown man. I shared with you about my son."[1] In this dialogue, Israel explains that hearing Johnson talk about Laramiun helped him to see him as a human, as someone real. Their conversation prompted him to acknowledge what he had done and to ask Johnson for forgiveness. Remembering that meeting, Johnson

1. Johnson, "Forgiving Her Son's Killer."

exclaimed, "I [had] just hugged the man that murdered my son, and I instantly knew that all that anger and animosity, all the stuff I had in my heart for 12 years for you, I knew it was over, that I had totally forgiven you."[2]

Johnson is a woman of faith. She credits God for helping her to forgive but acknowledges a selfish motive. "Unforgiveness is like cancer. It will eat you from the inside out. It's not about that other person, me forgiving him does not diminish what he's done. Yes, he murdered my son—but the forgiveness is for me. It's for me."[3]

On its own, a mother visiting her son's killer in prison is a remarkable thing. Who could expect more? Forgiving and hugging her son's killer goes even further. But Johnson didn't forgive Israel just so she could move ahead with her life, leaving him to move on with his. She did this because of her belief that Christians are called to forgive, deeply and completely, no matter the wrong. After release from prison, with Johnson's blessing, Israel moved into the apartment right next to hers—the two shared a roof! Amazingly, the two have grown very close, to the point where Johnson describes Israel as her "spiritual son" and says she looks forward to seeing him graduate from college and possibly get married—milestones she was unable to celebrate with her own son. And so, their story moves from terrible tragedy, hatred, animosity, and indifference, to perfunctory forgiveness, to contact and humanization, to apology and real forgiveness, to hugging, to love, and, finally, to the unqualified affection and contact that can happen when families are at their best.

Their NPR interview concludes: "I love you, lady." "I love you, too, son."[4] Later in 2015, Mary Johnson married Ed Roy in a ceremony where Oshea Israel served as a groomsman.[5]

From stranger to neighbor to family member.[6]

The Child God Planned for Us: An Adoption Story

As noted earlier, we, the Voses, are an adoptive family, with children from Bulgaria and China. The experience of traveling great distances to previously

2. Johnson, "Forgiving Her Son's Killer."
3. Hartman, "Love Thy Neighbor."
4. Johnson, "Forgiving Her Son's Killer."
5. Johnson, "In Marriage, a Bond of Love, Loss and Light."
6. For those interested in learning more about Mary Johnson-Roy and Oshea Israel, loss, grief, and forgiveness, visit the website of From Death to Life (http://fromdeathtolife.us/home.html), "an organization Johnson started in 2005 dedicated to ending violence through healing and reconciliation between families of victims and those who have caused harm," as well as that of the Forgiveness Project (https://www.theforgivenessproject.com/stories/mary-johnson-oshea-israel/).

unknown places and having a caretaker place a child in your arms is unparalleled in my life, and it is hard to describe. Although international adoption includes a mountain of bureaucratic paperwork, a lot of waiting, fingerprinting, vaccinations, agency and intercountry adoption fees, and anxiety, the "here's your child" moment is, I imagine, a bit like a birth. Whether a biological child (a strange term indeed!) or an adoptive one, meeting a new family member face-to-face for the first time is an enchanting experience. For a birth mother, I'm fairly certain (though a bit out of my depth here!) that the pain of labor and delivery quickly recedes as the child, safe and present, nurses for the first time. For an adoptive family, that "nursing moment" is different in character, yet also the same. I remember wondering whether I would feel attracted to our new child, whether I would bond quickly, and whether I would feel a protective instinct kick in. "Yes" on all counts. Adoption, to me anyway, seems more mysterious than having children in the usual way. Frequently, you know little about the child's backstory, birth parents, or circumstances while they were in utero. Holding a newly adopted child for the first time is like holding a mystery. Who are they? Who will they be? How did we all arrive at this moment?

We adopted our second daughter, this time from China, in 2005. We had completed the requisite paperwork with Bethany Christian Services, received a referral for a "healthy Chinese infant girl," and jumped through various bureaucratic hoops in preparation for our travel. Bethany, a very large agency, coordinated adoptions for twelve sets of parents, including us, in Beijing at the same time. From Beijing we flew on China Southern out to the province where the orphanage was located. Our infant daughters, ranging from about ten to eighteen months in age, were all from the same orphanage. When we arrived at the hotel where we would receive our daughters, we were ushered into a holding room, and doors were flung open, revealing twelve caretakers, each holding an infant girl wearing an identical red coat. Family by family, they called us forward, matched us to our new daughters, and instructed us to go directly to our hotel rooms to begin bonding. This experience was both exhilarating and sad. Some of the caretakers cried, mourning the loss of these girls with whom they had bonded.

After receiving the girls, our group remained in the province for about a week, then flew to Guangzhou, where the Chinese consulate is located, to complete more paperwork, acquire visas for the girls, and complete required health screenings. We all ate together, went on various tours, got to know each other, and bonded as a group. To the present day, some fifteen years later, we have a reunion in a different host family's city each year. Many of us are good friends, and the reunion is a high point of our year.

After returning from China, we all settled back into our lives and set about integrating a new child into our families and communities. International adoption has strange challenges that are difficult to anticipate. For example, at one point our doctor was concerned that our daughter's head circumference was too small. We worried about this a bit until we realized that height, weight, and head circumference charts vary by country and by racial group. Our daughter was just fine and right on track—unless you compared her to norm data derived from big-headed Caucasians!

As time passed, Jennifer and Dan, one of the couples in our adoption group, began to notice their daughter, Lillian, lagging behind developmental milestones.[7] Many of the small accomplishments families celebrate in their children—rolling over, crawling, first steps—simply did not happen for her. At first, they thought that perhaps her delays came from time spent in the orphanage, where she may have received only minimal stimulation and caretaker attention. Socially, however, she appeared quite advanced and impressed her parents as being very smart. This seemed to rule out orphanage life as the cause of her delays, as it would be unusual for institutional life to affect motor skills but not social development. Jennifer and Dan knew their daughter was delayed physically but thought that with physical therapy she might "catch up" with her same-age peers.

During a fifteen-month wellness check, Lillian's pediatrician raised the possibility that her delays may be a result of cerebral palsy (CP). After consults with various specialists, she received a CP diagnosis. CP refers to a group of disorders that affect motor ability, including movement, balance, and posture. *Cerebral* means "of the brain," and *palsy* is a word referring to weakness. Symptoms can range by type and intensity, and sometimes symptoms include intellectual disabilities, as well as hearing and vision problems. As you might imagine, a diagnosis like CP is disconcerting and involves reevaluating your plans and future. Jennifer and Dan were not new or inexperienced parents. Before adopting, they had three sons. But this was an entirely new challenge. Having a child with CP means purchasing a vehicle that can be retrofitted for a wheelchair lift, installing ramps on your house, being available 24/7, and meeting with a long list of medical and educational specialists. These things are expensive, time consuming, and emotionally and spiritually draining. Was this what they had signed up for?

For our friends Jennifer and Dan, it mattered little what they had "signed up for." When asked about how they reacted to their adopted daughter receiving a CP diagnosis, they'd smile and say, "We just believe that God planned for

---

7. Names have been changed for privacy reasons.

her to be with us." It might be overreach to say that they took it all in stride, but they do understand their adoption of an infant girl with CP as a calling from God. Jennifer told me, "It's never God's plan for a child to 'not' be with their family, but when that doesn't work out . . ." She also said, "We're not on earth to live for ourselves."

In Scripture, widows, orphans, and resident aliens (the *ger*) make up the "vulnerable triad." Members of each group, then as now, face unique challenges. To oppress, neglect, ignore, or exploit these "strangers" is to kindle God's wrath. To protect, embrace, advocate for, share resources with, and welcome strangers invites God's blessing. Any child who does not, or for some reason cannot, live with their parents is a vulnerable child. And God calls his people to take up the interests of these vulnerable ones. Adoption takes this call seriously, because the commitment is for life, and it involves the totality of a family's life and resources. The day we adopted each of our children was the day each received health insurance. Think about what that means for an orphaned child. Many of us take such resources for granted. What might health insurance mean for a child with CP? When Jennifer and Dan adopted their daughter and eventually learned about her CP, they simply saw caring for her as a calling—as the sort of thing that Christians should do and as something to embrace. Their attitude was, "Good thing she found her way into *our* family!"

Following the CP diagnosis, our friends busied themselves learning to apply for grants, familiarizing themselves with disability law, purchasing wheel-chairs, lifts, and other equipment, and signing up for various therapies. They have acquired a depth of knowledge about international transracial adoption, disability, educational benefits, and a host of other important topics related to the care of and advocacy for their daughter.

But this isn't the end of their story.

After learning so much about both international adoption and CP, Jennifer and Dan pondered adopting another young Chinese girl with CP. Most families don't *try* to adopt a child with such a serious disability. As a result, many of the neediest orphaned children are never adopted—they simply age out of the system or live institutionalized lives without families. One day while clicking through a Yahoo group online, Jennifer came across a woman who was advocating for a little Chinese girl with CP. She told Dan, and they looked into this situation a bit. While learning about this girl—who she was, her background, her circumstances—they began to feel drawn to her. Not long after, they started the adoption paperwork. There were hurdles to overcome and unanticipated problems to address. Oh well, such is life. They persevered, adopted the little girl, and today have two beautiful (and smart!) teenage daughters. None of this was easy. Not then; not now.

But this isn't the end of their story.

After adopting their second daughter, our friends adopted yet another child from China. This time a boy who was ten, older than what most adoptive families desire. When it comes to orphaned children, even age can function like a disability, reinforcing their stranger status. Now a young man in his early twenties, he is kind and winsome, and has a good sense of humor.

Faraway strangers become family members around Jennifer and Dan. Showing Christian hospitality to the least of these seems to be their normal.

And I'm guessing this isn't the end of their story.

Tamales with Immigrants

For more than a decade, our family attended Highlands Presbyterian Church, located on the edge of LaFayette, Georgia. The congregation began (prior to our involvement) as a denominational plant that initially met in a modest older house set on several acres in a low-income area. Neighborhoods surrounding the church included government-subsidized housing, low-rent apartments, and middle-class homes. After a time, the church built a simple log cabin–style building with a sanctuary that doubled as a fellowship hall, restrooms, and a small nursery. The house was converted to Sunday school classrooms, and its kitchen was retained for church functions. My wife and I were drawn to the informal worship style, relative lack of bureaucracy, friendly guitar-playing minister, and close proximity to our home. We liked it.

Over time, as the church moved beyond "mission church" status, more people joined, the minister and his family left to pursue overseas missions, and another minister was installed. Relying on significant volunteer labor, and the generous help of a contractor who was a member, we added a much larger log building to the existing one. We had hit the big time! Our minister felt strongly that a congregation with modest financial means should build as God provided resources and should refrain from borrowing money. He advocated this no-borrowing policy for a number of reasons, but two stand out. First, we were on the low end of the income spectrum, and we lacked certainty about our ability to meet monthly payment obligations. The average income of our members and regular attenders was about half of the average denominational income. We had a few wealthy members, but we were mostly made up of middle- and lower-middle-class families, with significant representation among the ranks of the working poor. Our minister jokes that an employed high school teacher represented what we thought of as well off! The second, and more important reason, was his conviction that financial debt would hamper our ability to meet needs in our own congregation and the surrounding area. The church never, and I suspect this is true to the present day, borrowed any money at all.

The economic and demographic characteristics of Highlands illustrate something important about hospitality and neighborliness. Surplus money and state-of-the-art facilities are not required for a church to embrace the vulnerable and marginal in their orbits. As a church, we had little money, yet were able to offer Christian hospitality in ways I haven't seen many other places. Perhaps having limited means translated to less concern with guarding resources. Perhaps the shared experience of having little contributed to the abundance of welcome that I remember. Here's the story:

Highlands Presbyterian was a mostly White church with a small but visible African American presence and a tacit commitment to multiracial ministry. In the late 1990s and early 2000s we began seeing a few Hispanic faces during Sunday morning worship. These people, who generally spoke Spanish and little, if any, English, came from at least two places. The first was the carpet industry. The church was not far from Dalton, Georgia, home to several large carpet mills, including Shaw Industries, Queen Carpet, and Mohawk, that hired significant numbers of immigrant workers from Mexico and other places. The second source was an elder at Highlands who owned a landscaping business and who employed a number of Mexican immigrants, whom he invited to church.

Noticing the Spanish-speaking people attending services, our minister and several other church members, some fluent in Spanish, began thinking about how to make our church more welcoming and hospitable to these brothers and sisters. Our minister taught, quite boldly, that majority-group members must always inconvenience themselves for the sake of the more vulnerable minority group. He simply saw that as what he called a "non-negotiable." That principle affects me still. Modifying our church to embrace these Spanish-speaking regulars, we purchased an inexpensive headphone system and began offering our weekly services in translation. Spanish speakers could pick up wireless headphones on the way into the sanctuary and hear the service in translation. We were blessed to have a number of college students, a few church members, and even a Spanish-language professor who sat at the back and translated into a microphone in real time.

In retrospect, the Spanish element permeating our church benefited more than just our Spanish-speaking friends. Spanish language and culture were also for "us." Furthermore, our fumbling efforts helped steer us away from a we/they church culture. We read the Bible in Spanish and English during the call to worship (we just read things twice!), prayer was offered in English, each phrase with a Spanish echo, and we alternated verses in Spanish and English as we sang hymns and praise songs together. No doubt our pronunciation left a lot to be desired (imagine Spanish with a Southern drawl!), but we belted out the words on the sanctuary screen and followed our bilingual music leader the best we could. The Spanish was for "us" in the inclusive sense of that term . . . not just for "them." And we slowly evolved into something new—something that transcended the old. What we orchestrated together was not benevolence for needy others but the gospel at work, the Spirit of God transforming the whole. To this day, I cringe whenever I hear someone say, in reference to immigrants, "If they're going to come here, they should learn our language." We versus they. What a missed opportunity for self-enrichment and the transformation of strangers into neighbors.

Occasionally, cultural differences arose that required a little adjustment all around. At one church potluck, when most had finished eating and were ready to head home, our minister spotted some of our Mexican members carrying trays of handmade corn-husk wrapped tamales toward the building. He began running around and shouting, "You have to stay and eat again. If you leave, you'll be sinning!" He was kidding, of course, but many of us dutifully reversed course and prepared to eat again. And the tamales, which were always great, were well worth the adjustment. Later I would learn that "they" weren't late, but rather were acting in conformity to the time norms of their culture of origin. Western cultures operate under a monochronic conception of time where "time is money," time can be wasted, and rigid punctuality functions as a moral imperative. Many countries in Latin America, sub-Saharan Africa, the Middle East, India, and parts of China, among others, manifest a polychronic conception of time. Time just is, relationships take priority over completing tasks, and "being on time" has little meaning. Mexico, where the majority of our Spanish-speaking members came from, falls into the polychronic category. Understanding that "lateness" is a culturally specific idea holding vastly different meaning in different places can help reduce tension that might arise in a blended culture such as the one at Highlands. But at the end of the day, "the majority group makes the concession for the sake of the minority group," and the question shifts from "Were they late?" to "Were we welcoming?" And over time, we/they becomes less and less important as it morphs into the more inclusive "us."

In addition to the worshiping and eating-together variety of hospitality, our relationship to a marginalized group in our fellowship afforded some the opportunity to protect our more vulnerable members. Animosity toward immigrants was very much alive then, as it is now. From time to time, some of our immigrant members would receive threatening materials in their mailboxes.

Some members on the church session (our term for the group of elders providing oversight) were in a position to offer assistance, investigate threats, and stand alongside. Once the aforementioned elder with the landscaping business had a brick thrown through a window of his home, probably because of his relationship to Mexican immigrants. This man was known to pay his workers well, somewhere north of double the minimum wage. When one of the Mexican men who worked for him and who also attended Highlands had something stolen and called the police to report it, he rushed over to his employee's home to make sure he received just treatment. When one suffers all suffer. When one rejoices, so do the rest.

Three other features of Highlands' approach to intercultural ministry bear mentioning. First, our church had little success offering ESL (English as a Second Language) classes to immigrant members. They had other avenues for accessing such services. However, we had some success offering SSL (Spanish as a Second Language) classes. When Highlands brought in a woman to teach Spanish in an evening class, even I showed up ready to learn! The fact that English speakers were willing to spend time learning "their" language—something that takes more effort than eating tamales!—demonstrated that walls were crumbling and that bridges were being built. Second, at one point Highlands put up a new church sign. In addition to English words, the sign contained Spanish words, "Traducción del Sermón y Clase de la Biblia en Español," which translates in English to "Translation of the Sermon and Bible Class into Spanish." In addition to offering information, this put a public and symbolic face on our commitment to multiracial and multicultural unity, and it communicated, "Strangers are welcome here." Look at your own church sign sometime, and ask yourself whether it proclaims "Welcome Strangers," or if it might deter immigrants, racial minorities, or others in marginal social locations from entering. Who is the stranger that is welcomed by your church sign? Is your church sign culturally and racially monolithic? Third (and another of our minister's really good ideas), we refrained from making reference to "Mexicans" in how we defined and communicated our ministry. Rather, we said that we had a ministry to "Spanish-speaking people." We had more nationalities represented than just Mexican in our church. The more inclusive term also helped us avoid a we/they emphasis on difference. "Ministry to Mexicans" sounds benevolent and may be stigmatizing to some. "Ministry to Spanish-speaking people" is broader and less racially specific. Perhaps by now Highlands is calling it "ministry *with* Spanish-speaking people"!

Epilogue: The minister described in the preceding story held the position that majority-group churches, except in very special circumstances, should not build daughter churches for minority groups. For the most part, there should not be a Mexican church five miles down the road. Instead, the majority-group congregation should adapt and inconvenience themselves to welcome in those "others"—the strangers. When he encountered arguments among his pastoral colleagues, such as, "They may feel more comfortable worshiping with their own people," he would respond, "But how then will your children ever become friends with their children?" At one point when one of our White members married one of our Mexican members, our minister exclaimed, "We've finally met the gold standard for interracial ministry!"

- Welcome the stranger
- Adapt to the stranger
- Inconvenience yourself for the stranger
- Protect the stranger
- Eat with the stranger
- Love the stranger

Care for the stranger invites the blessing of God.

The rest of this chapter examines the practice of Christian hospitality, explores social position in stratified systems, advocates for the common good, and concludes with a "strange(r)" perspective on the open gates and main street of gold in the city of God, the New Jerusalem.

Hospitality as Normative Christian Practice

A rising number of Christian theologians address what I have been calling the "stranger problem" under the banner of hospitality and the common good. In a recent book titled *Saved by Faith and Hospitality*, Joshua Jipp offers the following thesis, which captures the tenor of many similar books:

> The God of the Christian Scriptures is . . . a God who extends hospitality to his people, and who requires that his people embody hospitality to others. . . . God's relationship to his people is fundamentally an act of hospitality to strangers, as God makes space for "the other," for his people, by inviting humanity into relationship with him. This experience of God's hospitality is at the very heart of the church's identity. We are God's guests and friends. And it is because of God's extension of hospitality and friendship to us that the church can offer hospitality to one another *and* to those seemingly outside the reach of our faith

communities. . . . As we imitate God, we offer hospitality—particularly to "the other," the one who is not like us, the one outside.[8]

Jipp states that when asked by what means Abraham was justified, some early Christians would have responded, "By faith and hospitality to strangers." While this sounds like a clever "faith plus works" theology of justification, it's not. Drawing on material in Matthew, James, Luke-Acts, and 1 Clement (a letter penned from the church in Rome to the church in Corinth at the end of the first century), Jipp explores the connection between hospitality and salvation. Abraham demonstrates faith through his hospitality to the three men who came to his tent in Genesis 18. Lot's faith is evidenced in his hospitality to the divine visitors he refuses to surrender to the *inhospitable* men of Sodom in Genesis 19. Rahab's faith in the God of Israel is manifest in hospitality she offers to the Israelite spies seeking cover in Joshua 2. Concerning Lot, Jipp explains, "With respect to the claim in 1 Clement that Lot was saved by godliness and hospitality, we can see that whereas Sodom and Gomorrah are destroyed because of their flagrant inhospitality and abuse of strangers, Lot's hospitality to the divine visitors (Gen. 19:1–3) is the basis for God's rescuing of Lot and his family. Lot's hospitality is probably the sole reason 2 Peter refers to him as 'righteous Lot' (2 Pet. 2:7)."[9] Furthermore, Jipp writes, "Many Christians may assume they know exactly what the story of Sodom and Gomorrah in Genesis 19 is all about—sexual deviance! But in fact, Genesis 19 provides the negative counterpart to Abraham's hospitality, and it really makes the simple point that God will judge societies and individuals that abuse the vulnerable stranger."[10]

However one views the relationship between faith, hospitality, and salvation described in these biblical and extra-biblical texts, Scripture clearly presents hospitality as an essential part of what it means to be the people of God. When religious communities turn inward and forsake the needy (the poor, the widow, the orphan, the immigrant), they have good reason to question their status as God's people, and they would do well to reflect on what it *means* to be people of faith. "What good is it, my brothers and sisters, if you say you have faith but do not have works? Can faith save you? If a brother or sister is naked and lacks daily food, and one of you says to them, 'Go in peace; keep warm and eat your fill,' and yet you do not supply their bodily needs, what is the good of that? So faith by itself, if it has no works, is dead" (James 2:14–17). Can there be a clear dividing line between faith and the

8. Jipp, *Saved by Faith and Hospitality*, 2.
9. Jipp, *Saved by Faith and Hospitality*, 5.
10. Jipp, *Saved by Faith and Hospitality*, 130.

hospitality that testifies to the reality of that faith? Should there? Perhaps we can see faith and hospitality in dialectical relationship—"of a piece," where each defines the other.

According to Luke Bretherton, "Jesus relates hospitality and holiness by inverting their relations: hospitality becomes the means of holiness."[11] The New Testament story of Jesus is an account of one act of hospitality after another. For all the times I've heard some variant of "God cannot abide sin; his holiness prevents it," I can't help but notice the way that Jesus, the Son of God, moves toward those deemed sinful, pouring out hospitality on them. While those flanking Jesus worry about eating with sinners, Jesus is always looking for sinners with whom to eat. Bretherton writes,

> Instead of having to be set apart from or exclude pagans in order to maintain holiness, it is in Jesus' hospitality of pagans, the unclean, and sinners that his own holiness is shown forth. Instead of sin and impurity infecting him, it seems Jesus' purity and righteousness somehow "infects" the impure, sinners and the Gentiles. As Borg puts it: "in the teaching [and practice] of Jesus, holiness, not uncleanness was understood to be contagious." For example the hemorrhaging woman has only to touch Jesus and she is healed and made clean. Instead of Jesus having to undergo purity rituals because of contact with the woman, as any other rabbi would, it is the woman who is "cleansed" by contact with him.[12]

Holiness, it seems, is a quality most evident in lives spent pouring out hospitality on strangers and others on the margins, a quality unlikely to emerge in a life spent fortifying the boundaries between self and others. Oddly, holiness eludes the one who avoids contact with sinners and strangers. One is not holy, or "set apart," by setting oneself apart from others. The one truly "set apart" is the one "a part" of the lives of strangers.

Theologian Christine Pohl, in her beautifully titled book *Making Room: Recovering Hospitality as a Christian Tradition*, observes that the concept of hospitality is generally understood as something inward facing. "Today when we think of hospitality, we don't think first of welcoming strangers. We picture having family and friends over for a pleasant meal. . . . In any case, today most understandings of hospitality have a minimal moral component—hospitality is a nice extra if we have the time or the resources, but we rarely view it as a spiritual obligation or as a dynamic expression of vibrant Christianity."[13] She notes that people generally work to accumulate enough resources so they

11. Bretherton, *Hospitality as Holiness*, 130.
12. Bretherton, *Hospitality as Holiness*, 130.
13. Pohl, *Making Room*, 4.

can avoid relying on the hospitality of others. Working to avoid dependency on others, however, legitimates conventional views of social stratification and confuses hospitality with benevolence—something that bestows status on the one "giving" and maintains a fundamental separation between giver and receiver.

While serving on the board of Chattanooga Widows Harvest Ministries in the early 1990s, I found myself collaborating on a philosophy of ministry statement for the organization.[14] When one of the board members suggested we include some variant of the phrase "to provide for widows in their need," Andy Mendonsa, the ministry's director and driving force, kindly educated the group. He told us that the sentence sounded too much like benevolence. He explained that the more important ministry was the ministry of prayer led by the widows themselves. Our ministry, which provided food, paid electric bills, mowed lawns, and fixed front porches, was to better equip the widows to carry out their ministry—a ministry that should not be seen as less important than one that fixed roofs and plumbing! In fact, Mendonsa seemed to think that "we" were mostly support for the more essential ministry of prayer carried out by the widows. That distinction was helpful to me.

The ministry of Christian hospitality is not simply a transfer from the haves to the have-nots, with a tax deduction thrown in for good measure. Rather, Christian hospitality directed toward the poor, marginal, and stranger is part of God's more expansive vision for a 1 Corinthians 12 "many gifts, one body" church, where all play essential roles, none are excluded, and the trappings of social stratification are nullified. In her book *Making Room*, Pohl observes, "Paul urged fellow Christians to welcome one another as Christ had welcomed them. He challenged the early believers to 'pursue' hospitality; in fact, hospitality was a qualification for leadership in the early Christian communities. The writer of Hebrews reminded readers to offer hospitality to strangers for, like Abraham and Sarah, they might be entertaining angels. Indeed, Christian believers were to regard hospitality to strangers as a fundamental expression of the gospel."[15]

Elsewhere in *Making Room*, Pohl cautions against an exclusive focus on particular acts of hospitality or on larger structural concerns. Care for particular strangers should be accompanied by efforts to understand and address the larger social structures that exclude some people, label them, and reinforce their marginality. For example, while visiting someone as part of a prison

14. Widows Harvest Ministries offers an outstanding example of Christian hospitality (http://www.widows.org/).
15. Pohl, *Making Room*, 5.

ministry is very important, we must also keep an eye on the structures that, for example, contribute to the disproportionate imprisonment of African American men in the United States. Advocacy is required at both local and institutional/structural levels. Likewise, an exclusive focus on the structural problems that contribute to stranger-making, without standing alongside the flesh-and-blood strangers who languish at the margins, can lead us to think of strangers in the abstract and fail to enter into their pain.

Pohl notes it can be easier to extend hospitality to strangers who have something to offer us, like marketable skills, while it is sometimes more difficult to extend hospitality to those who have few resources or connections.[16] "What's in it for us?" should not be a factor in whether the body of Christ extends sacrificial hospitality to those in need. With some frequency, I hear Christian people say disparaging things about "illegal immigrants." The poor are almost always "illegal," as they rarely have opportunity or voice to affect the governments and policies that enforce their disenfranchisement. Requiring greater moral fortitude as a prerequisite for receiving our help really just amounts to a weak rationalization that allows us to maintain the injustice of the status quo. Remember that Rahab was commended for her faith and hospitality when she covered for illegal Israelite spies. Remember that Pharaoh's daughter hid the infant Moses, declared illegal in Egypt. To reserve our hospitality for those we deem worthy (say, the "good," "legal" immigrants) is to take a position against Jesus, who came for us while we were yet sinners with nothing to offer . . . and who most often comes to us in the guise of a stranger. Qualifying our hospitality by the merit of the recipient permits us to forsake the most vulnerable ones in society. Moral goodness, "theirs" and "ours," is not the basis for the hospitality that God requires of people.

In the book *Untamed Hospitality: Welcoming God and Other Strangers*, Elizabeth Newman discusses hospitality as a form of communion, explaining that the goal of communion is not moral perfection but rather learning to live with imperfection. Consider her summary: "God calls us to live lives of faithfulness in communion with each other. Faithfulness rather than perfection enables us to welcome the weak and the vulnerable even as we accept our own vulnerabilities, acknowledging our limitations as places of deep grace. Such hospitality is far from moral do-goodism. That we are limited and weak means we need others; we depend on others in order to receive, discover, and be the healing presence of Christ in the world."[17]

16. Pohl, *Making Room*, 100.
17. Newman, *Untamed Hospitality*, 182.

Coupling Christian hospitality with the distinctions of good/bad, legal/illegal, worthy/unworthy, or pure/impure does little more than further entrench us in the we/they distinctions to which we so easily anchor our identity. Having an identity that is "in Christ" frees us from the need to make these frequently self-serving qualifications about the worthiness of others. Consequently, our hospitality can be freely given to those in need—of resources, welcome, safety, encouragement, or hope—on the basis of nothing more than our shared humanity. Theologian and philosopher Miroslav Volf offers the following indictment of Christian hospitality based on "moral mapping": "*The will to give ourselves to others and 'welcome' them, to readjust our identities to make space for them, is prior to any judgment about others, except that of identifying them in their humanity.* The will to embrace precedes any 'truth' about others and any construction of their 'justice.' This will is absolutely indiscriminate and strictly immutable; it transcends the moral mapping of the social world into 'good' and 'evil.'"[18] Perhaps, while singing "Nothing in my hands I bring . . ." from the well-known hymn "Rock of Ages," we can extend the sentiment to those who stand on the margins with empty hands, thus making our theology a lived theology.

Standing Down from Privilege

In advocating for change on behalf of the marginal, it is important to understand one's own location in the social hierarchies of stratified systems. Letty Russell, in a book titled *Church in the Round*, explains the importance of knowing where the margin and the center are located, and where we ourselves stand in relation to those positions. While she is writing about ministry and the church, her ideas easily transfer to other institutions and power structures to which the church is connected. Consider the following:

- We make choices about moving from margin toward center or from center toward margin according to where we find ourselves in relation to the center of power and resources and of cultural and linguistic dominance in any particular structure. Our connection to the margin is always related to where we are standing in regard to social privilege, and from that particular position we have at least three choices: not to choose, to choose the center, or to choose the margin.[19]

18. Volf, *Exclusion and Embrace*, 29.
19. Russell, *Church in the Round*, 192.

- We may *decide not to choose*. Those who are marginalized may do nothing to challenge existing arrangements, and by so doing, internalize the oppression that structures their lives, perhaps accepting it as natural, deserved, and so on. If we are part of the privileged center of power, to not choose is to continue offering tacit support to the current system of oppression.

- We may *choose for the center*. Those on the margins may work to emulate those at the center, attempting to be like them and to be accepted among them, moving toward privilege and away from others on the margins. Sometimes those who choose the center work to acquire the "master's tools" and, once acquired, use them to "dismantle the master's house." Of course, those who choose the center may use their position to enhance their own privilege, at the expense of the marginal ones.

- We may *choose the margin*. Russell's third choice offers two possibilities. The first involves those on the margin "claiming the margin" and working in solidarity with other marginal ones in their effort to move toward the center. "They seek a transformed society of justice where they will be empowered to share the center, and no one will need to be marginalized."[20] The second possibility involves some who are related to the privileged center choosing to stand with the oppressed while working against the privilege of their own (central) group. This too is an effort aimed at challenging and transforming the center.

Russell's title *Church in the Round* offers a metaphor for an inclusive and transformed church/body that has self-consciously dismantled privilege and drawn all into the center. This vision becomes reality as people of faith in both central and marginal locations protest the injustice that is in the system, take a seat at the table, and begin sawing off its corners. A round table has no head, no hierarchy, no privileged position. A round table, structurally speaking, is a community where none are strangers and all are welcome.

Seeking the Common Good

Each spring I offer a course titled Interpersonal Communication. As you might imagine, I take a sociological approach to explaining various features of communication, such as "the self," "perception," "saving face," and "managing

20. Russell, *Church in the Round*, 193.

conflict." The authors of the text I assign employ the concept of "other-orientation" throughout their book.[21] They ask questions like, What does it mean be other-oriented as you work through interpersonal conflict? How might majority-group students and their professor demonstrate other-orientation in a college class containing first-year international students who may struggle to navigate an unfamiliar culture? How do you communicate care for the other but still recognize and voice your own needs?

Other-orientation finds expression in a host of related concepts and frameworks, such as "empathy," "social decentering," and "standpoint theory." Though without theological scaffolding in the secular-market text I use, the concept of other-orientation is remarkably similar to teachings found in the Old and New Testaments, which is perhaps most clearly expressed in the Golden Rule: "In everything do to others as you would have them do to you" (Matt. 7:12; cf. Luke 6:31). Among other things, the Golden Rule (itself not a term that appears in Scripture) calls a person to reduce the distance (both physical and social) between self and other by considering how the situation would look were they themselves in need of help, kindness, or encouragement. It calls us to ask, What if *I* were the poor migrant with hungry children standing at the border? What if my child were born with an intersex condition? What if I found myself arrested or in prison? What if I were a poor Indonesian woman making shoes in a factory that offered little hope for my future?

Embraced as a life ethic, the Golden Rule reflects a commitment to neighborliness and to "us," rather than to we/they. Living out a commitment to other-orientation, perhaps in conformity to the Golden Rule, contributes to the transformation of identity, reducing the (false) need for scapegoating and downward social comparison. Against conventional wisdom, a commitment to others functions as a commitment to oneself. We meet our own needs by acknowledging and addressing the needs of others.

As we explored in chapter 9, George Herbert Mead referred to viewing things from the others' perspective as "role taking," something he saw as the primary mechanism for the development of the self and, by extension, society. For Mead, the self and society reside not in you or in me but in our intersection, in the space where we meet and acknowledge each other, imagine things from the other's perspective, accommodate ourselves to each other, know ourselves because of the other, and are together changed. Likewise, Ken Gergen explains that the self is derivative of relationship.[22] We come into being through relationship(s) with God, with others. "I" am a *dependent* variable in the social equation. The whole (relationship) produces the parts

---

21. Beebe, Beebe, and Redmond, *Interpersonal Communication*.
22. Gergen, *Relational Being*, 29–59.

(the individual)—in that order. Seen thus, the entity we call "society" is only possible through role taking. Furthermore, role taking addresses the Hobbesian problem of order—what prevents the war of all against all? If the other remains stranger, then society unravels, and the self, severed from its relational roots, withers and dies. There is simply no "I" without "we." Conversely, as we collectively learn to treat the other as neighbor and friend—as an essential part of "us"—we stabilize society and the possibilities for human life on the planet expand considerably.

- As one interpersonal communication text frames our collective task, "Bridges, not Walls . . ."[23]
- As Jesus says, "Do to others as you would have them do to you" (Luke 6:31).
- As the apostle Paul writes, "If all were a single member, where would the body be? As it is, there are many members, yet one body" (1 Cor. 12:19–20).

Without prioritizing the common good—frequently through the mechanism of hospitality, and especially with an eye on the most disenfranchised among us—society dissolves. Without society (the group, neighborhood, institution, etc.), there is no individual—we simply do not survive, let alone thrive, apart from the social.

Arguably, most of the world's problems are sociological and theological in character. For example, as I write, the mask mandate has been lifted from Chattanooga, Tennessee, near where I live. While the Covid-19 viral pandemic has obvious connections to chemistry, biology, and other disciplines, at its most basic level, the pandemic represents a sociological problem. Masking became a symbol of "we versus they." In Chattanooga, some churches became known as "non-maskers" (sometimes defying the ordinances of local governments) in contrast with churches where masking protocols were followed. When blame for the virus was laid at the feet of the Chinese, "we versus they" violence against Asian Americans, irrespective of national origin, escalated sharply. Political allegiances further fueled we/they divisions, and conspiracy theories like the one suggesting that the new vaccines contained microchips that governments and other nefarious entities could use to track and control people abounded. As a result of such misinformation, many people refused vaccinations. As a public health issue, vaccine misinformation is not benign; it entails a cost disproportionately borne by the poor and racial minorities.

23. Stewart, *Bridges Not Walls.*

Some studies examine the problems that "vaccine nationalism" raises for addressing pandemics in a global society.[24] While rich countries may enjoy superior access to vaccines, their failure to help poor countries gain access will not be without cost to them. When the virus ravages vaccine-deprived poor countries, global supply lines and international travel are interrupted, and rich countries end up sustaining a significant portion of these economic costs. Additionally, a failure to address a global pandemic "globally" prolongs the pandemic.[25] "Vaccine nationalism is not just morally indefensible. It is epidemiologically self-defeating and clinically counterproductive."[26] In a globally interconnected society, the we/they of self-serving nationalism hurts everyone. You can have the world's most brilliant chemists, biologists, and epidemiologists working to solve the problem, but the benefits they offer are compromised when privileged countries prioritize self and tribe over the common good and the most vulnerable. The Covid-19 pandemic is mostly a sociological problem that requires hospitality, concern for the marginal, and a global focus on the common good if we are to achieve sustained solutions. It's the same for environmental problems, world hunger, immigration, genocide, prejudice, and racism. At their root, most of our problems are the problems of the stranger. How we treat the stranger reflects our commitment to the common good and, by extension, whether we act in obedience to Jesus's teaching to treat others as we ourselves would want to be treated.

This, of course, is not new information for God's people.

Where the Gates Are Always Open and the Streets of Gold Have No Name

With copious detail, Revelation 21:9–27 describes the holy city, the New Jerusalem, coming down out of heaven. The city seems ostentatiously ornate—to an extent I'm unaccustomed to in everyday life. Gold, precious stones, huge pearls, and other indicators of wealth adorn every facet of the New Jerusalem, so much that I wonder whether I would feel at home or comfortable in such a place. The city reminds me a bit of the houses of the wealthy, outfitted with white carpet and expensive furniture where I rarely feel at ease. During his earthly ministry, Jesus himself never seemed drawn to wealth, jewelry, gold, or the status and prestige that accompany such possessions. It wasn't Jesus who turned the cross into twenty-four-karat jewelry! He seemed far more

24. Goodman, "If Poor Countries Go Unvaccinated, a Study Says, Rich Ones Will Pay."

25. Ramgopal, Romo, and McFadden, "How 'Vaccine Nationalism' Could Prolong the Covid-19 Pandemic."

26. Ghebreyesus, "Vaccine Nationalism Harms Everyone and Protects No One."

concerned with what gold does to people—more interested in our willingness to share our gold with stranger and neighbor. Jesus gave us the Golden Rule, which, arguably, instructs us to give our gold to others!

Rather than "bring on the gold," Jesus focused on the spiritual reality of various forms of worldly wealth. Remember that the rich young man in Matthew 19 and Mark 10 (identified as a rich young "ruler" in the Luke 18 account) went away sad, for he had great wealth. For me this raises questions about why Jesus would sanction a city that could appear on *Lifestyles of the Rich and Famous*. Should the rich young ruler bide his time a bit, doing without in the present, so that (like Scrooge McDuck in his vault) he can return to swimming in gold in the city of God? Highly unlikely. Jesus represents a break with worldly value systems in general and with stratified economic systems in particular. Why does John the Revelator's description of the holy city contain so much of what we see as wealth?

This side of the New Jerusalem, gold is more important as a symbol than for its material properties or uses. Of course, gold is a valuable element, superior for conducting electricity, not affected by exposure to air (it does not rust), and highly malleable. But if you google "gold," you have to dig (mine?) a bit to find material related to its physical properties. Rather, a host of websites barrage you with information about the value of gold, gold as an investment, and whether it's a good time to buy gold. If you google "uses for gold," you get a bit more information about its various uses, properties, and so on, but much of this information relates to the symbolic value of this precious metal. Consider the following from Geology.com, the first website in the results hierarchy to my "uses for gold" Google query: "Throughout the history of our planet, almost every established culture has used gold to symbolize power, beauty, purity, and accomplishment. Today we continue to use gold for our most significant objects: wedding rings, Olympic medals, Oscars, Grammys, money, crucifixes and ecclesiastical art. No other substance of the same rarity holds a more visible and prominent place in our society."[27]

In short, gold is a symbol of wealth, and the media of stratification. Many spend the bulk of their lives searching for, working for, hoarding, and surrounding themselves with some form of gold, and gold (in its broader meaning) easily becomes a surrogate for God. Gold is the substance of idols. Gold derives value from its scarcity and uneven distribution among individuals and groups of people.[28] Furthermore, gold is valuable because it permits us

27. King, "Many Uses of Gold."
28. Diamonds derive much of their value from diamond monopolies (the social production of scarcity) and from the symbolic value that has been very craftily attached to them. Artificial or synthetic diamonds have the same properties as the natural variety, but they are considerably

to separate ourselves from others, enabling us to create and maintain strangers with whom we compare favorably on worldly (but not spiritual) measures. In a social system where gold holds priority, hospitality—reframed as entertaining—becomes the reciprocal showcasing of conspicuous consumption among those who have similar amounts of gold. Arguably, statistics on social stratification measure a group's access to, or possession of, gold—they identify who the strangers are in a society. In sum, gold is valuable because of its scarcity and the social currency it provides for those who have it, in contrast with those who don't. Gold permits downward social comparison. You can't turn lead into gold, but you can turn gold into strangers!

Human societies stratify around that which is scarce, whether gold, oil, Manhattan real estate, or social status. Resources are considered valuable when in limited supply—the so-called "law" of supply and demand. Drawing on the exodus narrative, Walter Brueggemann writes about the deep anxiety that permeates social systems that have deteriorated. He characterizes Egypt as a scarcity system of exploitation and oppression where everyone, from Pharaoh to the least of the Hebrew slaves, is consumed by anxiety and fear. In a scarcity system, both rich and poor are afraid there will not be enough. Rather than sharing, neighborliness, and other orientation, there is hoarding, maneuvering, anger, and violence. These behaviors are not limited to the Egyptians. The Israelites also operate under a consciousness that has been colonized by the nightmare system of scarcity found in Egypt. Brueggemann notes that when God provides the Israelites with miraculous abundance in the form of manna, they try to store it up, hedging their bets against a future of expected scarcity and lacking imagination for anything better.[29] The parallel with our own situation (I write as an American), where despite our wealth we anxiously build walls to keep out poor immigrants, disparage unaccompanied minors as threats to "our" resources, and scoff at sanctuary cities is unmistakable. Will we have enough? Can I afford to be neighborly? Will I be at risk if I offer my hospitality to sketchy freeloaders who want to take what is mine? So much of life revolves around negotiating a system of scarcity, hoarding for ourselves, and building walls to block strangers. However, God has called us out of the nightmare of scarcity and into abundance.

In the New Jerusalem, gold is anything but scarce. In Revelation 21:21, John describes the great street of the city of God as being of pure gold, like

---

less valuable and are commonly used in industrial applications such as drill-bit tips. For an interesting history of diamonds, their value, and their applications, see Goldschein, "Incredible Story." For an overview of the similarities between natural and synthetic diamonds, see With Clarity, "Buying Natural vs. Synthetic Diamonds."

29. Brueggemann, *Journey to the Common Good*, 7–17.

transparent glass. A street of gold! We might understand this to mean that gold is so plentiful there that it holds little social value. What then is the meaning of this heavenly gold in the city of Jesus, who values humility, generous giving, the first being last, taking the seat of lesser honor, and so on? Perhaps the reference to a street of gold is, in part, an announcement that God's presence negates any scarcity. In the city of God, the nightmare of scarcity (both real and imagined) ends, and human anxiety melts away. Want gold? Have a truckload of it, because gold is as common as gravel in this city. Have all you want. We pave with it here![30] In the city of God, identity will not rest on economic success, accumulated wealth, or social distance from others. Seen this way, the presence of so much gold testifies to its *lack* of social currency and power to divide. It's just not important; possessing it sets no one apart. When fashioned into a street, gold is something to be trampled underfoot. Furthermore, with gold's scarcity no longer at issue, its beauty, and perhaps other properties, can be valued and marveled at for their own sake. Like seeing a sunset. You really can't own one, anyone who wanders onto a beach or climbs up a hill can "have" one, and all you can do is marvel at its ethereal beauty while you share it with someone.

Curiously, the gold on the great street of the city of God is like transparent glass. Some commentators believe this means that it is highly polished rather than that it is see-through. Perhaps in this socially inert metal we will see the reflection of those who were formerly strangers, standing with us as "treasured" neighbors. Gold, so transformed, is no longer an end in itself but a means by which we apprehend that which is of real value—the neighborhood of those who were once strangers. No more we/they . . . just "us"—a neighborhood party on the street of gold.

Of the city of God, Revelation 21:25–26 states, "Its gates will never be shut by day—and there will be no night there. People will bring into it the glory and the honor of the nations." The image of gates that are never gated offers an intriguing sociological vision of a new kind of world—one with no strangers, where all are welcome.[31] The heading for this final section of the book, "Where

---

30. Gold being so plentiful that its value is changed reminds me of Roald Dahl's much-loved children's book *Charlie and the Chocolate Factory*. Before finding the golden ticket that gained him entrance into Willy Wonka's Chocolate Factory, chocolate was a scarce and extremely valuable commodity for young Charlie. When he was finally able to see the source of the chocolate he so desired, it was in the form of a huge river that flowed throughout the magical factory. Chocolate has little value to someone who has access to a river of it.

31. In his commentary on Revelation, M. Eugene Boring writes,

> The earthly Jerusalem had had a temple with a wall that separated men from women and Jews from Gentiles (cf. Acts 21:27–29; Eph. 2:14–16). The New Jerusalem has no temple, and its only wall is pierced by twelve gates that are always open and have only

the Gates Are Always Open and the Streets of Gold Have No Name," makes reference to the well-known U2 anthem "Where the Streets Have No Name," the opening track on the Irish rock band's 1987 album *The Joshua Tree*. Apparently, "The lyrics were inspired by a story that [singer] Bono heard about Belfast, Northern Ireland, where a person's religion and income were evident by the street on which they lived. He contrasted this with the anonymity he felt when visiting Ethiopia, saying: 'the guy in the song recognizes this contrast and thinks about a world where there aren't such divisions, a place where the streets have no name.'"[32] Open gates offering unfettered access to a city with a street of gold. If the gates are always open, why have gates at all? Perhaps as a symbol they serve a memory function, reminding us of how we used to shut gates on strangers, keeping "them" away from "our" gold. But never again, for the New Jerusalem, with its open gates, limitless and transformed resources, whose light is the Lord and in whom our identity finally rests, is a place without strangers or scapegoats.

---

one-way traffic—outside to inside (21:24, 26, 27). . . . Instead of sectarian separateness or astrological determinism, John makes the eternally open gates a powerful symbol of the radical inclusiveness of the city in which the hope of Isaiah 19:24–25 is finally fulfilled. "All" are there, because of the power and grace of the One who "makes all things new" (21:5)—the "all" is added by John to his Old Testament source (Isa. 43:19). (Boring, *Revelation*, 222)

32. Wikipedia, s.v. "Where the Streets Have No Name."

BIBLIOGRAPHY

Ackerman, Andy, dir. *Seinfeld*. Season 8, episode 1, "The Foundation." Aired September 19, 1996, on NBC.

Alexander, Michelle. *The New Jim Crow: Mass Incarceration in the Age of Colorblindness*. New York: New Press, 2010.

Allan, Kenneth. *The Social Lens: An Invitation to Social and Sociological Theory*. 3rd ed. Thousand Oaks, CA: Sage, 2014.

American Girl. "Nanea 1941." https://www.americangirl.com/shop/c/nanea.

American Girl Wiki. "Z Yang (doll)." https://americangirl.fandom.com/wiki/Z_Yang_(doll).

Anderson, Chris. "Cleveland Indians Stand in Solidarity during National Anthem Ahead of Monday's Game at Progressive Field." Cleveland 19, July 21, 2020. https://www.cleveland19.com/2020/07/21/cleveland-indians-stand-solidarity-during-national-anthem-ahead-mondays-game-progressive-field/.

Appelrouth, Scott, and Laura Desfor Edles. *Sociological Theory in the Contemporary Era: Text and Readings*. Thousand Oaks, CA: Pine Forge, 2007.

Bacote, Vincent, and Nathaniel Perrin. "Redemptive Rehabilitation: Theological Approaches to Criminal Justice Reform [In English]." *Christian Scholar's Review* 49, no. 1 (Fall 2019): 3–24.

Badenhausen, Kurt. "Michael Jordan Leads the NBA's Biggest Shoe Deals at $110 Million This Year." *Forbes*, June 9, 2017. https://www.forbes.com/sites/kurtbadenhausen/2017/06/09/the-nbas-biggest-shoe-deals/#6ed913291520.

Baum, Dan. "Legalize It All." *Harper's Magazine*, April 2016, pp. 22–32. https://harpers.org/archive/2016/04/legalize-it-all/.

Becker, Howard. "Relativism: Labeling Theory." In *Constructions of Deviance: Social Power, Context, and Interaction*, edited by Patricia A. Adler and Peter Adler, 40–44. Boston: Cengage, 2016.

Beebe, Steven A., Susan J. Beebe, and Mark V. Redmond. *Interpersonal Communication: Relating to Others.* 9th ed. Boston: Pearson, 2018.

Berger, Peter L. *Invitation to Sociology: A Humanistic Perspective.* Anchor Books. Garden City, NY: Doubleday, 1963.

———. *The Sacred Canopy: Elements of a Sociological Theory of Religion.* Garden City, NY: Doubleday, 1967.

Berger, Peter L., and Thomas Luckmann. *The Social Construction of Reality: A Treatise in the Sociology of Knowledge.* New York: Anchor Books, 1967.

Blackless, Melanie, Anthony Charuvastra, Amanda Derryck, Anne Fausto-Sterling, Karl Lauzanne, and Ellen Lee. "How Sexually Dimorphic Are We? Review and Synthesis." *American Journal of Human Biology* 12, no. 2 (2000): 151–66. https://doi.org/10.1002/(sici)1520-6300(200003/04)12:2<151::aid-ajhb1>3.0.co;2-f.

Bogardus, Emory S. "A Social Distance Scale." *Sociology and Social Research* 17, no. 3 (1933): 265–71.

Boring, M. Eugene. *Revelation.* Interpretation: A Bible Commentary for Teaching and Preaching. Louisville: Westminster John Knox, 1989.

Bourdieu, Pierre. *Distinction: A Social Critique of the Judgement of Taste.* Cambridge, MA: Harvard University Press, 1984.

Bretherton, Luke. *Hospitality as Holiness: Christian Witness amid Moral Diversity.* Burlington, VT: Ashgate, 2006.

Brice, Makini. "Trump Says Immigrants 'Unhappy' with Detention Centers Should Stay Home." *Reuters,* July 3, 2019. https://www.reuters.com/article/us-usa-immigration/trump-says-immigrants-unhappy-with-detention-centers-should-stay-home-idUSKCN1TY1A5.

Brueggemann, Walter. *Journey to the Common Good.* Louisville: Westminster John Knox, 2010.

———. *The Land: Place as Gift, Promise, and Challenge in Biblical Faith.* 2nd ed. Overtures to Biblical Theology. Minneapolis: Fortress, 2002.

———. *The Word Militant: Preaching a Decentering Word.* Minneapolis: Fortress, 2010.

Budiman, Abby. "Key Findings about U.S. Immigrants." Pew Research Center, August 20, 2020. https://www.pewresearch.org/fact-tank/2020/08/20/key-findings-about-u-s-immigrants/.

Bureau of Labor Statistics. "Women More Likely Than Men to Have Earned a Bachelor's Degree by Age 29." April 13, 2016. https://www.bls.gov/opub/ted/2016/women-more-likely-than-men-to-have-earned-a-bachelors-degree-by-age-29.htm#bls-print.

Burrows, James, John Ratzenberger, and Rick Beren, dirs. *Cheers.* Season 11. Aired 1992–93, on NBC.

Butler, Judith. *Bodies That Matter: On the Discursive Limits of "Sex."* New York: Routledge, 1993.

———. *Gender Trouble: Feminism and the Subversion of Identity*. Thinking Gender. New York: Routledge, 1990.

Canadian Down Syndrome Society. "Down Syndrome Answers." Accessed November 30, 2021. https://cdss.ca/awareness/down-syndrome-answers/.

———. "What Is Down Syndrome?" Accessed November 30, 2021. https://cdss.ca /resources/general-information/.

Carlisle, Belinda. "Heaven Is a Place on Earth." In *Heaven on Earth*, Edsel, 2015. Compact disc.

Carson, E. Ann. "Imprisonment Rates of Sentenced State and Federal Prisoners per 100,000 U.S. Residents of Corresponding Sex, Race, Hispanic Origin, and Age Groups, December 31, 2019." Bureau of Justice Statistics, February 2, 2021. https:// www.bjs.gov/nps/resources/documents/QT_age%20sex%20race%20distribution _rates_2019.xlsx.

———. "Prisoners under the Jurisdiction of State or Federal Correctional Authorities, December 31, 1978–2019." Bureau of Justice Statistics, October 7, 2020. https://www .bjs.gov/nps/resources/documents/QT_total%20jurisdiction%20count_total.xls.

Cavoukian, Raffi, and Ken Whiteley. *Singable Songs for the Very Young*. Universal City, CA: Shoreline/MCA/Troubadour, 1976. Audio recording.

Chase, C. "Hermaphrodites with Attitude: Mapping the Emergence of Intersex Political Activism." In *Sociology of the Body: A Reader*, edited by C. Malacrida and J. Low, 133–40. New York: Oxford University Press, 2008.

Chaves, Mark. *Ordaining Women: Culture and Conflict in Religious Organizations*. Cambridge, MA: Harvard University Press, 1997.

Chesney-Lind, Meda, and Lisa Pasko. *The Female Offender: Girls, Women and Crime*. Thousand Oaks, CA: Sage, 2013.

CleanClothesCampaign. "Foul Play 2: Sponsors Leave Workers (Still) on the Side- lines." 2018. https://cleanclothes.org/file-repository/resources-national-cccs-foul -play-ii-sponsors-leave-workers-still-on-the-sidelines/view.

Cockburn, Bruce. "Child of the Wind." In *Nothing but a Burning Light*. New York: Columbia Records, 1992. Compact disc.

"Comparison of Tanya McDowell and Felicity Huffman Sentences Misleading." Af- rica Check, November 1, 2019. https://africacheck.org/fact-checks/fbchecks/com parison-tanya-mcdowell-and-felicity-huffman-sentences-misleading.

Cornwall, Susannah. "The Kenosis of Unambiguous Sex in the Body of Christ: In- tersex, Theology and Existing 'for the Other.'" *Theology & Sexuality* 14, no. 2 (2008): 181–99. https://doi.org/10.1177/1355835807087061.

Coser, Lewis A. *The Functions of Social Conflict*. London: Routledge & Kegan Paul, 1956.

Creighton, Sarah. "Surgery for Intersex." *Journal of the Royal Society of Medicine* 94 (2001): 218–20.

DeFranza, Megan K. *Sex Difference in Christian Theology: Male, Female, and Intersex in the Image of God*. Grand Rapids: Eerdmans, 2015.

Dewhurst, Christopher J., and D. B. Grant. "Intersex Problems." *Archives of Disease in Childhood* 59, no. 12 (1984): 1191–94. https://doi.org/10.1136/adc.59.12.1191.

Diamond, Jared. "Race without Color: Basing Race on Body Chemistry Makes No More Sense Than Basing Race on Appearance, but at Least You Get to Move the Membership Around." *Discover*, November 1994, 82–89.

Disaster Center, The. "United States Crime Rates 1960–2019." Accessed December 1, 2021. https://www.disastercenter.com/crime/uscrime.htm.

Drake, Bruce. "Incarceration Gap Widens between Whites and Blacks." Pew Research Center, September 6, 2013. http://www.pewresearch.org/fact-tank/2013/09/06/incarceration-gap-between-whites-and-blacks-widens/.

Du Bois, W. E. B. *Darkwater: Voices from within the Veil*. Mansfield Centre, CT: Martino, 2014.

———. *The Souls of Black Folk*. Chicago: Dover, 1994.

Du Bois, W. E. B., and Eric J. Sundquist. *The Oxford W. E. B. Du Bois Reader*. New York: Oxford University Press, 1996.

Durkheim, Émile. *The Division of Labor in Society*. Translated by W. D. Halls. New York: Free Press, 1984. Originally published 1893.

———. *The Rules of Sociological Method and Selected Texts on Sociology and Its Method*. Edited by Steven Lukes. New York: Free Press, 1982.

"Ed Johnson Project, The." Accessed June 2, 2021. https://www.edjohnsonproject.com/.

Eiesland, Nancy L. *The Disabled God: Toward a Liberatory Theology of Disability*. Nashville: Abingdon, 1994.

Eitzen, D. Stanley. *Fair and Foul: Beyond the Myths and Paradoxes of Sport*. 6th ed. Lanham, MD: Rowman & Littlefield, 2016.

Emerson, Michael O., and Christian Smith. *Divided by Faith: Evangelical Religion and the Problem of Race in America*. New York: Oxford University Press, 2000.

End Slavery Now. "Half the Sky Movement: Turning Oppression into Opportunity for Women Worldwide." Accessed August 13, 2021. https://www.endslaverynow.org/half-the-sky-movement.

Farganis, James. "Georg Simmel: Dialectic of Individual and Society." In *Readings in Social Theory: The Classic Tradition to Post-modernism*, edited by James Farganis, 127–41. Boston: McGraw-Hill, 2004.

———. "Karl Marx: Alienation, Class Struggle, and Class Consciousness." In *Readings in Social Theory: The Classic Tradition to Post-modernism*, edited by James Farganis, 23–54. Boston: McGraw-Hill, 2004.

Federal Bureau of Investigation. "Arrests by Race/Ethnicity, 2017." Accessed December 1, 2021. https://ucr.fbi.gov/crime-in-the-u.s/2017/crime-in-the-u.s.-2017/tables/table-43.

Federal Bureau of Investigation Crime Data Explorer. "Arrests Offense Counts in the United States." Accessed December 1, 2021. https://crime-data-explorer.fr.cloud .gov/pages/explorer/crime/arrest.

Federal Bureau of Prisons. "Inmate Statistics: Offenses." Accessed December 1, 2021. https://www.bop.gov/about/statistics/statistics_inmate_offenses.jsp.

Felbab-Brown, Vanda. "Order from Chaos: Trump's Bogus Justifications for the Border Wall." Brookings, January 11, 2019. https://www.brookings.edu/blog/order -from-chaos/2019/01/11/trumps-bogus-justifications-for-the-border-wall/.

Fine, Cordelia. *Delusions of Gender: How Our Minds, Society, and Neurosexism Create Difference*. New York: Norton, 2010.

Fitzpatrick, Meagan. "Harper on Terror Arrests: Not a Time for 'Sociology.'" CBC, April 25, 2013. https://www.cbc.ca/news/politics/harper-on-terror-arrests-not-a -time-for-sociology-1.1413502.

Fromm, Erich, and T. B. Bottomore. *Marx's Concept of Man*. London: Continuum, 2004.

Frost, Natasha A., Todd R. Clear, and Carlos E. Monteiro. "Ending Mass Incarceration: Six Bold Reforms." In *Decarcerating America: From Mass Punishment to Public Health*, edited by Ernest M. Drucker, 21–40. New York: New Press, 2018.

Gabrielson, Ryan, and Topher Sanders. "Busted." ProPublica, 2016. https://www .propublica.org/article/common-roadside-drug-test-routinely-produces-false -positives.

Gergen, Kenneth J. *Relational Being: Beyond Self and Community*. New York: Oxford University Press, 2009.

Ghebreyesus, Tedros Adhanom. "Vaccine Nationalism Harms Everyone and Protects No One." *Foreign Policy*, February 2, 2021. https://foreignpolicy.com/2021/02/02 /vaccine-nationalism-harms-everyone-and-protects-no-one/.

Giese, Rachel. "How Immigration Helps to Lower Crime Rates." *The Walrus*, June 12, 2011, updated April 15, 2020. https://thewalrus.ca/arrival-of-the-fittest/.

Girard, René. *The Scapegoat*. Baltimore, MD: Johns Hopkins University Press, 1986.

Glanville, Mark R., and Luke Glanville. *Refuge Reimagined: Biblical Kinship in Global Politics*. Downers Grove, IL: InterVarsity Press, 2021.

Glassner, Barry. *The Culture of Fear: Why Americans Are Afraid of the Wrong Things*. New York: Basic Books, 1999.

Golding, William. *Lord of the Flies*. New York: Berkley, 2003.

Goldschein, Eric. "The Incredible Story of How De Beers Created and Lost the Most Powerful Monopoly Ever." *Business Insider*, December 19, 2011. https://www.busi nessinsider.com/history-of-de-beers-2011-12?op=1.

Goodman, Peter S. "If Poor Countries Go Unvaccinated, a Study Says, Rich Ones Will Pay." *New York Times*, January 23, 2021. https://www.nytimes.com/2021/01 /23/business/coronavirus-vaccines-global-economy.html.

Gramlich, John. "What the Data Says (and Doesn't Say) about Crime in the United States." Pew Research Center, November 20, 2020. https://www.pewresearch.org /fact-tank/2020/11/20/facts-about-crime-in-the-u-s/.

Gurney, Karen. "Sex and the Surgeon's Knife: The Family Court's Dilemma . . . Informed Consent and the Specter of Iatrogenic Harm to Children with Intersex Characteristics." *American Journal of Law & Medicine* 33, no. 4 (2007): 625–61. https://doi.org/10.1177/009885880703300403.

Handeyside, Hugh. "A Judge Just Reminded CPB That the Border Isn't a Rights-Free Zone." ACLU, October 1, 2018. https://www.aclu.org/blog/national-security /discriminatory-profiling/judge-just-reminded-cbp-border-isnt-rights-free-zone.

Hannah-Jones, Nikole. "The Problem We All Live with—Part One." Episode 562, July 31, 2015. In *This American Life*, produced by WBEZ Chicago, 30:00. https:// www.thisamericanlife.org/562/the-problem-we-all-live-with-part-one.

Hansen, Helena, and Julie Netherland. "Is the Prescription Opioid Epidemic a White Problem?" *American Journal of Public Health* 106, no. 12 (December 2016): 2127–29.

Hartley, Eugene L. *Problems in Prejudice*. New York: King's Crown, 1946.

Hartman, Steve. "Love Thy Neighbor: Son's Killer Moves Next Door." CBS, June 8, 2011. https://www.cbsnews.com/news/love-thy-neighbor-sons-killer-moves-next -door/.

Hauptman, Samantha. *The Criminalization of Immigration: The Post 9/11 Moral Panic*. The New Americans: Recent Immigration and American Society. El Paso: LFB Scholarly Publishing, 2013.

Hauslohner, Abigail. "U.S. Family Suing Federal Government after 11-Hour Detention on Canadian Border." *Washington Post*, May 13, 2017. https://www.washington post.com/news/post-nation/wp/2017/07/13/u-s-family-suing-federal-government -after-11-hour-detention-on-canadian-border/.

Hays, J. Taylor, MD. "What Is Thirdhand Smoke, and Why Is It a Concern?" Mayo Clinic, August 21, 2020. https://www.mayoclinic.org/healthy-lifestyle/adult-health /expert-answers/third-hand-smoke/faq-20057791.

Heddendorf, Russell, and Matthew Vos. *Hidden Threads: A Christian Critique of Sociological Theory*. 2nd ed. Lanham, MD: University Press of America, 2010.

Heim, S. Mark. *Saved from Sacrifice: A Theology of the Cross*. Grand Rapids: Eerdmans, 2006.

Hendricks, M. "Is It a Boy or a Girl?" *Johns Hopkins Magazine*, November 1993, pp. 10–16.

Hiebert, Dennis, and Valerie Hiebert. "Intersex Persons and the Church: Unknown, Unwelcomed, Unwanted Neighbors." *Journal for the Sociological Integration of Religion and Society* 5, no. 2 (Fall 2015): 31–44.

Hoffman, Shirl J. *Good Game: Christianity and the Culture of Sports*. Waco: Baylor University Press, 2010.

Hogg, Michael A. "Social Identity Theory." In McKeown, Haji, and Ferguson, *Understanding Peace and Conflict through Social Identity Theory*, 3–18.

Houston, Fleur S. *You Shall Love the Stranger as Yourself: The Bible, Refugees and Asylum*. Biblical Challenges in the Contemporary World. New York: Routledge, 2015.

Hubbard, Ben. "Saudi Arabia Agrees to Let Women Drive." *New York Times*, September 26, 2017. https://www.nytimes.com/2017/09/26/world/middleeast/saudi -arabia-women-drive.html.

Human Rights Watch. "Saudi Arabia: As Women's Driving Ban Ends, Provide Parity." September 27, 2017. https://www.hrw.org/news/2017/09/27/saudi-arabia-womens -driving-ban-ends-provide-parity.

Im, Jimmy. "Kevin Durant Sells Gorgeous $12 Million Malibu Beach House before Move to Nets." *USA Today*, July 2, 2019. https://www.usatoday.com/story/sports /2019/07/02/nets-kevin-durant-sells-malibu-california-beach-home-12-million /1631857001/.

Intersex Campaign for Equality. "Our Mission." https://www.intersexequality.com /mission/.

Isidore, Chris, and Ellie Kaufman. "We Have a Powerball Winner! Mavis Wanczyk Told Her Boss She's Not Coming Back." CNN Money, August 24, 2017. http:// money.cnn.com/2017/08/23/news/powerball-700-million-jackpot/index.html.

Jhally, Sut, dir. *No Logo: Brands, Globalization, Resistance*. Northampton, MA: Media Education Foundation, 2003. Videorecording.

Jipp, Joshua W. *Saved by Faith and Hospitality*. Grand Rapids: Eerdmans, 2017.

Johnson, Mary. "Forgiving Her Son's Killer: 'Not an Easy Thing.'" Interview by NPR, *Morning Edition*, May 20, 2011. https://www.npr.org/2011/05/20/136463363 /forgiving-her-sons-killer-not-an-easy-thing.

———. "In Marriage, a Bond of Love, Loss and Light." Interview by NPR, *Morning Edition*, January 27, 2017. https://www.npr.org/2017/01/27/511823122/in-marriage -a-bond-of-love-loss-and-light.

Kaeble, Danielle, and Mary Cowhig. "Correctional Populations in the United States, 2016." Bureau of Justice Statistics. https://bjs.ojp.gov/library/publications/cor rectional-populations-united-states-2016.

Kalin, Stephen, and Katie Paul. "'Rain Begins with a Single Drop': Saudi Women Rejoice at End of Driving Ban." *Reuters*, September 27, 2017. https://www.reuters .com/article/us-saudi-women-driving-idUSKCN1C217F.

Kelleher, Kevin. "Nike Shoes Close at All Time Record High after Controversial Colin Kaepernick Endorsement." *Fortune*, 2018. https://fortune.com/2018/09/14/nike -closes-another-record-high-wake-endorsement-colin-kaepernick/.

Kennedy, Merrit. "Saudi Arabia Says It Will End Ban and Allow Women to Drive." NPR, September 26, 2017. https://www.npr.org/sections/thetwo-way/2017/09/26 /553784663/saudi-arabia-says-it-will-end-ban-and-allow-women-to-drive.

King, Hobart M. "The Many Uses of Gold." Geology.com. https://geology.com /minerals/gold/uses-of-gold.shtml.

Knepper, Lisa, Jennifer McDonald, Kathy Sanchez, and Elyse Smith Pohl. "The Abuse of Civil Asset Forfeiture." Institute for Justice. https://ij.org/report/policing-for -profit-3/pfp3content/introduction/#postlanding.

"Lest We Forget Slavery Museum." Accessed June 2, 2021. http://lwfsm.com/.

Lewis, Danny. "This Map Shows over a Century of Documented Lynchings." *Smithsonian Magazine*, January 24, 2017. https://www.smithsonianmag.com/smart-news /map-shows-over-a-century-of-documented-lynchings-in-united-states-180961877/.

Lewis, David Levering. *W. E. B. Du Bois: A Biography*. New York: Holt, 2009.

Light, Michal T., and Ty Miller. "Does Undocumented Immigration Increase Violent Crime?" *Criminology* 56, no. 2 (2018): 370–401. https://doi.org/10.1111/1745-9125 .12175.

Macaray, David. "Nike's Crimes." In *Sport in Contemporary Society: An Anthology*, edited by D. Stanley Eitzen, 320–21. New York: Oxford University Press, 2015.

Marx, Karl. *Capital*. Vol. 1 of *A Critique of Political Economy*, edited by Friedrich Engels. London: Lawrence & Wishart, 1996.

Marx, Karl, and Friedrich Engels. *The Communist Manifesto*. New York: Penguin, 2002.

Mazur, Tom. "Ambiguous Genitalia: Detection and Counseling." *Pediatric Nursing* 9, no. 6 (1983): 417–22.

McClendon, David. "Gender Gap in Religious Service Attendance Has Narrowed in U.S." Pew Research Center, May 13, 2016. https://www.pewresearch.org/fact-tank /2016/05/13/gender-gap-in-religious-service-attendance-has-narrowed-in-u-s/.

McKeown, Shelley, Reeshma Haji, and Neil Ferguson, eds. *Understanding Peace and Conflict through Social Identity Theory: Contemporary Global Perspectives*. New York: Springer International Publishing, 2016.

Melfi, Theodore, dir. *Hidden Figures*. Beverly Hills, CA: Twentieth Century Fox Home Entertainment, 2017. DVD.

Merleau-Ponty, Maurice. *Phenomenology of Perception*. Atlantic Highlands, NJ: Routledge, 1981.

Merrill, William Pierson. "Rise Up, O Men of God." In *The United Methodist Hymnal*, #576. https://www.hymnsite.com/lyrics/umh576.sht.

Merton, Robert K. "The Unanticipated Consequences of Purposive Social Action." *American Sociological Review* 1, no. 6 (1936): 894–904. https://doi.org/10.2307 /2084615.

Milgram, Stanley. *Obedience to Authority: An Experimental View*. New York: Harper & Row, 1974.

Miller, Barbara D. *Cultural Anthropology in a Globalizing World*. 3rd ed. Boston: Prentice Hall, 2010.

Miller, Barbara D., P. van Esterik, and J. van Esterik. *Cultural Anthropology*. 4th Canadian ed. Toronto: Pearson Education Canada, 2010.

Miller, Reuben. *Halfway Home: Race, Punishment, and the Afterlife of Mass Incarceration*. New York: Little, Brown, 2021.

Mita, Theodore, Marshall Dermer, and Jeffrey Knight. "Reversed Facial Images and the Mere-Exposure Hypothesis." *Journal of Personality and Social Psychology* 35 (1977): 597–601.

Montpetit, Jonathan. "As Fight over Quebec's Religious Symbols Law Shifts to Courts, Legal Experts Debate Best Way to Challenge It." CBC, July 8, 2019. https://www.cbc.ca/news/canada/montreal/as-fight-over-quebec-s-religious-symbols-law-shifts-to-courts-legal-experts-debate-best-way-to-challenge-it-1.5204112.

NAACP. "History of Lynching in America." Accessed June 2, 2021. http://www.naacp.org/history-of-lynchings/.

Natarajan, Anita. "Medical Ethics and Truth Telling in the Case of Androgen Insensitivity Syndrome." *Canadian Medical Association Journal* 154, no. 4 (1996): 568–70.

National Down Syndrome Society. "Down Syndrome Facts." Accessed November 30, 2021. https://www.ndss.org/about-down-syndrome/down-syndrome-facts/.

National Safety Council. "Make Fall Safety a Top Priority." Accessed October 14, 2021. https://www.nsc.org/workplace/safety-topics/slips-trips-and-falls/slips-trips-and-falls-home.

Newbigin, Lesslie, and Paul Weston. *Lesslie Newbigin: Missionary Theologian; A Reader*. Grand Rapids: Eerdmans, 2006.

Newman, Elizabeth. *Untamed Hospitality: Welcoming God and Other Strangers*. Grand Rapids: Brazos, 2007.

Nike. "Nike Better World." Posted March 17, 2011. YouTube video, 1:59. https://www.youtube.com/watch?time_continue=11&v=7sggmRi_xx0.

O'Connell, Liam. "Brand Value of the Sports Company Nike Worldwide from 2016–2019." *Statista*, March 7, 2019. https://www.statista.com/statistics/632210/nike-brand-value/.

Palma, Bethania. "Did Tanya McDowell Get 5 Years for Sending Her Son to a Better School While Felicity Huffman Got 14 Days?" *Snopes*, September 19, 2019. https://www.snopes.com/fact-check/tanya-mcdowell-felicity-huffman/.

Paris, Jenell Williams. *The End of Sexual Identity: Why Sex Is Too Important to Define Who We Are*. Downers Grove, IL: InterVarsity, 2011.

Park, Robert E. "Human Migration and the Marginal Man." *American Journal of Sociology* 33, no. 6 (May 1928): 881–93.

Pereira, Pedro. "Top 5 Nike Endorsements." *Football Finance*, January 9, 2021. https://financefootball.com/2021/01/09/top-5-nike-athlete-endorsements/.

Perkins, Julia. "Felicity Huffman Sentencing Compared to Bridgeport Mom Tanya McDowell." *New Haven Register*, September 15, 2019. https://www.nhregister.com/news/article/Felicity-Huffman-sentencing-compared-to-14441185.php.

Peters, William. *A Class Divided, Then and Now*. New Haven: Yale University Press, 1987.

Peters, William, dir. *The Eye of the Storm*. 1970; Pound Ridge, NY: Admire Productions, 2008. DVD.

Pew Research Center. "Religious Landscape Study." Accessed August 30, 2021. http://www.pewforum.org/about-the-religious-landscape-study/.

Philips, Emo. "The Best God Joke Ever—and It's Mine!" *The Guardian*, September 25, 2005. https://www.theguardian.com/stage/2005/sep/29/comedy.religion.

"Phil Knight: Real Time Net Worth." *Forbes*, accessed June 3, 2020. https://www.forbes.com/profile/phil-knight/#df5d98c1dcbd.

Pohl, Christine D. *Making Room: Recovering Hospitality as a Christian Tradition*. Grand Rapids: Eerdmans, 1999.

Potok, Chaim. *The Chosen: A Novel*. New York: Simon & Schuster, 1967.

Quan, Douglas. "Years after Two Ships Brought 568 Migrants to Canada, Seven Acquittals and One Conviction." *National Post*, July 27, 2017. https://nationalpost.com/news/canada/years-after-two-ships-brought-568-migrants-to-canada-seven-acquittals-and-one-conviction.

Rajendra, Tisha M. *Migrants and Citizens: Justice and Responsibility in the Ethics of Immigration*. Grand Rapids: Eerdmans, 2017.

Ramgopal, Kit, Christine Romo, and Cynthia McFadden. "How 'Vaccine Nationalism' Could Prolong the Covid-19 Pandemic." NBC, January 23, 2021. https://www.nbcnews.com/news/us-news/how-vaccine-nationalism-could-prolong-covid-19-pandemic-n1255417.

Reinarman, Craig. "The Social Construction of Drug Scares." In *Constructions of Deviance: Social Power, Context, and Interaction*, edited by Patricia Adler and Peter Adler, 159–70. Boston: Cengage, 2016.

Riesman, David. *The Lonely Crowd: A Study of the Changing American Character*. Garden City, NY: Doubleday, 1953.

Ritzer, George. *Sociological Theory*. 4th ed. New York: McGraw-Hill, 1996.

Ritzer, George, and Jeffrey Stepnisky. *Modern Sociological Theory*. 8th ed. Thousand Oaks, CA: Sage, 2018.

Roberts, Keith A., and David Yamane. *Religion in Sociological Perspective*. 6th ed. Los Angeles: Sage, 2016.

Russell, Letty M. *Church in the Round: Feminist Interpretation of the Church*. Louisville: Westminster John Knox, 1993.

———. *Just Hospitality: God's Welcome in a World of Difference*. Edited by J. Shannon Clarkson and Kate M. Ott. Louisville: Westminster John Knox, 2009.

Sabanoglu, Tugba. "Nike's Advertising and Promotion Costs from 2014 to 2020 (in Billion U.S. Dollars)." *Statista*, February 4, 2021. https://www.statista.com/statis tics/685734/nike-ad-spend/.

Sage, George H. "Corporate Globalization and Sporting Goods Manufacturing: The Case of Nike." In *Sport in Contemporary Society: An Anthology*, edited by D. Stanley Eitzen, 391–410. Boulder, CO: Paradigm, 2009.

Salcedo, Andrea. "Police Told a Man a Container in His Car Tested Positive for Drugs. It Was His Daughter's Ashes." *Washington Post*, May 21, 2021. https://www.wash ingtonpost.com/nation/2021/05/21/dartavius-barnes-daughters-ashes-mixup/.

Sanders, Bernie (@BernieSanders). "We have a criminal justice system which is rac ist, broken, and must be fundamentally reformed." Twitter. September 13, 2019. 8:08 p.m. https://twitter.com/berniesanders/status/1172663320169668609?lang=en.

Sargent, Greg. "The Walls around Trump Are Crumbling: Evangelicals May Be His Last Resort." *Washington Post*, January 2, 2019. https://www.washingtonpost.com /opinions/2019/01/02/walls-around-trump-are-crumbling-evangelicals-may-be-his -last-resort/?noredirect=on.

Sawyer, Wendy, and Peter Wagner. "Mass Incarceration: The Whole Pie." *Prison Policy Initiative*, March 24, 2020. https://www.prisonpolicy.org/reports/pie2020.html.

Seinfeld, Jerry, writer. *I'm Telling You for the Last Time*. Directed by Marty Callner. New York: Funny Business Productions, 1998. DVD.

Shelden, Randall G., and Pavel V. Vasiliev. *Controlling the Dangerous Classes: A His tory of Criminal Justice in America*. 3rd ed. Long Grove, IL: Waveland, 2017.

Shetterly, Margot Lee. *Hidden Figures: The American Dream and the Untold Story of the Black Women Mathematicians Who Helped Win the Space Race*. New York: William Morrow, 2016.

Simmel, Georg. *On Individuality and Social Forms: Selected Writings*. The Heritage of Sociology. Chicago: University of Chicago Press, 1971.

Smithsonian National Museum of American History. "Separate Is Not Equal: Brown v. Board of Education." Behring Center, accessed July 10, 2019. https://american history.si.edu/brown/history/1-segregated/jim-crow.html.

"Somali-American Family Sues after Detained for 11 Hours at U.S.-Canadian Border." Fox, July 13, 2017. https://www.fox9.com/news/somali-american-family-sues-after -detained-for-11-hours-at-u-s-canada-border.

"Sports Industry to Reach $73.5 Billion." SportsMoney. *Forbes*, October 19, 2015. https://www.forbes.com/sites/darrenheitner/2015/10/19/sports-industry-to-reach -73-5-billion-by-2019/#670d4cbc1b4b.

Stecker, J. F., Jr., C. E. Horton, C. J. Devine Jr., and J. B. McCraw. "Hypospadias Crip ples [In Eng.]." *Urologic Clinics of North America* 8, no. 3 (October 1981): 539–44.

Stellin, Susan. "Is the 'War on Drugs' Over? Arrest Statistics Say No." *New York Times*, November 5, 2019. https://www.nytimes.com/2019/11/05/upshot/is-the-war -on-drugs-over-arrest-statistics-say-no.html.

Stewart, John Robert. *Bridges Not Walls: A Book about Interpersonal Communication*. 11th ed. Dubuque, IA: McGraw-Hill, 2012.

Stone, Bryan P. *Evangelism after Christendom: The Theology and Practice of Christian Witness*. Grand Rapids: Brazos, 2007.

Strauss, Anselm L. *George Herbert Mead on Social Psychology: Selected Papers*. Chicago: University of Chicago Press, 1964.

Swardson, Anne, and Sandra Sugawara. "Asian Workers Become Customers." *Washington Post*, December 30, 1996, A1. https://www.washingtonpost.com/wp-srv/inatl/longterm/poverty/poverty2.htm.

Synnott, Anthony. *The Body Social: Symbolism, Self, and Society*. New York: Routledge, 1993.

Tajfel, Henri, ed. *Social Identity and Intergroup Relations*. European Studies in Social Psychology. Cambridge: Cambridge University Press, 1982.

Tajfel, Henri, Michael G. Billig, R. P. Bundy, and Claude Flament. "Social Categorization and Intergroup Behaviour." *European Journal of Experimental Social Psychology* 1 (1971): 149–78.

Tepfer, Daniel. "Tanya McDowell Sentenced to 5 Years in Prison." *CT Post*, March 27, 2012. https://www.ctpost.com/news/article/Tanya-McDowell-sentenced-to-5-years-in-prison-3437974.php.

Thomas, Gordon, and Max Morgan Witts. *Voyage of the Damned*. Chelsea, MI: Scarborough, 1990.

Thompson Day, Heather. "Evangelicals Are Less Likely to Welcome Refugees Than Non-believers: How Did We Sink So Low?" *Newsweek*, July 11, 2019. https://www.newsweek.com/christians-acceptance-refugees-evangelicals-1448757.

Tikkanen, Amy. "MS *St. Louis* German Ocean Liner." In *Encyclopedia Britannica*, July 3, 2017. https://www.britannica.com/topic/MS-St-Louis-German-ship.

Topp, Sarah S. "Against the Quiet Revolution: The Rhetorical Construction of Intersex Individuals as Disordered." *Sexualities* 16, nos. 1–2 (2013): 180–94. https://doi.org/10.1177/1363460712471113.

Treisman, Rachel. "American Girl's 1st Chinese American 'Girl of the Year' Doll Aims to Fight AAPI Hate." NPR, January 5, 2022. https://www.npr.org/2022/01/05/1070616965/chinese-american-girl-doll-corinne-tan-aapi-racism.

Turner, B. S. "The Sociology of the Body." In *21st Century Sociology: A Reference Handbook*, edited by C. D. Bryant and D. L. Peck, 90–97. Thousand Oaks, CA: Sage, 2007.

Turner, John. *Rediscovering the Social Group: A Self-Categorization Theory*. New York: Blackwell, 1987.

———. "Towards a Cognitive Redefinition of the Social Group." In Tajfel, *Social Identity and Intergroup Relations*, 15–40.

University of Tennessee. "Chattanooga Dedicates a Place of Remembrance, Reconciliation at Walnut Street Bridge." September 19, 2021, University of Tennessee.

https://blog.utc.edu/news/2021/09/chattanooga-dedicates-a-place-of-remem
brance-reconciliation-at-walnut-street-bridge/.

U.S. Immigration and Customs Enforcement. "Keeping America Safe." Accessed October 14, 2021. https://www.ice.gov/.

Vedantam, Shankar. "Zipcode Destiny: The Persistent Power of Place and Education." November 12, 2018. In *Hidden Brain*, produced by Jennifer Schmidt, Parth Shah, Rhaina Cohen, Thomas Lu, and Laura Kwerel, 52:00. https://www.npr.org/2018/11/12/666993130/zipcode-destiny-the-persistent-power-of-place-and-education.

Volf, Miroslav. *Exclusion and Embrace: A Theological Exploration of Identity, Otherness, and Reconciliation.* Nashville: Abingdon, 1996.

Vos, Matthew S. "Competing in Cedar: Nike, Superstar Athletes, and the Unseen Strangers Who Make Our Shoes." *Journal of Sociology and Christianity* 9, no. 2 (Fall 2019): 7–28.

———. "Prizes and Consumables: The Super Bowl as a Theology of Women." *Comment*, February 1, 2013. https://www.cardus.ca/comment/article/3864/prizes-and-consumables-the-super-bowl-as-a-theology-of-women/.

———. "The Way That You See." *Journal of Sociology and Christianity* 10, no. 1 (2020): 7. https://sociologyandchristianity.org/index.php/jsc/article/view/170.

———. "Who Is My Neighbor?" *Pro Rege* 47, no. 4 (2019): 27–35.

Wallerstein, Immanuel Maurice. *The End of the World as We Know It: Social Science for the Twenty-First Century.* Minneapolis: University of Minnesota Press, 1999.

———. *The Essential Wallerstein.* New York: New Press, 2000.

Waskul, Dennis D., and Phillip Vannini. *Body/Embodiment: Symbolic Interaction and the Sociology of the Body.* Burlington, VT: Ashgate, 2006.

Waters, Mark, dir. *Mean Girls.* Los Angeles, CA, Paramount Pictures, 2004. DVD.

Watts, Isaac. "Alas! And Did My Savior Bleed." In *The United Methodist Hymnal*, #294. https://hymnary.org/hymn/UMH/294.

Weir, Peter, dir. *Witness.* Hollywood, CA: Paramount Home Video, 1986. DVD.

Wells-Barnett, Ida B., Mia Bay, and Henry Louis Gates. *The Light of Truth: Writings of an Anti-Lynching Crusader.* New York: Penguin, 2014.

West, Candace, and Don H. Zimmerman. "Doing Gender." *Gender & Society* 1, no. 2 (1987): 125–51. https://doi.org/10.1177/0891243287001002002.

Wikipedia. S.v. "Augusta National Golf Club." Last modified August 27, 2021. https://en.wikipedia.org/wiki/Augusta_National_Golf_Club.

Wikipedia. S.v. "Lynching of Ed Johnson." Last modified August 20, 2021. https://en.wikipedia.org/wiki/Lynching_of_Ed_Johnson.

Wikipedia. S.v. "Where the Streets Have No Name." Last modified June 17, 2021. https://en.wikipedia.org/wiki/Where_the_Streets_Have_No_Name.

Willigan, Geraldine E. "High Performance Marketing: An Interview with Nike's Phil Knight." *Harvard Business Review*, July/August 1992. https://hbr.org/1992/07/high -performance-marketing-an-interview-with-nikes-phil-knight.

Winerip, Michael. "Revisiting the 'Crack Babies' Epidemic That Was Not." *New York Times*, May 20, 2013. https://www.nytimes.com/2013/05/20/booming/revisiting -the-crack-babies-epidemic-that-was-not.html.

With Clarity. "Buying Natural vs. Synthetic Diamonds." Accessed October 25, 2021. https://www.withclarity.com/education/diamond-education/natural-vs-synthetic -diamonds.

Wokutch, Richard. "Nike and Its Critics: Beginning a Dialogue." *Organization and Environment* 14, no. 2 (June 2001): 207–37.

Wolf, Z. Byron. "Trump Basically Called Mexicans Rapists Again." CNN, April 6, 2018. https://www.cnn.com/2018/04/06/politics/trump-mexico-rapists/index.html.

"Women Can Be on Council of Senior Scholars." *Arab News*, July 2, 2016. http:// www.arabnews.com/node/948181/saudi-arabia.

Woodward, John. "Canada Deported Man to Torture in Sri Lanka: Affidavit." CTV News, October 8, 2013. https://bc.ctvnews.ca/canada-deported-man-to-torture -in-sri-lanka-affidavit-1.1489741.

World Population Review. "Incarceration Rates by Country, 2021." Accessed November 12, 2021. https://worldpopulationreview.com/country-rankings/incarceration -rates-by-country.

Wright, N. T. *Surprised by Hope: Rethinking Heaven, the Resurrection, and the Mission of the Church*. New York: HarperOne, 2008.

Zeiler, Kristin, and Anette Wickström. "Why Do 'We' Perform Surgery on Newborn Intersexed Children? The Phenomenology of the Parental Experience of Having a Child with Intersex Anatomies." *Feminist Theory* 10, no. 3 (2009): 359–77. https:// doi.org/10.1177/1464700109343258.

INDEX